Wildcatters

TEXAS INDEPENDENT OILMEN

NUMBER TWENTY
Kenneth E. Montague Series in Oil and Business History

Joseph A. Pratt, General Editor

Wildcatters

TEXAS INDEPENDENT OILMEN

by Roger M. Olien & Diana Davids Hinton

Texas A&M University Press
College Station

LIBRARY OF CONGRESS CATALOGING-IN-PUBLICATION DATA

Olien, Roger M., 1938–
    Wildcatters : Texas independent oilmen / Roger M. Olien, Diana Davids Hinton. — 1st pbk. ed.
        p. cm. — (Kenneth E. Montague series in oil and business history; no. 20)
    Includes bibliographical references and index.
    ISBN-13: 978-1-58544-606-3 (pbk. : alk. paper)
    ISBN-10: 1-58544-606-8 (pbk. : alk. paper)
    1. Petroleum industry and trade—Texas—History.   I. Hinton, Diana Davids, 1943– II. Title.
    HD9567.T3O45 2007
    338.2'72820976409047—dc22   2006102739

For

Conrad and Kathlyn

CONTENTS

PREFACE

For more than a decade, we have lived and worked in a rapidly changing Texas oil town. We have watched a business cycle in the petroleum industry unfold over the course of a decade, running from slow times to booming prosperity to abrupt decline. As the cycle ran its course, new ventures were launched, new careers begun, and new fortunes made, all in response to rapidly changing conditions. Then, in a sudden reversal, we saw some new ventures founder and some fortunes sink more quickly than they had appeared. Most recently, the city's principal bank collapsed. Its fall still sends shock waves through independent oil and banking circles. At the same time that the downturn brought catastrophe to some, other oilmen and other banks have survived and even prospered.

During this decade of boom and bust, it was clear that neither independent oilmen nor their methods are understood by the public, which often seems unaware that there is more to oil than Exxon. In response, we decided to explain the important role independents play, in an industry dominated by giant multinational corporations, by explaining how they do business and by telling their story.

Our approach to the independents is historical; unlike the economists and financial analysts who have also written about independents, we have studied broad changes over time. In order to describe independent oilmen as a group and delineate their approaches to business over more than six decades, we have investigated a variety of oilmen and companies. To have written of only one man or company would have limited the number of approaches we could describe and might have offered a misleading view of the activity of independents in general.

We have also gone beyond the scant records of individual companies to describe business strategies. The independents, most of whom are accountable only to themselves and to the members of their business circles, are not prone to keep records of transactions long past (with the exception of the growing volume of records that must be kept for state and federal authorities). Most independents are also reluctant to open their papers on current or pending projects. For these reasons, we have supplemented information from company papers with data from other sources, including interviews, scout reports, and Texas Railroad Commission records. We have placed these data in national and regional contexts by referring to industry publications, journals, and reports.

Though we intend to provide an accurate description of independent activity in general, we have chosen to limit the context of our story in terms of both time and place. The elements of business opportunity necessarily include national and international developments. Prevailing financial conditions, regulation, and applied technology, as well as domestic and world prices, affect the approaches and operations of all independents. But in order to go beyond these general considerations and examine specific opportunities and the use made of them, we have placed them in the context of regional and local conditions. The general way West Texas independents do business, for example, is not significantly different from the way independents do business in Houston, Dallas, or Tulsa; but specific strategies are keyed to local and regional opportunities, and they can differ significantly from place to place.

Our story is set in one of the most interesting arenas of independent activity, the Permian Basin of western Texas and southeastern New Mexico. The region stretches over a quarter of Texas and beyond, from Sweetwater on the east to Artesia, New Mexico, on the west, and from central Pecos and Crockett counties on the south to Hale and Lamb counties on the north. The Permian Basin is of considerable importance in the American petroleum industry because it produces about one fifth of the nation's domestic oil. Its sixty-year history contains vivid examples of the profound effects of technological change, government regulation, and economic fluctuation on the oil and gas community. The area's complex geology and its thick potentially productive rock sequences have provided opportunities for independents with a wide variety of specializations and approaches. Independents have brought in shallow oil with cable tool rigs and tapped ultradeep gas with the largest and costliest rotary drilling equipment. In recent years, major companies and large independents have undertaken highly sophisticated, multimillion-dollar enhanced oil recovery projects in the region. In short, a wide variety of oil and gas activity may be viewed in the history of the Permian Basin.

Our work was eased by many considerate people, and we have space to name only a few of them. Mrs. J. H. Penson, William Landreth, John J. Redfern, Jr., John B. Gunn, Jr., and Clyde Barton permitted us to use materials in their possession.

Professors Henrietta M. Larson, Forrest McDonald, and David Prindle read the manuscript. These colleagues and Kelly Bell, Leo and Betty Byerley, J. Conrad Dunagan, Tom Scott, and Wilbur A. Yeager, Jr., provided important suggestions and critiques as our work progressed. We have not always adopted the suggestions of our readers, and thus, whatever errors or other shortcomings remain in this book are our responsibility.

We received especially strong encouragement to undertake this project from Ford Chapman, John Hendrix, Robert Leibrock, Joseph B. McShane, William D. Noel, John J. Redfern, Jr., and the directors of the First National Bank of Midland, Texas. Research and writing were supported by the Texas Historical Foundation and the University of Texas of the Permian Basin.

Scott Lubeck, our editor at Texas Monthly Press, and Chris Kindschi have helped us make our story of independent oilmen understandable and available to a greater number of readers. Librarians in the Southwest Collection at Texas Tech University were generous with time and attention, as were Sancy Harris and Sandra Wegner at the Midland County Library and Betty Orbeck at the Permian Basin Petroleum Museum. Jean Tims and Gayla Carbajal gave valuable aid in the preparation of our manuscript.

In earlier books, we have acknowledged the unflagging encouragement and sound advice of J. Conrad Dunagan; we are delighted to do so again.

Midland, Texas
December 1983

INTRODUCTION TO THE 2007 EDITION

Wildcatters are more important now than ever. Since 1983, when the original manuscript of *Wildcatters* went off to press, independent oil companies and independent oilmen, long responsible for most American oil and gas exploration, have been part of a remarkable transformation of the domestic petroleum industry. Major companies, those giant integrated multinational firms that once dominated oil at home and abroad, have merged, downsized, and spun off operations. The majors have shifted their primary exploration and production focus offshore and overseas. They have sold domestic assets, leases, prospects, and reserves worth billions of dollars as they have assumed a larger presence in the global arena. Undoubtedly, in 2006 the best prospects for spectacular petroleum finds lie overseas. But many of those prospects, like giant production already on line, are located in places like Iran, Nigeria, and Venezuela—places where the political risks of doing business are high. To the extent we satisfy our voracious appetite for energy with petroleum from overseas, we risk being at the mercy of the ups and downs of global politics. Our alternative is to do more to develop the energy resources we have at home. In this respect, independents are more vital than ever to our future. They have taken over where the majors have left off.

In 1983, however, no one could have predicted how great the changes of the next twenty years would be. At that time it was clear that the great boom of the late 1970s and early 1980s was over. Independent oilmen, in the Permian Basin and elsewhere, faced uncertain times. Some of the firms we studied were in trouble and not likely to recover. Others hunkered down, debts paid, waiting for better opportunities. Among independents, there were industry adventurers beginning to move from acquiring reserves and profits out in the field to finding them on Wall Street, targeting large, underperforming companies for takeover. Nonetheless, the major companies still dominated production. There were still the so-called Seven Sisters—Exxon, Mobil, Shell, British Petroleum, Texaco, Standard Oil of California (Chevron), and Gulf. Among energy lenders, Penn Square and the First National Bank of Midland failed, but a tidal wave of nonperforming loans had not yet swamped most other banks on the boom time bandwagon. One could still find a few oil patch optimists who talked about "$85 in '85"—$85 a barrel oil in 1985—though fewer people believed them. Even the pessimists did not foresee how calamitous the events ahead would be.

As usual in the petroleum industry, prices drove change. Prices of crude oil slid downward, from a high averaging over $30 a barrel (spot market prices could be higher) in 1981, to under $26 a barrel in 1984 and less than $24 in 1985. At that point, the Saudis, disgusted at widespread cheating on production quotas by fellow OPEC members, moved to regain market share. They elevated their production and cut prices for their customers. Crude prices responded with a dramatic plunge in November 1985, and crashed to $12–$15 a barrel levels in March 1986. By that time, anyone who borrowed to fund projects framed with the economics prevailing only months earlier was in trouble.

While disaster overtook many oil producers, gas producers were hardly much better off. In the Natural Gas Policy Act of 1978, the federal government moved toward deregulation of interstate natural gas prices and offered price incentives to those who would go after gas reserves that were more challenging and expensive to bring in. Federal policy encouraged high levels of gas exploration for the remainder of the decade and beginning of the next. Unfortunately, prospectors' success meant more gas on the market than the market could absorb, a prolonged "gas bubble." Average natural gas prices began moving down in 1984 and had fallen 32 percent by the end of 1986. Thereafter, gas prices stayed relatively flat at low levels. At the same time producers coped with low prices, purchasers were in even worse shape. The energy crisis mentality of the late seventies led them to buy gas with "take or pay" contracts—agreements to take producers' gas at high prices or to pay for a percentage of potential output without actually taking the gas. That locked them into buying gas they did not want or paying for it anyway, losing money in either event.

Whether looking at either oil or gas, then, there were few grounds for upstream industry optimism by the end of 1986. Of course, there was scant incentive to pursue exploration and development, and many drilling and service contractors faced bankruptcy. A hot commodity in boom times, rigs sat idle and rusting in equipment yards, while roughnecks and roustabouts applied for unemployment benefits. In April 1986 alone, the oil and gas industry lost 35,000 jobs. The crash spared neither petroleum professionals nor refinery workers. By October 1986, one out of four petroleum geologists was out of work; unemployment in Port Arthur, a refining center, reached almost 21 percent. The decade between 1982 and 1992 saw fifty-one percent of exploration and production jobs eliminated, and the American petroleum industry as a whole lost over 400,000 jobs. Foreclosure signs peppered oil-town neighborhoods. In all, the crash of 1986 ushered in the most severe depression ever experienced by the American petroleum industry, a depression far worse than that of the 1930s.

The entire petroleum industry sustained tremendous damage, but independents, particularly those whose operations included contract drilling, were hit especially hard. By the end of October 1986, only 59 of the *Oil and Gas Journal's* list of the 170 largest firms showed a net profit for the year, and, of these, 35 showed a sharp decline in profits from the previous year. Independents coped through

Chapter 11 bankruptcies, layoffs and salary freezes, office closings, and sales of assets. Perhaps the most dramatic bankruptcy proceedings were those involving Herbert, Bunker, and Lamar Hunt and their companies Placid Oil and Penrod Drilling. The Hunts sued First National Bank of Chicago and twenty-two other banks, claiming the bankers tried to destroy Placid and Penrod; First National of Chicago countersued to collect loans to Placid and Penrod. At the end of the year, the *Dallas Morning News* reported that between their various ventures, the Hunt brothers had lost close to $5 billion. Some observers suggested this was the largest personal loss in history. A sign of the times, *Texas Monthly* magazine ran a cover story, "Lifestyles of the Rich and Bankrupt" in March 1988.

The bust took a heavy toll on oil-patch banks. Between 1987 and 1990 bank failures soared, and many banks, including some of the largest Texas institutions, changed hands. During 1988 more than half all Texas banks were rated as problem banks, undercapitalized and with a host of non-performing loans. Those banks surviving concentrated on collecting old loans and were understandably reluctant to make energy loans. Thus, when North Carolina National Bank took over Republic Bank in Midland, local oilmen joked that its NCNB stood for "No Cash for No Body." Worse yet, the Reagan Administration's 1986 adjustments in tax law dropped maximum tax brackets down from seventy percent, thus tending to discourage private investors from making substantial industry investments with a view to improving their tax position. Independents with cash, however, could pick up oil reserves for as little as $1.50 a barrel.

With an estimated $400 billion in value lost by the end of 1986, industry recovery from the downturn was uneven and very slow. Independents in a position to take on new projects had to cope with low and volatile crude oil prices. In the decade following 1987, average wellhead prices ranged between $12 and $20 a barrel, generally hovering in the $15–$16 range, but in 1999 they crashed once more to $10.80. Some of the volatility resulted from trade in crude oil futures on the New York Mercantile Exchange (NYMEX), trading which began in 1983. As they responded to every change in global economy and politics, NYMEX traders made crude prices gyrate far more than they had when major company purchasers simply posted field prices. Unpredictable prices not only got in the way of responsible planning of project economics, but they also encouraged a "wait-and-see, better safe than sorry" mentality among independents who might otherwise have gone ahead with exploration and development.

In the 1980s and 1990s, as usual in industry downtimes, there were a great number of mergers and acquisitions, with a large volume of reserves changing hands. This time, however, hard times meant profound changes for the twenty-odd major and lesser major companies visible in 1980. Even before the crash of 1986, ranks of the top twenty companies began to thin as underperforming and/or ineptly managed firms became targets for hostile takeovers. Two of the more dramatic instances involved takeover attempts by independents and acquisition of target companies by another major.

The man who gained most industry notice for pursuing large companies for takeover was Mesa Petroleum's T. Boone Pickens. In 1981–1982 Pickens moved to take over faltering Cities Service, only to be blocked, first by Gulf and then by Occidental; the latter eventually acquired Cities Service. Nothing daunted, Pickens went after Superior Oil and Dallas-based General American Oil. Ultimately, Phillips picked up General American, and Mobil took over Superior, but Pickens and his circle profited from trading in the two target companies' shares. Pickens next turned his attention to Gulf, whose shares had long failed to reflect the value of its assets. In 1983 the Mesa group of investors began to buy large blocks of the major's stock. As Pickens would sum up his strategy, at a time of falling oil and gas prices, the odds of making money on Gulf shares were a lot better than they were in exploration. By October 1983, Pickens and the Mesa circle owned more Gulf shares than the Mellon family. To escape Pickens, Gulf accepted takeover by Standard Oil of California (Chevron). One of the great Seven Sisters absorbed another.

Pennzoil's J. Hugh Liedtke was as ambitious and ready to take over underperforming majors as Pickens. One of the "Ivy Leaguers" who came to Midland in the late 1940s and went into business with fellow newcomer George H. W. Bush, Liedtke was a takeover veteran by 1983. He had built Pennzoil through purchase of South Penn Oil, Wolf's Head Oil, and the United Gas Corporation in the 1960s. While Pickens pursued Gulf, Liedtke trained his sights on Getty Oil. Just when Liedtke thought he had secured the company, Texaco stepped in and purchased the California firm. No quitter, Liedtke hired Houston attorney Joe Jamail and sued Texaco for $14 billion. In 1985 a Houston jury awarded Pennzoil $10.53 billion and interest—the largest judgment in United States history and one driving Texaco to seek bankruptcy protection. Pennzoil settled for a $3 billion payment in April 1988. Ironically, Pennzoil would place over $2 billion of the payment in Chevron stock, the company that had acquired Gulf and would acquire Texaco in 2001.

Mega mergers also thinned the ranks of the majors. In 1998 Exxon and Mobil joined forces. BP, which acquired Standard Oil of Ohio in 1987, swallowed up Amoco in 1998 and ARCO in 2000; the former was the old Standard Oil of Indiana and the latter the product of the 1960s merger of Atlantic and Richfield. In 2002 Conoco merged with Phillips. More recently, in 2005, Unocal, pursued by the China National Offshore Oil Corporation, became part of Chevron. Mega mergers have allowed giant American oil companies to compete more effectively with other global giants like Rosneft, Petrobras, and Statoil. Each merger and acquisition, however, meant downsizing, dispensing with redundant employees, and paring back staff in overlapping arenas. The majors closed many of their domestic regional offices, and the majority consolidated operations in Houston, making it truly the oil capital of the United States, if not the world. In effect, in this part of their transformation, the majors emulated the traditional strategy of independents, doing more with fewer people, or, as the industry has it, "being lean and mean."

In response to hard times, the majors also restructured their operations, entered into operational alliances with other companies, spun off less profitable segments to focus on better money-makers, and geographically consolidated field operations. For example, before BP acquired Amoco, Amoco and Shell tried joint management of Permian Basin production by setting up Altura in 1997. Two years later they sold Altura to Occidental, making Oxy the largest oil producer in Texas. Having acquired Cities Service, Oxy shed that company's refining and retailing operations, Citgo, selling it to the Southland Corporation, which, in turn, passed it on to the Petroleos de Venezuela SA (PdVSA). Shell tried a joint venture with Exxon in California exploration and production, Aera Energy. It entered into another joint venture, in refining and marketing, Motiva Enterprises, with Texaco and Saudi Aramco in 1998. Texaco had earlier launched a joint refining venture with Saudi Aramco, Star Enterprise, which included operation of Texaco's Port Arthur refinery.

In spin-offs, giant companies identified and parted with less profitable sectors of their operations. For example, Sun spun off its exploration and production as an independent company, Oryx, acquired by Kerr-McGee in 1998. ARCO created Lyondell from some of its refining and chemicals assets in 1985. Lyondell tried a joint refining venture with Citgo in 1993 and bought Occidental's polyethylene business in 1995. In the early 1990s, ARCO restructured its exploration and production, creating ARCO Permian to manage Western Texas and New Mexico operations, and Vastar to go after Gulf of Mexico gas. It consolidated its field and regional exposure, cutting the number of fields in which it had leases by 1400, and closed its Dallas office building. Gone were the days when a major like ARCO would try to be everywhere and do everything; cost cutting and efficiency were the new goals, and they often mandated what amounted to disintegration.

Like the oil giants, large gas companies resorted to mergers, acquisitions, and spin-offs. Thus, Panhandle Eastern spun off its exploration and production subsidiary, Anadarko, in 1986, in response to threat of hostile takeover. Trying to evade competition from Oscar Wyatt's Coastal States Gas, Panhandle Eastern took over Texas Eastern in 1989 and dismantled it. Much earlier, Coastal created Valero as a corporate successor to its ill-fated Lo Vaca Gathering Company; a quarter century of expansion in refining has seen Valero become the largest refiner in North America. That most ill-fated of gas companies, Enron, was the product of the combination of Houston Natural Gas and Internorth in 1985; the new company's CEO was HNG's Kenneth Lay. Across the domestic petroleum industry horizon, then, the largest players undertook dramatic transformations.

As major oil companies rationalized their operations and focused on their most profitable sectors, they began to part with a significant proportion of their domestic reserves of both oil and gas. They aimed at geographical rationalization of production, keeping a presence in areas with especially large and profitable reserves and selling off scattered, less important properties. Sales served the main element in the majors' exploration and production strategy, that of moving away from the domestic arena to find and exploit much larger reserves offshore and overseas. For independents of all sizes, the majors' strategy opened opportunities to grow by picking up properties long locked in major company inventories at bargain basement prices, reflecting low prices of oil and gas. At the same time, as the majors downsized their professional staff, independents were often able to pick up highly trained professionals as well as properties. Independents thus positioned themselves to take on the smaller, more challenging projects that did not appeal to the majors—getting more production from old wells, bringing in oil and gas from narrower pay zones bypassed in earlier years, taking on technologically challenging tight formations with less certain returns. They could see profits in what the majors passed up.

Since 1983, a new group of mega independents has emerged, firms like Anadarko, Apache, Devon, and Chesapeake Energy. Most of the mega independents have grown large by going public and acquiring other companies as well as reserves discarded by majors. Oklahoma City's Devon Energy, for example, was founded by John and Larry Nichols in 1971 and became a publicly held company in 1988. In 1992 it acquired Hondo Oil and Gas; in 1996 it bought Kerr-McGee's North American onshore oil and gas properties; and in 1998 it acquired Northstar Energy. Picking up PennzEnergy in 1999 let Devon enter Gulf of Mexico action. The following year it merged with Santa Fe Snyder to become one of the five largest independent companies. Devon intensified focus on natural gas by picking up Anderson Exploration in 2001, which gave it extensive Canadian production, and Mitchell Energy in 2002, which made it a leading independent natural gas processor. Merger with Ocean Energy in 2003 saw Devon reach a firm size of over 4000 employees and operations in Brazil, Russia, China, and Egypt, as well as North America.

As the Devon example illustrates, mega independents have followed the majors in trying their luck abroad. Apache has branched out in Canada, Egypt, western Australia, and the North Sea. Anadarko has developed reserves in Canada and Algeria. Pioneer Natural Resources, formed in 1997 with a merger of Midland's Parker and Parsley with MESA, Inc., has projects in Argentina, Canada, South Africa, and Tunisia as well as the United States. But if the mega independents are like the majors in looking overseas, in other ways they remain very much in the traditional independent model.

Though mega independents like Anadarko and Apache employ several thousand persons, they carry on operations with far fewer employees than the majors. In the Permian Basin, where both companies had an important presence by 2000, Anadarko employed 30 office workers and 100 field hands; Apache employed 7 office workers and 99 field hands. Mega independents have also tended to stay in the petroleum industry's upstream sector of exploration and production, leaving refining and marketing to others; as they have picked up other firms, they have generally taken on those in exploration and production. They may produce both oil and gas, but they generally emphasize one or the other. Devon and Chesapeake Energy, for example, have emphasized natural gas, increasingly attractive to independents with the last few years' high prices. Company strategies often have geographical focus, and companies commonly seek to grow by extending a successful regional strategy to other geologically similar regions. Thus Chesapeake Energy has been successful at finding gas in the Permian and Fort Worth Basin shale formations; it is now looking to expand its gas exploration in the Appalachian Basin and has bought properties from Columbia Gas with that strategy in view. One of the strategies of Parker and Parsley lay in acquiring proven Spraberry Trend properties and enhancing their production, an approach its "descendent," Pioneer Natural Resources, uses in a far wider geographical context. Many independents have thus enlarged a niche strategy to fit broader horizons. These broader horizons still emphasize domestic, rather than foreign, operations, notwithstanding ventures overseas. In many ways, the independent business approach is still distinctive from that of the majors.

Limitations on the scale of operations of even the mega independents are obvious in their involvement offshore, in the Gulf of Mexico and other places. On the Gulf of Mexico Continental Shelf, for example, mega independents have a highly significant presence and produce large quantities of gas from leases no longer attractive to major companies. They are able to do so economically, however, because the majors put infrastructure like gathering systems and pipelines in place much earlier. Even mega independents must rely on the majors to construct the dauntingly expensive infrastructure permitting production of the dazzling finds of Deep Water Gulf of Mexico. As for their exploration in Deep Water, they look to participate in projects with majors like Exxon Mobil, BP, or Chevron, rather than shoulder staggering costs of drilling by themselves. Early in September 2006, Devon announced a spectacular Deep Water find, Jack 2; Devon's partners in the project were Chevron and Statoil. In a high-cost arena like Deep Water Gulf of Mexico, where a well can cost $100 million to drill, there is no place for the old-time poor boy independent. Those prospecting in this part of offshore action have to be ready to come forward with many millions of dollars to do so.

The expense of Deep Water exploration is still prohibitively high for the majority of independents of lesser size, but, thanks to advances in petroleum technology, the expense of finding a barrel of oil or oil equivalent on shore fell dramatically between 1983 and 2000. Technological progress has made it possible to get much more accurate information about what lies underground and be much more efficient at getting it out. Better yet, the cost of that technology, extremely expensive in 1983, has dropped to a tenth of what it once was, making it affordable even to relatively small independents. The most significant breakthroughs have come in three-dimensional seismic imaging; horizontal and multilateral drilling; steerable, downhole drilling offering information while drilling; and the application of computer technology to operations. Though the cost of doing business in present-day boom times has offset technological savings to some extent, technological change has opened up new and affordable opportunities to independents.

The industry experimented with 3-D seismic imaging as early as the mid-1960s, but processing huge amounts of information generated in these early efforts required investment in room-sized mainframe computer systems at a staggering cost. For that matter, simply doing the seismic work necessary to gather information for 3-D seismic imaging was extremely costly, perhaps some eight to ten times as expensive as it might be today. Spectacular advances in computer technology in the late 1980s and 1990s meant that more information could be processed at lower cost. With refinement of the personal computer, this technology became available on a grand scale. Developed into desktop workstations, computer technology lets petroleum geologists and engineers use 3-D seismic data to find the likeliest places to look for petroleum and calculate how best to produce it. It is now affordable and essential to independent companies. Computers also revolutionized daily office operations in a cost-saving direction, letting one employee do record-keeping and reporting in a fraction of the time it once took a number of employees to carry out. But whether applied in exploration and production or in office routine, computer technology has meant a tremendous breakthrough in independent operations.

Perfecting horizontal drilling has let independents produce oil and gas from pay zones long passed up because of their thinness. A pay formation only four feet thick is not likely to produce enough from a vertical hole to be economically attractive to anyone, but if the hole extends several miles horizontally along productive rock, production from it may be very profitable. By the early 1990s horizontal drilling technology was not only capable of such extended hole projects, but it could be used to drill down to a pay and extend multilaterally into a producing formation, letting one vertical hole tap production in a number of horizontal directions. Beyond this, by the 1990s drilling became much faster and more accurate by application of polycrystalline diamond compact bits, powered by steerable downhole motors and returning a constant stream of immediate downhole information to the driller, measurement while drilling. Faster, more accurate drilling meant dramatic reduction in both exploration cost and project risk. For independents of all sizes, keeping costs as low as possible is as crucial to business success as it ever was. Technology lets independents be meaner and leaner, and at less risk than ever before.

Despite challenging times since 1983, there have been opportunities for independent growth, not only for veterans surviving the crash of '86 and the new mega independents but also for newcomers of all sizes. Midland-based Mexco Energy Corporation's history shows how a Permian Basin-focused independent company found ways to grow and prosper in an uncertain and volatile industry environment.

Emerging from the Miller Oil Company, which was organized by Midland geologist Harry Miller in 1972, Mexco was a small public company in 1983 when
Midland attorney Nicholas C. Taylor became its president. Taylor's first element
of strategy was cutting costs—dispensing with club memberships and a company
car, lowering office rent from $800 to $250 a month by subletting office space,
and doing Mexco's legal work in-house. Rather than hire its own landmen, geologists, and engineers, Mexco hired consultants as needed; Taylor did much of
Mexco's non-scientific work himself. Even today, Mexco is so "lean" in terms of
employees—two full-time and several part-time persons on the payroll—that
the American Stock Exchange recently called the company to ask if there had
been an error in company reporting with regard to staff. Taylor recalled, "We
said, 'No, there's no error. That's all we've got.'" That Mexco's treasurer and chief
financial officer is Tammi McCommic is another sign of change in the independent sector since 1983: more women now fill higher positions in independent
companies than before.

Keeping debt to a minimum is a key element in Mexco's business strategy.
Mexco paid off its debt as soon as possible and began acquiring properties, for
sale at reasonable prices during the downtimes. In 1993 it acquired another independent company, Forman Energy, a firm which, like Mexco, focused on oil
and gas exploration and development. At present, Mexco has properties in ten
states, but its largest holdings are in the West Texas Permian Basin. While the
company's proven reserves include some 183,000 barrels of oil, its main focus
is gas; total proven gas reserves are close to 6.7 billion cubic feet. High natural
gas prices of recent years are not the only reason for Mexco's gas emphasis. Less
influenced by global politics, gas prices have been more stable than oil prices,
making project economics more predictable. Drilling for and producing natural
gas usually involves fewer mechanical problems and lower operating costs than
the same operations for oil, and it is far less likely to result in environmental
complications or damage. With a view to better positioning in downtimes, Mexco
has diversified by owning royalties, a strategy which allows it production revenues
without operating expenses. As Taylor put it, "It's a good anchor to a company
through a difficult period."

Much of Mexco's gas production is in that long-time area of petroleum bonanza,
Pecos County, with especially significant holdings in the Viejos and Gomez gas
fields. In the Viejos field, Mexco has gone in where others found production, but
used different well stimulation techniques as well as 3-D seismic technology to
improve production levels and identify new sites for developmental drilling. Its
next developmental step will be horizontal drilling on some of these leases.

Like many other independents, Mexco has tended toward geographical
concentration of its projects, but that has not kept the company from looking
at possibilities for gas exploration and development overseas. Several years ago
it moved to enter Russia, a strategy it found attractive because of the expertise
of one of its directors, former U.S. Ambassador Thomas Graham Jr. What followed, however, amounted to a demonstration of overseas political risk. A Russian

firm stepped in to head off Mexco's finalizing a project just when the American company thought it was ready to close its deal. The discouraging outcome of its Russian venture has brought Mexco back to its domestic focus.

Now that the oil patch is booming, Mexco, like all other operators, faces the kind of problems that were common in former boom times like those of the early 1980s. Drilling and workover rigs are in even shorter supply than they were twenty-five years ago, so there are long waits for a rig, and costs are much higher when one is available. Prevailing royalty rates have risen, now ranging from one-fifth to nearly one-quarter; gone are the days of the standard one-eighth royalty. The presence of relatively inexperienced professional and blue-collar workers out in the field means unexpected expenses as green employees make costly mistakes. Nor are boom time problems the only source of mounting costs. Like other companies, Mexco has had to adjust to the ever-escalating expense of complying with state and federal regulation; its audit fees alone have quadrupled since 1983. Costs that would be a minor item in a major company budget loom large in the economics of a small independent company.

Tremendous improvements in technology offset some of these problems. They have allowed an independent company like Mexco to cut costs and pursue new exploration and development opportunities with diminished risks. As Taylor observed, 3-D seismic imaging, horizontal and directional drilling, more accurate well logging, and the ability to drill much deeper have marked significant advances in what independents can do. For that reason, when asked where American independents, the wildcatters, might be headed, Taylor said, "I think the future's pretty terrific."

As a group, then, independents remain a dynamic and increasingly important part of the American petroleum industry. It is all the more essential to understand who they are and what they do.

Sources for this introduction include, but are not limited to, periodicals like the *Oil and Gas Journal* and *Texas Monthly;* newspapers including the *Wall Street Journal, Dallas Morning News, Houston Chronicle, New York Times,* and *Midland Reporter-Telegram;* Hart Energy Publishing, LP's *America's Independents: From Black Gold to Diamond Jubilee;* the Federal Reserve Bank of Dallas's newsletter, *The Southwest Economy;* and publications of the Energy Information Administration. Information about major and independent companies includes material from company websites. Information about Mexco Energy Corporation came from the company's annual report for 2006 and from an interview with Nicholas C. Taylor, by Diana Davids Hinton, September 15, 2006, Midland, Texas.

1: WHO THEY ARE AND WHAT THEY DO

One of the most durable caricatures of American life as portrayed on television and movie screens is the larger-than-life, go-for-broke, mean-as-a-polecat oilman. J. R. Ewing, the ruthless wheeler-dealer of Ewing Oil, and the rest of the not-so-good ol' boys of the Texas Oil Cartel on *Dallas* enter millions of homes around the world every week, dramatizing what is supposed to be the world of the independent oilman. J. R.'s business methods are as unscrupulous as his morals are deplorable, a combination that appeals to popular taste at home and abroad. After all, the public has never expected oilmen to be ordinary, and since the days of John D. Rockefeller, they have never been presented so. Before J. R., Hollywood exploited popular interest in oil tycoons. In *Boom Town*, Clark Gable and Spencer Tracy, heroes rather than the usual oilmen-villains, fought runaway wells and gushers of fire. In *War of the Wildcats*, John Wayne took on oilman James E. Gardener, "a fast-talkin', double-crossing four-flusher," and, with the fortuitous help of Teddy Roosevelt, saved Oklahoma Indians from an unfair oil lease. More recently, in *Oklahoma Crude*, George C. Scott helped oilwoman Faye Dunaway fight the murderous Pan-Oklahoma Oil Company. Whatever else television and motion pictures have taught the public about the oil industry, they have made it clear that gushers and greedy men add up to a doubly dirty business.

Oilmen have not fared much better at the hands of popular novelists. Jett Rink, Edna Ferber's wildcatter in *Giant*, was a "modern version of the old buccaneer type," a "twentieth-century Paul Bunyan" who wore a vicuña topcoat, owned Cadillacs and airplanes, fought dirty, and spoke ungrammatical English. Departing from the image of the swashbuckling oilman, Larry McMurtry portrayed Gene Farrow, the independent in *The Last Picture Show,* as an ordinary, dull, undersexed, small-town businessman, and he showed Vernon Dalhart, in *Terms of Endearment,* as a lonely eccentric wedded to his work. Neither novelist paid as much attention to the way oilmen actually make money as did Upton Sinclair in his long, preachy novel *Oil!* Sinclair's oilman, J. Arnold Ross, was neither villain nor eccentric: he signed leases, worked with a geologist, drilled wells, including dry holes, and produced oil. Sinclair's oilman is a caricature, the focus of Sinclair's political and economic theories, but he was drawn from field observation.

The average reader would find what has passed for the truth about oilmen a great deal racier than fiction. Indeed, the authors of a host of popular biographical sketches of oilmen have, by and large, chosen subjects to fit the swashbuckling cinematic caricature. Thus, Houston's Glenn McCarthy emerged as a character worthy of the many roles of Errol Flynn in Wallace Davis's *Corduroy Road.* Of the growing literature about H. L. Hunt, whose domestic arrangements made him of as much interest to the *National Enquirer* as to the *Oil and Gas Journal,* the less said, the better. While his lifestyle has been catalogued in lavish detail, the reasons Hunt was a vastly successful businessman remain largely unexplained. Hunt fit the swashbuckling caricature.

The obsession popular writers have had with oilmen's lifestyles, as the literature on Hunt and others so amply illustrates, is understandable, if somewhat tiresome. How appealing to the reader's imagination is the rags-to-riches tale of the grubby roughneck living on beans suddenly catapulted to wealth beyond his wildest dreams, to live ever after on champagne and caviar! How different from the ordinary person's surroundings is the milieu of the oil super-rich, the world of private jet planes, flashy foreign sports cars, palatial homes, swimming pools in the shape of exotic objects, and diamonds as big as golf balls — the world in which the price of anything is of no consequence. As for the oil business, the source of these untold riches, that, if considered at all, is seen as a treasure hunt rather than a rational enterprise. In the popular caricature, the oilman does nothing to earn his wealth; he merely enjoys what amounts to the windfall of dumb luck. If he should be so hapless as to go bankrupt, that too is just a matter of luck — of luck that ran out.

There have been independent oilmen who have chosen to live up to or beyond the lifestyle of the caricature of the oilman; they have served to obscure the basic role of the independent oilman in the American petroleum industry. Independents are far more numerous and important in the United States than in other countries, in large part because in the United States minerals are not the exclusive property of the sovereign power but may be held by private individuals. Thus, it has been possible to enter oil exploration by leasing a small tract of acreage with a modest amount of capital — a circumstance very different from obtaining a large concession with a vast sum.

Private ownership of minerals in the United States has also meant that while the petroleum industry is generally dominated by giant companies, independent oilmen have long played important roles in its upstream sector, that of exploration and production. Independents have drilled most of the tests for oil and gas, successful and unsuccessful. Between 1969 and 1978, for example, they drilled almost nine times as many wells as the sixteen largest integrated oil companies. During the same period they drilled 89.5 percent of new field wildcats and made 81.5 percent of all oil and gas discoveries. Since 1920, independents have done most of America's wildcatting and have found vast amounts of domestic petroleum.[1] The statistics on independent activity, moreover, do not reflect the projects independents originated but passed on to major companies; if anything, independents have been more important in American oil exploration than the figures suggest. Not only have independents found new oil, but they have also kept oil in production from stripper wells, whose small output lacks economic appeal to major companies. Independents have been highly important to America's supply of oil, yet so little has been written about their role in the petroleum industry or how they have done business during the twentieth century.

Of particular importance to the domestic petroleum industry, for example, are the amounts and sources of capital independents have used to carry out their specific industry functions. Independents have always found some support for projects from within the industry, from other independents and from major oil companies. They have also raised funds outside the industry, though approaches to fund-raising have changed along with most important features of business. These changes, tied to changes in technology, economics, and regulation, have prompted the most adaptable independents to modify their approaches to business from time to time. Precisely what independents do in the industry at a given time reflects their ability to raise funds and seize opportunities.

Basic to any discussion of energy questions is a workable definition of "independent," as the term is understood in the petroleum industry, and this is no easy matter. In 1946, Senator Joseph O'Mahoney, chairman of the Special Senate Committee on Petroleum Resources, tried to get industry members to define the term. What he heard forced him to recall the oilman who said that the Standard Oil Company (New Jersey) was independent "because they did what they pleased." The great petroleum geologist Everette L. De Golyer, a founder of the Amerada Petroleum Corporation, met the problem of defining an independent by wittily reflecting that the independent was "one who always believes that the posted prices for crude oil, whatever they are, are too low."[2] The main barrier to precise definition of "independent" is its traditional use as an umbrella term in the industry; it has been applied to wildcatters, mail order promoters, lease brokers, producers, stripper well operators, royalty owners, refiners, and retailers, and to giant corporations with production in many countries as well as to one-man operators working in shared offices. No wonder the oil industry representatives quizzed by O'Mahoney's committee fumbled for words when they were asked to define the term.

"Independent" came to cover so wide a variety of petroleum industry businessmen because, in its early usage, the word described any corporation, firm, or individual in the oil business that had never been part of the Standard Oil holding company, which was broken up in 1911. "Independent" meant independent of Standard Oil. This usage, long adhered to by the Federal Trade Commission, took no notice of size or scope of business operations. In 1930, one industry observer, Leonard Logan, remarked that some independent companies were larger than companies of Standard ancestry; among his "large independent companies" were Royal Dutch Shell, The Texas Company, and Gulf.[3]

By 1930, however, to most persons in the petroleum industry, the term "independent" had a more specific meaning than that used by Logan. In June 1929, for example, the Independent Petroleum Association of America organized and self-consciously separated what it called "the rank and file of the petroleum industry" from "a few large companies," importers of South American oil to the United States. In this context, "independent" was to be interpreted in the context of public policy — specifically, the politics of tariff protection. The following February, the newly formed Independent Petroleum Association of Texas limited its membership to operators who were "strictly independent of major company connections."[4] IPAT meant to exclude men from Humble and Magnolia as well as men from The Texas Company and Gulf; in IPAT's context, as De Golyer's witticism implied, the difference was between majors who could set crude oil prices and independents who could not. Function, company size, and scope of operations had begun to enter into the meaning of "independent." Small operators distinguished themselves from major companies.

Since the thirties, independents have been commonly defined as the oil companies and firms remaining after major and "lesser major" companies are subtracted from industry ranks.[5] The majors — known now as Exxon, Gulf, Texaco, Mobil, Shell, Standard Oil of Indiana, and Standard Oil of California — are the largest of the vertically integrated American oil companies. Their globe-spanning operations are capable of bringing petroleum from geological prospect to the gas pump. In addition to great reserves of oil in the ground, these companies have massive investments in pipelines, refineries, storage facilities, and marketing operations. The lesser majors, like Atlantic-Richfield, Phillips, Getty, Union of California, and Amerada-Hess, are also integrated companies, differing from the majors only in the value of their assets, the number of their employees, and, in some instances, the extent of their involvement in foreign operations. There are few significant differences between their methods of business operation and those of the industry majors.

A list of major and lesser major American oil companies would not amount to more than twenty companies. By contrast, on March 31, 1982, the *Dallas Morning News* told its readers that there were more than 18,000 independent oil producers and/or operators in the United States. Three and a half decades earlier, Senator O'Mahoney's special committee decided that there were twenty major oil companies and over 20,000 independents.[6] The number of independents doing business has varied considerably, but at any time during the twentieth century, independents have vastly outnumbered the major companies that dominate the American petroleum industry. There are obvious problems with generalizations about so many independents. Quite apart from their large numbers, many have been highly creative in adopting strategies to meet narrowly specific and often unique opportunities. Though the diversity of independents bars simple definition, it is possible to make some general distinctions between major oil companies and independents, and between large, intermediate, and small independents.

Major and so-called lesser major companies share a number of important characteristics. They are fully integrated, with investments in production, transportation, refining, and marketing. These operations, together with long-term borrowing and the sale of equity interests, provide most of the revenue of these large companies. Most of them have foreign operations of considerable magnitude. All of them are managerial: they are operated by professional managers who do not necessarily hold a significant number of shares in the corporation.[7]

An independent is an individual, partnership, or corporation primarily engaged in exploring for and producing petroleum. Most independents are not integrated, and compared to the major oil companies, they are smaller in size, less managerially organized, and more limited in both geographical scope of operations and access to capital. Unlike the majors, the independents raise much of their risk capital from investors, who receive significant tax incentives to place their money in relatively speculative ventures. Most independents are specialists in exploration and production; the majority of them also limit their activity geographically. Finally, independents tend to be less managerial than the majors; most often the founding entrepreneur is the chief executive officer, and he participates in all significant decisions. Though scientists and other specialists may have staff responsibilities, the founder rarely delegates authority.

Within the broad category of independents, the legal, scientific, and economic contexts of their activity, as well as the strategies they devise, also tend to be significantly different for independents of large, intermediate, and small size. Large independents, like the greater and lesser majors, control sizable assets and are legally structured as corporations. They receive operating capital from retained earnings, sale of stock, and long-term borrowing. They, too, tend to be managerial, because the scale of their investments and the scope of their operations place effective operational control beyond the reach of the founder or his heirs. Like the majors, they have been active in most domestic provinces and in a number of foreign countries, though their foreign ventures tend to be less important than their domestic activity. They have, so to speak, fewer eggs than the majors, and they put them in fewer baskets.

Large independents can be further divided into two categories, the integrated and the nonintegrated companies. This distinction is an important one: companies such as Signal, Ashland, and Murphy have fully integrated operations. They differ from the majors in that their refining and marketing operations are restricted to a single section of the United States. Like the majors, their assets are spread over production, transportation, refining, and marketing, and their income is drawn from both upstream and downstream activity. The nonintegrated large independents, such as Superior, have limited their activity to exploration and production, which both absorb their capital and provide their income. Like the majors and the large integrated independents, they have sufficient capital to undertake long and costly projects abroad and in domestic offshore areas.

The independents of intermediate size are, as a group, more narrowly committed to domestic activity than large independents. Many of them invested some funds abroad when leases or concessions could be obtained on terms they could meet, but their activity has been largely limited to the contiguous states. In terms of forms of corporate organization and control, the intermediates are a mixed lot. Some of them, like the Midland, Texas, corporations of John Hendrix, John Cox, and Clayton Williams, Jr., are privately held, though most of them are incorporated for legal purposes. Other intermediates, such as Anderson Petroleum of Denver, Tesoro Petroleum of San Antonio, and the Adobe, MGF, and Flag-Redfern corporations of Midland, have been controlled by a relatively small number of large stockholders.

A few of the intermediates, like Tesoro, are fully integrated; most are not. Like the majors and large independents, they have often invested in transportation and processing operations, but these facilities are usually located in a relatively small number of locations. Thus, to a greater extent than either the large independents or the majors, the intermediates obtain their income from the sale of oil and gas. They may also sell equity in their companies, borrow from financial institutions, and sell interests in their ventures and programs to other independents and to investors outside the oil industry. Their sources of capital are generally the same as those of small independents, with whom they share appeal to tax-motivated investors. Like the large independents, all the intermediates have sizable professional staffs. In some instances, however, they prefer to limit the size of their organizations by paying retaining and other fees to consulting geologists, landmen, and attorneys. In either case, the principal financial and personnel decisions are typically made by the chief executive officer, who is commonly the company founder. Intermediates are less likely than large independents to delegate responsibility and authority.

It is considerably more difficult to generalize about the thousands of small independents. Over the sixty-year span of this study, there were a wide variety of types of small independents and many distinctive approaches to business. Some small independents were merely mail order promoters who peddled dreams of quick riches to gullible and greedy investors. This type of independent has appeared with every upswing in the fortunes of the oil industry and disappeared during subsequent contractions, as well as during sporadic legal crackdowns. In the interval, such small operators prey on the victims of oil fever; they create a widespread and unfavorable image of promoters that is detrimental to the legitimate promoter. For the latter, the solicitation of outside funds from tax-motivated investors has long been a means of reducing risk in exploration projects. Commonly, the small independent who promotes a drilling or development deal contributes his managerial and entrepreneurial skills while the investors assume some or even all of the direct costs of the venture. When he "promotes" a deal in this fashion, the legitimate small independent provides the basket and gathers eggs from others to fill it.

For decades the most numerous independents were the driller-promoters who owned drilling rigs, acquired leases, promoted deals, drilled wells, and managed whatever production resulted from their ventures. From Pennsylvania during the nineteenth century to Texas during the first half of the twentieth century, many an independent started as a driller-promoter; men like Sid Richardson, Ford Chapman, and Aere "Peanuts" Bradford drilled the lion's share of wildcat wells and, hence, of dry holes as well. Some of them, like Richardson and Chapman, were highly successful; others, like Bradford, simply made a comfortable living. As a group, the driller independents have been the legendary figures of the industry, the much-acclaimed wildcatters who have captured popular imagination.

Less colorful and seldom studied are the members of a more recent group within the industry, the scientifically and technically trained small independents. Beginning with the geologists in the late twenties and continuing with the engineers and financiers of subsequent decades, these independents applied their professional skills to the development of highly specific and narrowly limited opportunities. In the Permian Basin, for example, William Y. Penn became known as the King of Pecos County because of his successful work in the complex geological formations of that area. Similarly, W. W. West carried out four decades of successful exploration in a small part of Runnels County. Many such specialists started small but grew as their skills brought them substantial production. John L. Cox of Midland, for example, used engineering knowledge to extract commercially profitable oil from the difficult formations of the Spraberry Trend; Earle M. Craig, Jr., and others with training in economics and finance applied financial strategy and analysis of economic trends to build prosperous businesses through management of production. Beginning during the Depression, specialists accounted for an increasing proportion of small independent activity and an increasing proportion of those who graduated into intermediate ranks. As the petroleum industry has grown steadily more scientific and technical, scientists and technicians have become a larger segment of the independent ranks.[8]

Regardless of their size or skills, the inescapable reality for all independents is the dry hole. It is entirely possible for an investment of hundreds of thousands or millions of dollars to be a total loss. It may not return a single dollar. Moreover, if something dire and unexpected happens — if, for example, the would-be oil well yields only thousands of barrels of brine — it may be necessary to spend even more money cleaning up a losing venture. Nor does a well have to be bone-dry to be a financial calamity. If an operator drills a wildcat well that produces only a thousand cubic feet of gas per day, that gas will not pay his cost of drilling and operating the well. It would be, to say the least, highly unlikely that any company would agree to buy so little gas, let alone build gathering lines to the well. But having found that gas, the operator may be obliged by contract terms to drill more gas wells. He has something worse than a dry hole.

Even with all the highly sophisticated technology at the disposal of an oil prospector today, oilmen must accept these risks to find new oil. It remains true that only the drilled test confirms the presence of petroleum and its quantity. Many a dry hole has been drilled in a producing field, in the middle of producing wells; unexpected anomalies of underground formations are commonplace. In oil exploration, every field is different from the next, every new well distinct from the last. That is what makes exploration a high-risk business. A dry hole cannot be turned into a bonanza producer; it cannot be peddled at a discount, sold at a loss, or put to some other profitable use. Its cost, like that of the Broadway play that never opens or the unreleased Hollywood film, is borne by the operator and investors: a painful discovery for many fledgling participants in oil deals. The independent whose exploration results in a dry hole cannot pass its cost along to consumers.

Because no two oil or gas wells are exactly alike in geology or drilling conditions, exploration costs of individual tests differ widely. Since World

War II, moreover, the variable costs of exploration have been increasingly high. The expenses of leasing properties, drilling wells, and completing them for production have increased steadily, raising the ante to the point that oil is universally a high-stakes game. At the same time, the typical small independent's fixed costs — what it costs him to run his business by renting an office, hiring a secretary, and paying the telephone bill — may be exceedingly low. Depending on the individual independent's scale of operations, the fixed costs of operation may be so low as to have no significant bearing on his business strategy. Some large and intermediate independents have their own office buildings, hundreds of employees, fleets of company vehicles, and all the visible trappings of modern corporate affluence. Whether such bigness is an asset in finding oil is debatable: larger scale does not necessarily increase success at finding oil, and large and small operators alike drill dry holes. In oil exploration it is doubtful that conventional theories of economies of scale can be generally applied.

The independent who is successful at exploration and retains ownership of his properties is a producer of petroleum. As a producer his business assumptions are more akin to the economic assumptions of the conventional manufacturer than is characteristic in exploration. Variable costs, for example, are not as high in production as in exploration; fixed costs, in the form of equipment, gathering lines, and storage facilities, may come to a substantial sum, depending on the size of producing properties and the producer's management of them. The risks in exploration are, therefore, significantly different from those in production. There is little likelihood that a producer will ever lose all of his investment, but there is always the possibility that the return he realizes on producing properties will not measure up to the return he might receive on other types of investments. It is possible that the payout period will be long and that production investments, such as those in stripper wells, will be returned so slowly as to require considerable financial skill to plan. In production, managerial skills are applicable to business operations and economies of scale are possible.

The typical independent oilman is engaged in both exploration and production, but unlike a manufacturer of finished goods, in neither area does he have significant control over either the quality of his product or his market. He cannot change a well that produces heavy sour crude into one producing light sweet crude commanding a better price. He sells his oil or gas at the price set by its purchasers, usually the major oil companies or gas purchasers; he himself cannot determine price. He cannot be sure the oil or gas he discovers will be purchased at all; since 1981, for example, many gas producers in the Southwest have been subject to severe curtailments by purchasers. The independent does not even exercise complete control over the quantity of petroleum he can produce. He is subject to natural limitations upon what he can extract from a given well. Practically speaking, when the independent wishes to increase his production, he has to find new oil. He cannot double his production to respond to a rising market without finding new oil or undertaking costly programs to enhance production from his properties. If he finds a bonanza, regulatory agencies and purchasers may keep him from producing at peak capacity. If he responds to a declining market by shutting down production, neighboring lease owners may drain petroleum from his property as they continue to produce their wells. His contractual obligations to partners and royalty owners may commit him to full-scale production.

The limitations of the independent's control over his product and its market mean that competition among independents is of a substantially different character than competition in conventional manufacturing and sales. Independents compete for geological prospects — leads or ideas on where and how to explore for oil — and for promising land, leasable for exploration. But they mainly compete for capital for new ventures, capital beyond what their own income generates. They compete for the funds other independents wish to invest outside their own ventures; they compete for the dollars of other tax-motivated investors; and they compete for loan funds available from financial institutions. The large and intermediate independents who form public companies compete for dollars in the securities markets. This generalized competition for capital reflects the high risk of independent ventures, exploration in particular. The typical small independent shares out risk by securing most, if not all, of the costs of drilling exploratory wells from investors. His own funds, produced by the sale of oil and gas, are used to secure prospects and leases, to pay the small overhead expenses of ventures, and to pay his share of the costs of developing producing properties. The successful independent usually invests his surplus capital in the ventures of other independents to increase his "exposure" and spread his risks; he also uses surplus revenues to increase his inventory of leases, as a basis for further exploration work. Given the real possibility of a total loss in a single exploration venture, independents rarely drill "straight up," assuming all of the costs. Even development projects, including drilling in proven areas and secondary recovery projects, are undertaken only with other investors, who absorb some of the costs and risks. Like the operators, these investors commonly finance development costs with loans from banks and other financial institutions.[9]

While intermediate-sized independents have been raising an increasing amount of capital through public funds in recent years, most independents still raise the bulk of the money for their projects within the oil and gas community, in the business circles to which they belong. Understandably, the independent whose success at business is known

in his community has an advantage in competing for the money of investors and banks. An independent who has been successful over long periods
often has his own circle of preferred investors who regularly buy into
his projects. Belonging to such a circle not only affords access to capital
but also diminishes the risk of investing capital, the risk faced by anyone
in letting someone else use his money; the members of a circle know
one another's character, resources, methods of doing business, and past
business history. In an arena of high risk, they rely on one another's
judgment.

The economic realities of the world of the independent oilman thus
present considerable contrast to modern capitalism as practiced by Exxon,
DuPont, and General Motors. Seen beside the industrial giants, the small
independent, with his small-scale operations and his distinctive approach
to conducting ventures, seems a historical anachronism, a reversion to
the preindustrial world of fifteenth-century Venice or seventeenth-century
Holland. In the context of small business, the small independent oilman
is an anomaly. Like the large transportation and manufacturing corporations, the activity of the independent is technologically complex and
capital-intensive. Like the smaller businesses that still proliferate in the
service sector of the American economy, the operations of the small independent oilman are high-risk, owner-operated, and nonmanagerial. The
business world of the independent oilman is both traditional and modern,
competitive and cooperative; it was so in the twenties and it remains
so today.

2: WILDCATTERS AND TRENDOLOGISTS

There have been few times when the economic future of the petroleum industry seemed as rosy as it did in 1920. As Lord Curzon's famous statement that "the Allies floated to victory on a wave of oil" reflected, World War I demonstrated the importance of oil in international affairs. Vital in war, oil was just as essential in peacetime, for the age of the automobile was under way.[1] Whether enough oil could be found to meet the burgeoning demand was far less certain. That uncertainty made the twenties a decade of unprecedented exploration and speculation in oil. Big companies grew bigger, small companies proliferated, and wildcatters of every description searched avidly for oil.

Highly publicized warnings that the United States was running out of oil indirectly encouraged the search for new oil fields. In 1908 David T. Day, director of the Petroleum Division of the U.S. Geological Survey, warned that the nation might have no more than 10 to 25 billion barrels of recoverable oil reserves. This early warning was repeated in 1919 by Van H. Manning, director of the U.S. Bureau of Mines, who estimated that domestic oil production would peak within five years. Statistics added credibility to such dire predictions, for production was increasing faster than the industry could replace reserves. Between 1911 and 1921, for example, production rose 145 percent, but reserves increased only 56 percent. In 1920 production rose 17.2 percent over 1919 levels, but reserves rose only 7.5 percent. In 1924 those who feared that the nation would run out of oil in the near future succeeded in pushing President Calvin Coolidge to establish the Federal Oil Conservation Board. The apprehension that the country would use up oil vital to meet future need became an enduring aspect of federal oil policy.[2]

The widespread belief in an approaching supply crisis and the higher prices it would bring prompted investment in exploration, even among oilmen who did not share the federal government's alarmist opinions. After all, even if the worst fears of future oil shortages were discounted, there was no doubt that demand for refined products would continue to increase and that refineries would need greater quantities of crude oil as feedstock. In the relatively long run, it was likely that independents who found oil could dispose of it in a seller's market. This optimism was reinforced by experience. In 1920, for example, producers received $2 to $3 a barrel for crude produced from the Mid-Continent and Gulf Coast regions, and as much as $6 for Pennsylvania crude.[3] Such record prices, though they lasted but a brief time, provided experienced independents with additional revenues for exploration and attracted new entrants to the independent sector of the industry.

By contrast with the present, the business world in which the independent oilman of 1920 moved was one of freewheeling operation. The man who became an independent oil operator in 1920 could join the search for oil with very little capital. Cable tool rigs sufficient to drill shallow wells in many areas were inexpensive to purchase and operate; vast unexplored reaches of the Southwest and the Rocky Mountains contained hundreds of thousands of acres that hard-pressed farmers and ranchers were willing to lease for rock-bottom prices. Few oilmen outside the scientific avant garde of the major companies troubled to make use of new and expensive apparatus to find oil in 1920.[4] Nor was it necessary for the independent to make frequent visits to attorneys or accountants. Whether or not most business deals were, as folklore has it, sealed with a handshake, the independent of 1920 did not design his business deals to fit a jungle of legal tangles, regulatory red tape, and complex tax laws. State regulation of oil was in its infancy in such places as Texas and Oklahoma; most states did not regulate the industry at all. The operator who did not lease federal land or raise capital by mail was unaffected by federal regulation — save for the possibility of paying income tax in a good year. There were indications during the twenties that this business environment would change — that prospecting at greater depths would mean higher operating costs, that applied science would be increasingly useful in lowering the risks of exploration and production, that regulation would come to affect operations — but such portents had little effect on the average independent oilman's daily operations and immediate plans.

The individual wishing to enter the independent oil business could expect to raise the capital he needed in a wide variety of ways. If he had personal assets he could offer as collateral for a commercial loan, he might raise his initial stake by that means. R. R. Penn, a young Dallas newspaper reporter, called his wife from Corsicana in 1921, telling her to borrow on "everything but her wedding ring" and bring him the funds for a promising deal.[5] Apart from flirtation with individual bankruptcy, this method of capital formation had the liability of yielding only limited amounts and being desirable only for a lucky sort of prospector. If a man had enough capital, a common way of building up funds was to buy leases on cheap acreage and resell them at a profit. A prospector interested in a specific area, for example, might lease a "spread," a large block of acreage, and sell off portions of it to major companies or other operators interested in having a test made for oil. The money raised by selling parts of a spread could cover the costs of drilling a wildcat well. When low-cost acreage was available, this method of financing wild-catting worked well for the man who started out with a little money.[6]

Even a man with next to no funds of his own could enter the oil busi-ness if his prose style was eloquent enough to wring funds from other people. Here the man who could offer fabulous opportunities to the out-side investor came into his own, especially if his projects escaped the notice of the United States postal authorities. The new attention given the strategic and economic importance of oil, the popular magazine stories of "black gold" and fortunes made overnight, the postwar get-rich-quick mentality, all served the promoter of oil ventures, whether legitimate or not. One journalist, commenting upon the superabundance of oil pro-motion schemes in 1923, observed that oil stocks seemed to have "become the psychological magnet for that portion of the investing public that likes to gamble. They provide the quickest and surest route to a thrill, financial and emotional."[7] Legitimate and less than legitimate com-panies alike took names calculated to appeal to the gambling instinct. Thus, when the oil and gas fields of the Texas Panhandle opened up, among the 110 corporations doing business in Hutchinson County were the Double Five Company, the Straight Eight Oil Company, the Lucky Ten Oil Company, and the Magic Eighty Oil Company.[8]

Promoters approached all varieties of potential investors, but wealthy persons ignorant of oil—doctors and lawyers and their widows—were favorite clients. Sharp promoters would send potential investors carefully doctored photographs of gushers and brochures full of visions of fabulous wealth. One promoter told the Yale graduates of the class of 1923:

> How would you like to get started by investing $100 in an oil company and have it later worth over $50,000? If you had invested in The Texas Company when it was first organized you would today have an investment worth over $50,000. . . . History repeats itself. There will be another oil investment which will return just as much money. . . . Your chance to ride with us and be with us as we accumulate a momentum of success is now.[9]

Some promoters took prospective investors on oil field tours, filling them with "cold lunch and hot air." Others stuck strictly to the mails, as longtime *Oil Weekly* columnist H. H. King recalled:

> There was a big promoter . . . he would send out a mass of letters with wild promises, and the postman would come in and just dump a huge stack of return envelopes contain-ing cash, money orders, and checks, and he would sit down there—he and that girl, that's all he had for an office—and

open that mail and throw the envelopes in the waste paper basket.

They lived high on a cash basis, come easy, go easy.[10]

All did not go easily with such dishonest promoters, however, when federal authorities cracked down on postal fraud in 1923. Among those nailed by federal inspectors were Dr. Frederick Cook, who had been given the keys to New York City after he claimed that he had climbed Mount McKinley and beaten Admiral Peary to the North Pole, and promoters Charles Sherwin and Harry Schwarz, organizers of the General Lee Development Interest, who found a would-be descendent of Robert E. Lee, one Robert A. Lee, and had him tell investors, "I would rather lead you and a thousand others to financial independence than to have won Fredericksburg or Chancellorsville." The number of names on promoters' sucker lists astounded federal investigators; one Fort Worth list contained over two million names. Dr. Cook was thought to have sent out over 300,000 letters a month, from which he grossed roughly $2 million in 1922.[11] The American public was indeed ready to invest in oil, but not all promoters intended to find it.

Those who raised capital with the genuine intention of looking for oil could choose from a wide variety of unexplored regions of interest to the oil prospector. Among the relatively untested areas in 1920 was the vast expanse of Texas west of Abilene. During the previous decade oil discoveries in North Texas and West Central Texas caused oil booms in many a small town and made many an independent rich. By 1920 these areas had been active for several years; land was largely leased, and the oil pools accessible with the current technology had been found. But to the west it was a different story. Though scientists differed on the region's promise for exploration, oilmen knew that there was at least some oil in the arid reaches of West Texas and southeastern New Mexico; there were oil seeps in the area, and small production had been found near the Reeves County town of Toyah. No one, however, had found any production of commercially attractive size.[12]

As a region, in 1920, the Permian Basin did not seem a likely place for anyone to make a fortune, in oil or other endeavors. Taking its name from the Permian rock formations found within it, the region was a considerable distance from major population centers. Except for isolated army forts, there were no sizable settlements in the central part of the Permian Basin until the Texas Pacific Railroad laid its tracks and gave birth to town sites in the early 1880s. Thereafter, Colorado City, Big Spring, Midland, and Pecos emerged as local agribusiness centers, joining San Angelo, which had grown slowly around Fort Concho until the completion of the Kansas City, Mexico, and Orient Railroad connected it with outside markets. There was little industry in the region other than railroad shops in Big Spring and San Angelo.

Before 1920 regional prosperity depended upon the vagaries of weather and commodity markets. On any terms, it was hard to eke out a living on the arid terrain. Few farmers and ranchers hung on for long; most of those who did were desperately poor by 1920. The extreme bleakness of their circumstances spawned grim humor:

> In the days before oil was discovered in West Texas, a traveling man stopped for the night at a dry-land ranch near Wink. . . . He became more and more puzzled as to how the little ranch paid its way. At last he ventured the question, "How in the world do you make a go of things at all?"
>
> Indicating the hired man, who was sitting at the far end of the supper table, the host replied, "You see that fella there? Well, he works for me and I can't pay him. In two years he gets the ranch. Then I work for him till I get it back."[13]

In the light of existing knowledge on oil finding, the Permian Basin did not look any more attractive as a source of wealth from oil than it did from ranching or farming. Most professional geologists did not think the Permian rock formations, thick throughout the basin, were likely to yield oil in quantity. Geologists, however, really knew very little about the region. Even the University of Texas geologists who surveyed its minerals listed the resources of a great many Permian Basin counties as "unknown." Nor would it be easy to find out what they were, for the methods and techniques employed by the new discipline of petroleum geology were not readily usable in West Texas.[14]

Much of the science of oil prospecting in 1920 depended upon the analysis of geological structures that could be mapped from evidence on the earth's surface. In 1917, J. A. Udden, professor of geology at the University of Texas, attempted to apply the technique in West Texas. Studying what remained of the ancient Marathon Mountains in Brewster County, he suggested that an underground fold of rock might run from the Marathon area through Pecos County and on into Upton and Reagan counties. Overlying this Marathon Fold, Udden noted, were relatively undisturbed layers of rock — red beds and Comanche limestone — which he thought would make "excellent cover" for an oil pool.[15] These same top layers of rock that Udden thought likely to trap oil, however, effectively obscured underground strata from the geologist who worked with surface mapping. In many parts of West Texas there were few surface features of use to prospecting. Indeed, shifting sand dunes in parts of Crane, Ward, and Winkler counties in Texas and Lea County, New Mexico, made accurate surface mapping impossible.[16] For the most part, the Permian Basin offered limited scope for use of the best-developed geological prospecting technique of the early twenties.

To West Texas landowners struggling to survive the worst drought in memory, Udden's suggestion that there might be oil under their arid land offered hope of financial salvation. It prompted a number of searches for oil, conducted by persons with little experience in either science or oil. The first notably successful effort was initiated by several of the town fathers of Colorado City in Mitchell County, located on the eastern edge of the Permian Basin. Mitchell County's oil fields produced in modestly profitable quantities, but they were nowhere near as prolific as oil fields being developed elsewhere.[17] Still, the widespread publicity given Mitchell County production encouraged imaginative oilmen to try exploration in West Texas.

Were a prospector to consider looking for oil in the Permian Basin, there was a good economic incentive for finding it an attractive place to explore: acreage could be had in large blocks, easily leased at stunningly low prices. Because economically viable ranches were of necessity large, lease agents could obtain huge blocks of acreage through negotiations with a handful of landowners. Landowners, willing to settle for almost any sum that would help them stave off financial disaster and keep their land, accepted as little as 10 cents an acre for leasing their property.[18] Cheap acreage appealed not only to the independent oil operator looking to build a spread from which he could finance a test but also to traders and speculators in leases. On the heels of the Mitchell County discoveries, C. W. Webster and J. W. Grant, both Fort Worth brokers, did a lively business in West Texas properties. Grant, for example, leased 31,440 acres of the T. G. Hendrick ranch in Winkler County for 10 cents an acre in 1925.[19] Not even cheap acreage and aggressive salesmanship, however, could give the Permian Basin a high priority in Southwestern oil exploration in advance of discovery of an oil field of great size and profitability. That discovery came in Reagan County, with the opening of the Big Lake oil field.

It fell to a small-town lawyer with time on his hands to launch exploration in the area, for there was no strong scientific or practical reason to think there was oil in Reagan County. In 1919 young Rupert Ricker, newly discharged from the United States Army, returned to his hometown of Big Lake, Texas, to practice law. With ample leisure in his fledgling practice, Ricker happened to read Udden's speculation about the Marathon Fold. How tempting it was to think that under the desolate Reagan County countryside there might lie a fortune in oil, for there seemed little prospect of making a fortune practicing law in the dusty West Texas village. Ricker convinced himself and several friends that they should apply for a lease on a vast tract of 431,360 acres owned by the University of Texas, which held the major part of the land in Reagan County, and interest an oil firm in exploring for oil. He obtained the preliminary state lease forms, completed the necessary paperwork, and began to look for $43,136, which, at the rate of 10 cents an acre, was what a lease on the university land would cost.[20]

When he visited Fort Worth, then the oil center for North and West Texas, however, Ricker found that other people could not readily be brought to share his conviction that land in Reagan County had to be good for something. Ricker could show a prospective investor a chance to lease a huge block of acreage at a low price, but he could offer little else. There never had been any sign of oil in Reagan County; there was no nearby production, and there were no surface structures or other concrete scientific evidence indicating the presence of oil. Neither major companies nor Fort Worth independents were interested in Ricker's proposal to sell his wonderful idea for $50,000. But by luck, Ricker ran into an old army buddy, Frank Pickrell, on the streets of Fort Worth. Pickrell and a wealthy dry goods merchant, Haymon Krupp, came to Fort Worth to try their luck at oil promotion. Ignorant of informed opinion on the Permian Basin, they decided Ricker's scheme could be promoted as well as any other; they bought his lease applications and planned to make money by selling small parcels of leases to investors.[21]

When Krupp was unsuccessful in selling leases, however, the partners decided they would have to drill a rank wildcat well in order to make their venture more credible to investors. To finance the test, they issued stock in a new corporation, the Texon Oil and Land Company. But even at a time when the American public seemed mad to buy oil stock, Texon's shares did not move readily. In 1921, Pickrell and Krupp decided to sell "certificates of interest" in future production from their acreage to raise funds. Among the small investors they found to buy into this scheme were some ladies in a Catholic sodality in New York; the ladies, perhaps not overly persuaded of success by Pickrell's sales pitch, told him to name the test well after Saint Rita, patron saint of the impossible and hopeless.[22] By hand-to-mouth methods, the promoters of the Texon Oil and Land Company raised money for a project no experienced oilman would touch. Though they hired a geologist to select a site for their test, they staked their location near the railroad in order to cut the cost of transporting material. And on May 28, 1923, these amateur oilmen learned that their test, Santa Rita No. 1, was gushing oil.[23] Overnight, what had been foolhardy became visionary.

Unfortunately for the managers of Texon Oil and Land, their financial problems were greatly magnified by their success, for they now had to raise enough money to go ahead with development of their holdings. The money would not come from the sale of the newly discovered oil; their discovery emerged as a modest-sized producer of roughly 100 barrels a day, and even if Texon could find a purchaser willing to pay the prevailing Mid-Continent price, the income would be little more than $100 a day. Texon's only access to market from remote Big Lake, moreover, was by railroad, and that meant facing relatively high shipping costs. What Texon needed was a big oil purchaser to assist in financing development, to undertake pipeline construction, and to buy what Big Lake could produce. Pickrell, Krupp, and their friends had to persuade experienced oilmen that Reagan County was the site of something big.

Unlike Rupert Ricker, Pickrell and Krupp could at least show prospective investors a producing well. They soon found, however, that a 100-barrel well was not sufficient to overturn years of oil industry skepticism about the profitability of Permian Basin ventures. Gulf, The Texas Company, Humble, Magnolia, and Sinclair all looked at Texon's find, but none found it tempting, for a variety of reasons. Though Texon found oil, the principal question posed by the discovery was that of where to drill next on the company's vast tract. Contemporary science offered scant help, for surface features yielded few clues to underground formation.[24] For this reason, most oilmen viewed prospects at Big Lake as more than ordinarily risky. Worse yet, Big Lake's remote location meant that the cost of drilling would be higher than in other places; it would be expensive to guess wrong. If much oil was found, hundreds of miles of costly pipelines would have to be built to arrange efficient transport. From a major-company perspective, only evidence that Santa Rita No. 1 was the discovery well of a big oil field — a field that would yield millions of barrels of oil in a short time — would justify such an expensive project. Pickrell and Krupp thus found it as difficult to secure capital to develop their vast leases as it had been to find the money to drill a test.

Turned down by major companies, Pickrell and Krupp searched the independent ranks for participants in Big Lake development and eventually interested Pittsburgh independent Michael L. Benedum in their project. Benedum, whose remarkable success at wildcatting was well known, had taken part in the spectacular Ranger-Desdemona boom in West Central Texas several years earlier, but he had gone several years without a major discovery; he was tempted to try his luck at Big Lake. The directors of his own Transcontinental Oil Company did not share his urge to gamble on long odds, so Benedum sidestepped them by forming a new company, the Big Lake Oil Company, to do business with Texon. Big Lake and Texon worked out an agreement to cooperate in developing Texon's acreage that involved an exchange of cash and properties that one observer compared to the tossing of "plates in the hands of a Japanese juggler," and Big Lake hired the Richmond Drilling Company to start work. The initial results were anything but promising. Just as the Big Lake Oil Company seemed about to exhaust its credit with the regional junk dealers from whom it bought secondhand materials, its ninth and eleventh tests came in, with production of thousands of barrels of high-quality crude per day.[25] Benedum, Pickrell, Krupp, and their friends were jubilant: their long shot had proved to industry skeptics that the Permian Basin contained at least one major oil field.

Once Big Lake's great wells came in, the field attracted national attention, not only because its production was so large, but also because the field was amazingly profitable to its developers. In typical independent fashion, the Texon and Big Lake companies made their capital investment go as far as possible by keeping costs low. They obtained their land cheaply, and they developed prolific production at relatively shallow depths. Since they drilled near the center of their sixty-four section tract, they avoided the expense of competitive drilling with other companies along lease lines. Better yet, the timing of their development coincided with a period of strong industry demand for the high-quality crude they produced. In 1923, when Texon made its discovery, high-grade production from the Mexia-Corsicana fields was at a peak. Major-company purchasers like Humble, which had constant need of large amounts of high-grade crude to meet supply contracts with the Standard Oil Company (New Jersey), enjoyed an abundance of oil from that source. But by the time Big Lake's giant wells came in, production in Mexia-Corsicana had tapered off, and the most plentiful crude oil on the market was heavy, less desirable Arkansas crude.[26] Just as major purchasers began looking for new sources of refinery stock, the Texon and Big Lake companies brought in a big field.

Before major company purchasers could act on the new bonanza, a large Oklahoma independent, Marland Oil, entered the Big Lake picture. Quick to see that bigger firms would be eager to purchase such prolific and desirable production, E. W. Marland set up a subsidiary firm, the Reagan County Purchasing Company; in October 1924, that firm agreed to buy Texon and Big Lake oil at the rate of 10,000 barrels a day for the first year and 20,000 barrels a day thereafter. It would pay the prevailing Mid-Continent price for high-gravity crude. Marland then made a deal with crude-hungry Humble: the Reagan County Purchasing Company would sell its Big Lake crude to the major company for what it had paid plus a gathering fee. Once this agreement was reached, Humble began to construct the first major pipeline outlet from the Permian Basin to the Gulf Coast.

For Texon and Big Lake, the arrangement eliminated the problem of marketing production in a remote new region, a problem other wildcatters often face but seldom resolve so easily, and ensured a steady flow of capital for further field development. But for the Marland subsidiary, as well as for the Texon and Big Lake companies, the key to long-run profit making was to be the part of the agreement that tied the price paid for Big Lake oil to the average Mid-Continent price for high-gravity crude. Half a dozen years later, subsequent Permian Basin discoveries would reduce the posted regional prices to levels well below those prevailing in the Mid-Continent producing area as a whole, but in the agreement, Humble had committed itself to purchase Big Lake oil at premium prices till April 1, 1940! With good reason, one industry observer called the terms of the agreement "the most satisfactory ones ever realized by independent producers on a major crude deal." Humble came to view the deal as the worst one the company ever made.[27]

The profits that Permian sandy lime yielded for the owners of the Big Lake oil field not only caused major companies to reevaluate Permian Basin prospects but also encouraged wildcatting for comparable bonanzas throughout the Permian Basin. Independent wildcatters from older oil regions — California, Oklahoma, Pennsylvania, and West Virginia — suddenly appeared in West Texas to try their luck. The greatest volume of wildcatting, of course, took place as near as prospectors could get to existing Reagan County production; given the size of the block held by the Big Lake and Texon companies, there was no close-in acreage. Within five years of Texon's original discovery, hopeful wildcatters drilled fifty-eight dry holes in Reagan County, but no one struck a bonanza in oil. No one located a production trend running from the Big Lake field beyond the holdings of the Big Lake and Texon oil companies. Prospectors broadened the scope of exploration to include adjoining Sterling, Glasscock, Upton, and Crockett counties, and in Crockett County oil was discovered on the L. P. Powell ranch, sixteen miles southeast of Big Lake, in 1925.[28]

Like the Big Lake discovery, the Crockett County find was an independent venture whose antecedents included amateur exposure to science and the availability of cheap acreage. Beyond this, the similarity of the two ventures ended. The discovery well on the Powell ranch was not the work of a conventionally organized oil firm; it was the result of a bizarre promotional scheme conducted by mail. Chester R. Bunker, a Fort Worth oil promoter who published a promotional magazine called *Western World,* offered new and renewal subscribers an interest in a wildcat venture managed by his World Oil Company on properties leased by his Marathon Fold Drilling Club and Marathon Fold Lease Club. Having leased 2900 acres of the Powell ranch, Bunker started a test, selling leases on adjoining acreage to raise additional operating funds. Bunker was not an experienced oilman, and the Powell lease had little allure for veteran wildcatters, but Bunker had both funds and a legal obligation to drill a well. Whether or not he expected it, Chester Bunker found oil.[29]

The World Oil discovery well came in at a meager twenty-five barrels a day, disappointing compared to the prolific Big Lake wells but strong enough to encourage a frenzied lease play in Crockett County. Humble, Gulf, and Roxana (Shell) purchased leases at $100 an acre in the vicinity of the discovery well; C. W. Webster, who had originally sold the Powell acreage to Bunker, peddled leases on 150 acres adjoining Bunker's well to major companies for more than $200,000. In all, more than $5 million changed hands in lease and royalty trading in Crockett County during the two weeks after the discovery well sprayed oil. Shortly thereafter, Chester Bunker's World Oil Company sold its Crockett County holdings to Humble and Marland for $1.4 million. The major companies were determined not to repeat the mistake they had made in 1923 when they passed up the chance to enter Big Lake development. Unfortunately for Humble, Gulf, and Roxana, subsequent field development showed that they had overreacted. Crockett County wells in the World field were relatively small producers, the oil produced was of lower gravity than that of Big Lake, and wells tended to produce great quantities of sulphur water with oil, an expensive complication.[30] But Chester Bunker had made his profit — on the sale of properties rather than oil.

Chester Bunker's World Oil discovery shows that the early sale of promising property can be as good an independent profit strategy as selling oil, and it is also a reasonably typical example of the cooperative roles played — in the twenties as in the eighties — by major companies and independents in new producing regions. Major companies like Humble were happy to let wildcatters like Chester Bunker turn a profit; they let him and his investors assume the risks of buying acreage and drilling a test, in the absence of compelling scientific evidence. Once the major companies acquired an interest in an area, they assumed the high costs of applying science and technology. By the time Humble and Marland bought out Chester Bunker, scientists employed by major companies had advanced beyond surface mapping to two new techniques, geophysical testing and subsurface geological analysis. Geophysical data, gathered from the use of such devices as the torsion balance, the refraction seismograph, and the magnetometer, could locate subsurface irregularities in rock formations where oil might collect. Gathering geophysical data was time-consuming and expensive, but by the end of the twenties such large companies as Amerada, Humble, Roxana, Gypsy, and Midwest Exploration were using geophysics as an aid to determining what acreage to lease in Lea and Roosevelt counties, New Mexico. Subsurface geological analysis involved the microscopic study of cuttings or core samples taken from drilling; geologists used paleontological evidence to identify, correlate, and map underground formations. Major companies like Humble perfected the use of subsurface analysis in the twenties, but there was a drawback to its use: the rock cuttings necessary for study had to come from drilling, either for oil or for core samples, and correlation required a number of tests in an area.[31] Where there had been no drilling, there could be no subsurface analysis. In 1925 neither scientific technique was as useful to major companies as the optimistic independent wildcatter who was willing to "prove up" leases by assuming the risk and expense of drilling a test. For this reason, the work of independents in the twenties effectively led major companies to oil in the Permian Basin and many other regions.

While major companies would incur the expense of applying science in especially promising areas — indicated by independent exploration — independent wildcatters of the twenties were, by and large, rather casual about the use of science in oil prospecting. Large independents like Michael Benedum regularly employed geologists, but smaller fry were unlikely to pay for a scientist's services, unless they wished to impress investors. The smaller independents seldom gathered geophysical data or had staff trained in subsurface analysis; such refinements used up capital that was needed to lease properties and drill for oil. At a time when overhead costs were low, moreover, many an independent did business quite successfully without the risk-cutting aid of science. The small operator did not report to a board of directors with a sheaf of scientific data to persuade them to take on a project; he was usually responsible to few investors and able to follow his hunches. Thus the early Permian Basin oil discoveries in the Big Lake field, the Shipley field in Ward County, and the Hendrick field in Winkler County were the result of random drilling and fortunate hunches.[32]

Because independents did not rush to apply science to exploration, much of the exploratory activity that took place in the Permian Basin and elsewhere in the late twenties was the result of geographical, rather than geological, speculation — known as yardstick geology or trendology. Those who let trendology be their guide in effect measured inches on county maps and drew straight lines between the oil discoveries. This procedure was no more scientific than the creekology — exploration on creek banks — that had guided the Pennsylvania wildcatters of half a century earlier. As Roy Westbrook explained his test site in Winkler County, "I noticed that the place where I was drilling was just about as far from the Pecos River as the Big Lake field." Majors and independents alike leased acreage on the basis of geographical guesses about trends of underground oil accumulation, for in many parts of the Permian Basin there was little else on which to base a decision. Discoveries made by independents in 1925 and 1926 seemed to indicate a trend of production extending from Upton County through Crane County and into Ector County, roughly southeast to northwest. Accordingly, leasing activity followed a northwestward direction into southeastern New Mexico. When the great Yates and Hendrick fields were discovered in 1926, those who studied county maps envisioned a trend running from Pecos and Crockett counties up through Lea and Eddy counties, New Mexico. Lease trading was brisk in this corridor in the late twenties. An incredibly large amount of oil would eventually be produced from fields along these trends; among the oil pools discovered by independents following trends were the Church and Fields in Crane County, the Fuhrman in Andrews County, the Kugle in Ward County, and the Bashara in Winkler County. But cheap acreage and good guesses played a greater part than science in these discoveries. As one journalist remarked, most Permian Basin exploration in the twenties was largely a matter of "shooting in the dark."[33]

When it had been demonstrated that Permian formations could hold profitable amounts of oil, major oil companies began to channel exploration capital into buying leases on great tracts of acreage in various parts of the region. Gulf and Humble were the most extensive purchasers; Gulf picked up gigantic tracts extending in contiguous blocks through Crane, Ector, Ward, and Winkler counties, and Humble leased over two million acres in a number of West Texas counties by 1926. Dixie Oil, a Standard of Indiana subsidiary, leased large tracts in Crockett, Pecos, and Reeves counties, while Pure Oil gambled on acreage farther west in Culberson County. Prices were commonly $1 to $1.25 an acre. Because there was not the slightest chance that they could test all this land in a short time, the majors leased tracts for ten years, rather than three or five, a strategy that would result in unusual opportunities for independents in the mid-thirties, when the leases neared expiration.[34] Despite these mammoth leasing campaigns by major companies, the Permian Basin was so large that independents could still find ample cheap land for lease in all but the busiest areas. The majors' purchases did not shut independents out of the region; indeed, the very size of the tracts the majors leased created opportunities for independents interested in prospecting in the Permian Basin.

Once they had leased great tracts of land, major companies encouraged independents to take the drilling risks that would show what acreage might profitably be developed; they retained the option of purchasing the oil independents found. In turn, independent oilmen looked to major companies for cash, which they received both directly — in the form of dry-hole or bottom-hole money, investments in drilling ventures, income from the sale of crude oil produced, or money from the sale of producing properties — and indirectly, in the form of acreage the independents could sell to raise capital.

The discovery of oil in Upton County by J. P. Johnson and George B. McCamey, independent Fort Worth drilling contractors, offers a good example of this interdependence of majors and independents in the opening of a new oil region. The discovery took place in one of the few parts of the Permian Basin where there was a surface indication of a promising underground structure. Both Marland Oil and Dixie Oil had leased acreage in a checkerboard pattern in the area. George McCamey, believing the area worth testing, approached Marland with an offer to drill a test if the company would "farm out" the necessary acreage to him. Marland agreed to give Johnson and McCamey a three-fourths interest in 1250 acres in return for their undertaking a test; Dixie Oil, as interested as Marland in seeing someone else assume the risk and expense of looking for oil near its property, contributed 480 acres to the project. Johnson and McCamey then proceeded to sell tracts from this acreage to other oil companies to finance drilling. Once they discovered oil, they sold their well to the Republic Production Company, thus avoiding the expense of storage tanks and gathering systems and at the same time acquiring capital for other ventures. The Marland and Dixie Oil companies came away from their subsidy of the venture with proof that their leased acreage was well worth further exploration and development.[35]

The cooperative relationship between major companies and independents with respect to risk taking and venture financing had a direct effect on the level of exploratory activity in the Permian Basin during the late twenties. When major companies bought adjoining leases from independents or donated leases for the wildcatters' projects, and when they offered dry- or bottom-hole money, they financed independent risk taking; when that financial support slackened, exploratory activity declined. In response to a national oversupply of crude oil and falling prices, for example, exploration and development slowed down greatly in Crane and Upton counties in early 1927. Nevertheless, reserve-hungry major companies did not wish to be left out when new flush fields were opened; by midyear, when the Yates and Hendrick fields' development indicated how huge the production of Permian Basin oil pools could be, exploration and its subsidy by major companies picked up throughout the region. Activity continued high until mid-1929, when major companies began to show increasing reluctance to help finance tests that were not of special interest to company geologists.[36] By that time, giant finds had brought the supply of West Texas crude to a level far in excess of pipeline capacity. As crude prices fell, independents active in regional exploration were financially pinched from two directions: their production generated less income that could be directed to new ventures, and opportunities to raise venture capital through cooperation with major companies diminished. The ebb and flow of exploratory activity in the Permian Basin during the late twenties reflected the large measure to which prospectors depended upon major companies.

Most risk capital for independent exploration and development in the Permian Basin and other regions was generated within the petroleum industry, but major companies were not the independents' only source of funds for ventures. As the history of Mike Benedum's participation in the development of the Big Lake field illustrates, independents invested in one another's ventures. Like major companies, independents leased spreads and purchased interests in wells, often with the aim of proving their own acreage or participating in promising areas where they did not drill on their own. With such participation, the individual independent could minimize his risk by spreading capital over a greater number of prospects than he could promote or manage, at the same time increasing his exposure to a greater number of geological opportunities in a region. Thus, when C. P. Watson undertook a wildcat well in Andrews County, he received backing from the Argo Royalty Company, which owned royalty interests in sections adjoining the site of his proposed well. Argo gave Watson part of its interest in one section, retaining eleven thirty-seconds; Watson kept one eighth of what Argo gave him and sold the balance of it to the Rector Oil Company of New York, the Landreth Production Company of Fort Worth, and Barron Kidd, a Midland royalty and lease broker.[37] The independent seeking to raise cash, then, could look to other independents as buyers and investors.

When it came to selling the crude oil they produced, whether in the Permian Basin or elsewhere, the independents' most important customers were major companies. This was especially true in the Permian Basin, which relatively few independent refiners entered. Much of the Permian Basin oil found after 1925 was sour (heavily laced with sulphur) and heavy (of relatively low gravity). Sour crude caused tremendous corrosion problems in pumping equipment, pipelines, and storage facilities. Refiners needed to use special, expensive processes to handle sour crude; heavy crude had a lower yield of gasoline and other light and profitable products. In short, a refiner could not make as great a profit on Permian Basin crude as on crude oils from many other areas. Prices for Permian Basin crude, with the exception of Big Lake production, were among the lowest in the nation in the late twenties and remained so until the late forties. Price, moreover, was not the only gauge of the competitive disadvantage of Permian Basin crude in the marketplace. The region's remoteness from existing population and refining centers meant that purchasers and producers had to meet substantial costs in getting oil to market. After an initial construction spurt in the twenties, major pipeline companies had scant incentive to build and enlarge lines to carry some of the nation's least desirable crude oil. Pipeline outlets were not sufficient to carry all the oil the Permian Basin would normally produce until after World War II, and pipeline proration, the restriction of production to pipeline capacity, was a familiar fact of business life to regional producers.[38] To a greater extent than in other regions, the peculiarities of production in the Permian Basin made regional independents vulnerable to changes in major-company crude oil purchasing policies.

In planning ventures, independents had to weigh regional conditions as well as major-company policies, but apart from such general considerations, independent business strategies exhibited a wide variety of approaches. Promotional ability, attitude toward risk, access to capital,

familiarity with scientific thinking, assessment of narrow local opportunities, and business connections within the petroleum industry all helped
shape the independents' approach to doing business. There was no simple business strategy common to all independent oilmen, no universal
method for making money in a given region at a given time. Thus the
Texon Oil and Land Company, Chester Bunker, and Johnson and
McCamey used three different ways to finance wildcat ventures. Similarly, the Permian Basin operations of two independent oilmen especially
prominent in regional exploration in the late twenties, Edward A.
Landreth of Fort Worth and Robert R. Penn of Dallas, demonstrate
two quite different approaches to business.

Ed Landreth, born in Illinois and raised in Joplin, Missouri, entered
the oil business in Breckenridge, Texas, shortly after the end of World
War I. Sent to the oil town to sell the machinery produced in Joplin
by his brother Will, Landreth caught oil fever and aimed for larger
rewards than his salesman's commission. A large, burly, gregarious man,
Ed Landreth was easy to like, so much so that one of his friends, Breckenridge Walker, sold him a proven lease and then lent him the money
to drill an oil well on it! In short order the well came in, Landreth paid
his creditor, and the newly minted oilman returned to Joplin to raise
more money to acquire additional leases to drill. His aggressive enthusiasm for his prospects spread oil fever through Joplin; local merchants and boyhood friends subscribed to Landreth's venture, which was
organized as a common-law trust. With full control over invested funds,
Landreth purchased unproven acreage and drilled four dry holes. Oil
fever in Joplin subsided into suspicion and mistrust. But Ed Landreth,
though his personal capital was much depleted, was not about to beat
a retreat from oil.[39]
    It is possible that Ed Landreth's Joplin experience led him to be wary
of partners outside the oil industry; in later years he also avoided deals
in which large numbers of investors shared interests. But if he were not
to take in partners, Ed Landreth had to raise venture capital from some
other source. He tried selling shares by mail and then hit upon a way
to raise money through bank loans. For an oilman to get money from
a banker in the twenties was no small achievement. Few banks customarily made loans for oil ventures, whose risky nature was fully appreciated
by prudent bank directors. Those few that did lend money to oilmen
would not accept their major asset, oil-producing properties, as collateral;
bankers knew that there was no reliable way to determine a property's
future production level, that production could decline precipitously in
a short time, and that crude oil prices were notoriously unstable. When
bankers agreed to lend money to an oilman like Ed Landreth, they looked
for collateral above the ground: equipment, like drilling rigs or storage

tanks, or oil in storage.[40] Borrowing from bankers on his equipment
and stored oil became a staple part of Ed Landreth's business strategy
as his operations increased in size.

With equipment he had used near Breckenridge as collateral, Landreth
borrowed to purchase additional leases in Stephens County. The development of these properties during 1921 and 1922, financed by mail order
promotion, made Landreth a handsome profit. He went on to parlay
it into greater gains. With extensive oil production, he approached
Humble with an offer to sell out; Humble accepted his offer, and he
made a substantial gain on the venture. He then turned his attention
to Shackelford County, where the Ibex Oil Company had brought in
a promising discovery well; with capital from his sellout to Humble,
he bought leases from Ibex and drilled the field's second well, which initially produced almost 1700 barrels a day from roughly 3570 feet. The
well also produced up to a million cubic feet of gas a day, so Landreth
built a gasoline plant to extract liquids from the gas; he sold residue
gas to the Lone Star Gas Company. In 1924, having drilled about half
the proven locations on his Ibex leases, opening two new producing
horizons in the process, Landreth sold his wells, undrilled acreage, and
gasoline plant to Phillips Petroleum Corporation for the spectacular price
of $3 million cash and additional payments in oil.[41]

Such a bonanza might have led another businessman to relax, but
it had the reverse effect on Landreth; without hesitation, he bought the
discovery well and 1400 acres in the heart of what became the Noble-
Dyson field in Wilbarger County. Within several weeks, Landreth spent
$2.5 million to become the largest lease owner in the field and to sup-
plant Humble as the dominant producer in the area. He spent the money
he obtained from his Shackelford County sellout on the grand scale of
a major company. After his initial fling at wildcatting, moreover, he
acted like many a major company, buying leases only after another prospector had taken the initial risk and found something promising. Using
several of his own strings of drilling tools and contracting additional work
to other drillers, Landreth completed seventeen wells and pushed his
production up to 3800 barrels a day. Rather than continue development
by drilling the more than seventy additional wells his lease agreements
required and running the risk of dwindling production or dry holes,
Landreth repeated his Ibex coup in 1926 by pulling his Wilbarger County
properties together into the Landreth Production Company, through
which he sold them to Phillips for $3.25 million in cash and an equal
amount to be paid out of production revenue.[42]

The spectacular sellout thus became an essential part of Ed Landreth's
dashing business strategy. With the cash from the Wilbarger County
sale, Landreth paid his creditors and distributed the remaining funds
and properties among his stockholders, all of whom were either employees

or relatives. Landreth himself obtained substantial cash and producing properties. With his cash and with money borrowed from banks in Fort Worth and Chicago, he was ready to look for another promising property in the middle of something big. It did not take him long to find one.

The opportunity that Ed Landreth found in Crane County, a newly opened area of the Permian Basin, was one that only an operator with imaginative daring and large quantities of ready cash could have pursued. By virtue of a surveyor's error, there was a vacant, unleased strip of land 4 miles long and 200 to 1000 feet wide in the heart of the newly developing Gulf-McElroy field, which straddled Crane and Upton counties. Though anyone who leased this strip would be reasonably sure to face litigation from Gulf, the owner of adjoining leases, and royalty owners, Landreth paid $72,500 to do so.[43] In response to Landreth's first location of a rig on the vacancy, Gulf moved in six derricks overnight to drill offsetting wells along the property line. Landreth, in little more time, brought in six rigs to offset Gulf's rigs and six more to offset Gulf's flowing wells. Typically, Landreth met the challenge of his competition and raised the stakes. Within two months, he had completed fourteen wells on the strip at a cost of about a half-million dollars. He found an enormous quantity of oil; his No. 9 well produced 7000 barrels a day, his No. 14 well was good for 3000 barrels a day, and the remaining wells averaged 300 barrels a day. By contrast, each of Gulf's offset wells brought in 200 to 300 barrels a day.[44] Ed Landreth's phenomenal production, without rival in the vicinity, was a clear demonstration of that omnipresent variable in the oil business, luck. Landreth managed to tap a part of a formation that happened to be many times more productive than anything around it, and he did so purely by chance; there was no obvious reason why there was so much more production from Landreth's property than from Gulf's offset wells, nor could this bonanza have been predicted.

As Landreth had foreseen, Gulf and others, including Dallas independent Robert R. Penn, challenged the title to the strip and Landreth's leasing of it. As Landreth also expected, Texas courts recognized the validity of his claim to the vacancy, and they settled its width at 400 feet. Legal problems dragged on for more than a year, but Landreth was able to hire legal talent to match that of Gulf.[45] It was much more difficult to sell the oil produced on the strip than it had been to win the case in court. No one, least of all Gulf, was willing to accommodate Ed Landreth by buying great quantities of his sour, low-gravity Crane County crude at the posted area price of $1 a barrel. In another move requiring abundant capital, Landreth chose the only alternative to shutting in his production; he erected vast storage tanks down the center of the strip, spending another million dollars to store his oil until he found a purchaser for it.[46]

At the same time that he was tying up capital in Crane County storage tanks, Landreth faced financial problems from having plunged into another promising area in the Permian Basin, Winkler County. He had spent heavily to acquire leases on 1360 proven acres in the Hendrick field, discovered in 1926. He had drilled on part of the land, found strong production, and invested in a twenty-mile pipeline and a loading rack on the Texas and Pacific Railroad, only to find that a weakening market for regional production would not absorb his crude oil at a profitable price. His immediate solution to his shortage of capital and weak cash flow was to sell a half-interest in his Hendrick field properties to Roxana (Shell), realizing a $700,000 profit on the transaction. He used the better part of these funds to build storage facilities, intending to wait for prices to rise before he sold his oil. Then, arriving at an imaginative tactic to try to pass along part of his costs for his pipeline and storage system, Landreth turned to Winkler County royalty owners; late in 1927 he informed them that he and Roxana would deduct 10 cents a barrel from royalty payments to cover transportation costs. In the uproar that followed, the royalty owners organized an effective pressure group, refused to accept the 10-cent-a-barrel levy, and told Landreth and Roxana they were free to give up their leases if they wished to do so. The two companies hastily backed down.[47]

At this juncture, Landreth needed a Wilbarger County–style coup to meet cash flow problems. Unfortunately, the price of Winkler crude continued to decline until, by March 1928, much of it was selling at the distress price of 50 cents a barrel. So Landreth once again turned to his bankers; he borrowed $1 million on stored oil and equipment in Crane County from the Mercantile Trust of St. Louis and permitted local creditors to take out liens against his equipment. By mid-1928, however, it was clear that his creditors would force him to sell some of his producing properties. Interest on notes was due, payrolls had to be met, and income from the sale of oil was inadequate to meet his operating expenses.[48]

With no reasonable alternative, Landreth set about dismantling his fledgling empire. He sold 800,000 barrels of stored oil and some properties in Winkler County at distress prices. This step took care of his most pressing debts and met his 150-man payroll, but it was not sufficient to generate the amount of capital Ed Landreth would need to enter new ventures in the style to which he was accustomed: purchase of leases on a large scale, at high prices; rapid development; and investment in storage facilities as needed. If he wished to continue to operate on an impressive scale, moreover, he could not settle into complacent enjoyment of the income generated by the Crane County strip, assuming he found a purchaser for its oil. Like other oilmen of the twenties, Ed Landreth had learned through experience that production rarely held up for long; before such refinements in oil field operation as mandatory well spacing and production limitations geared to maintaining oil reservoir pressure, the oil operator produced his properties with a view to getting the oil before the fellow on the adjoining lease got it, and getting as much oil as he could before the pressure declined enough to make the wells stop flowing. Under any circumstances, each barrel of oil he produced was one less barrel of reserves; and a producer who does not replace reserves is in the process of going out of business. So Ed Landreth once again embarked on a sellout campaign. He succeeded in selling his daily production in Crane County to Magnolia Oil, for 5 cents a barrel below the posted price. Then, with the knowledge that The Texas Company was looking for producing properties, he traveled to New York, where, after two days of negotiation with the president of that company, he sold the Crane County strip, its stored oil, and his remaining Winkler County properties for $6.5 million, a sum that placed him in the ranks of large independents. Once again, Landreth dazzled the oil world with the amount of money he received in his deal. He paid his bankers, issued dividends to his stockholders, and was all ready for the next spectacular plunge.[49]

It did not take Landreth long to find two ventures tailor-made to his approach. In Pecos County two independent partnerships found oil on what seemed to be a southeast-to-northwest oil production trend running from Crockett and Pecos counties in Texas to Lea and Eddy counties in New Mexico. In the first venture, J. L. Taylor and C. P. Link, San Angelo operators, decided in May 1929 to drill on leases they held about twenty miles west of McCamey, "uptrend" from the giant Yates pool discovered in 1926. They covered their $18,000 drilling cost by selling acreage adjoining the initial location to W. A. Moncrief, an energetic new independent who had previously worked for Marland Oil; to Walter and Paul Henshaw, San Angelo independents; and to the Marland Oil Company. When their discovery well came in a month later, its location seemed to vindicate the trendologists. Within two weeks the well was making 140 barrels of oil a day and four additional wells were under way in the vicinity. In mid-August, Moncrief's test produced 160 barrels of oil in fifteen hours, confirming high expectations for what came to be known as the Taylor-Link field.[50]

Though lease bonuses in the Taylor-Link area rose as high as $500 per acre, Landreth plunged into the play. He bought out Moncrief's 40 acres and producing well for $125,000 and bought a half-interest in another 282-acre lease for $175,000. On the strength of the initial production of the discovery and Moncrief wells, and his own confidence in the trend, Landreth committed himself to drill on thirteen locations on his leases. Wells were inexpensive to drill in the field, costing less than $20,000 on the average, and judging from existing production, it was expected that they would pay out in less than one month. Landreth's plans, however, went far beyond projecting the payout on thirteen wells. He purchased a forty-car loading rack in McCamey, built an eight-inch pipeline from the Taylor-Link field to it, and erected 800,000 barrels of storage. Thus, on the strength of two wells producing less than 200 barrels a day each, Landreth constructed facilities to meet the kind of production he had owned in Crane and Winkler counties. By the time the Landreth Production Company transport and storage system was complete, Ed Landreth had staked nearly a million dollars on his ventures in the Taylor-Link field.[51]

Not far from Taylor-Link lay the site of Ed Landreth's second Pecos County venture, a test undertaken by two San Antonio operators, J. V. Rowan and F. W. Tong. In August 1929, their discovery came in at roughly 1600 feet and flowed the equivalent of 3060 barrels per day. Humble and Gulf had protection acreage in the area; Simms Oil, a large Dallas-based independent, and Fred Turner, a Midland independent who had made a fortune on a vacancy in the Yates field, held tracts adjoining the discovery well. Ed Landreth's response to this discovery, which was thought to be an extension of the Taylor-Link field, was swift: he immediately hired an airplane in Fort Worth and flew to Pecos County, where he spent more than $1.6 million in two days of frenzied lease buying. It took big money to buy into an area where strong production had been discovered, and Rowan-Tong was no exception to this rule. Even Oklahoma independent Josh Cosden, generally regarded as a prince among plungers, invested only $70,000, for which he acquired Fred Turner's eighty-acre tract. Landreth was not the only oilman who scented something big, but he spent more spectacularly than the others. He invested in royalties as well as leases, purchasing more than 2000 full royalty acres around the Rowan-Tong well at a time when royalty prices topped $150 an acre, long before he had the opportunity to begin his own tests for oil.[52]

Within two weeks of leasing property in the Rowan-Tong area, Ed Landreth committed funds for six tests. Before long, however, he faced expensive operating problems that would have daunted a less optimistic operator. His first well in Rowan-Tong came in not as an elephant-sized producer of crude oil but as a massive gasser. Enthusiasm undampened, Landreth made plans to sell the gas rather than flare it off, as was the common practice when there was no obvious purchaser for gas close at hand. Then the well caught fire, burning 5 million cubic feet of gas per day for four days: Landreth hired Tex Thornton, the most famous well shooter and fire fighter of the era, to snuff it out. When the discovery well in Rowan-Tong subsided to pumped production of 99 barrels a day, in October 1929, Landreth nonetheless remained committed to development of the field. Even when offsets to the Rowan-Tong discovery well by Tidal Oil and Independent Oil and Gas proved dry, Landreth persisted. He did not swerve from his course when Independent's third offset to the discovery well proved dry, but when his McDonald No. 1 test failed in December, he finally had no alternative to cutting his losses by abandoning the once-promising area.[53] He had gambled big and he had lost big on Rowan-Tong.

By December 1929 it was also clear that two other speculative forays had gone against Landreth. His massive investment in storage, pipelines, and loading racks to handle a flood of oil from the Taylor-Link field was in serious trouble, for the flood failed to materialize. Indeed, the field never produced more than one quarter of its expected 5000-barrel-a-day output. Neither Landreth's storage tanks nor his pipeline, parallel to a Humble line, ever filled. The bottom had fallen out of Ed Landreth's oil empire. Worse yet, during the final months of 1929 Ed Landreth, like so many other American investors, suffered financial losses when his speculations in stocks and bonds fell through; in all, Landreth was said to have lost nearly $8 million in a matter of months. From the time of his sellouts in Crane and Winkler counties, when he was at least $3 million to $4 million ahead, to the end of 1929, when he was as much behind, he saw his tried-and-true strategy fail. He was by no means ruined, but he was no longer in a position to effect the grand coup. He paid some of his creditors by selling his surface equipment in Pecos County at distress prices. Shell purchased his pipeline system for $330,000, while Tidal bought his tank farm and other McCamey facilities for $180,000, about half Landreth's cost. His lease and royalty investments were a total loss.[54]

In surveying the fortunes of Ed Landreth, it is tempting to shrug off his losses in 1929 as simple misfortune; certainly his Pecos County plunge proved unlucky. Apart from luck, however, there were compelling practical reasons why Ed Landreth's strategy was not a long-run success. Perhaps its most telling flaw was the concentration of risk it involved. Ed Landreth did not spread his risk widely, either financially or geographically. He developed a pattern of conducting his ventures without sharing financial risk with partners or shareholders outside his immediate circle of family and employees. When a deal went sour, therefore, the full financial burden fell squarely upon Landreth's shoulders. His failure to share risks might not in itself have proved to be a serious liability if he had found ventures that were relatively safe. In looking to buy into areas with proven production, he avoided the high risks of rank wildcatting. But the safest ventures seldom offer huge profits, and Landreth based the financial elements of his strategy on capital acquired in sellouts and raised through interest-bearing loans, both of which led him to look for the spectacular return rather than the slow steady payout. When

Landreth found a venture he liked, moreover, he was inclined to throw everything he had into it; he shunned the strategy of diversifying investments in favor of the big plunge, the preemptive purchase of an expensive, usually large chunk of property. In Shackelford, Wilbarger, and Crane counties, that approach gave him impressive properties to sell at handsome prices; in Pecos County a similar concentration of effort yielded dry holes and a lot of gas for which there was limited demand. Landreth's habit of committing great sums of capital to storage and pipelines met short-run marketing problems that other Permian Basin independents with less money found a great handicap, but it also tied up his capital and led to cash flow problems of awesome proportions. Landreth's investment in pipelines and storage in the Taylor-Link venture showed a free hand with capital comparable to the style of a major company — and Landreth did not have the assets of a major company.

Even if Landreth had not made two unfortunate guesses in Pecos County, however, by 1929 his business strategy was ill suited to changing industry conditions, especially to falling crude oil prices. At the beginning of the twenties, when the supply of oil seemed barely capable of meeting the continually rising demand, the strategy of making a quick profit on producing properties and selling out for a substantial gain worked beautifully; Landreth had no trouble finding purchasers for what he developed. In 1928, however, he had to work harder to find a purchaser for the strip and its oil. Gulf did not rush to buy him out, Magnolia took his crude oil only at a reduced price, and The Texas Company eventually bought him out because it wished to fill its pipeline. By 1929, Landreth was not the only oilman with property and crude oil for sale. At the same time, falling crude prices cut into his profits from investments in oil. That meant lower income from sale of production for Landreth, cutting into the income needed to pay interest on debts and meet the increasing cost of operation. As prices continued to fall, moreover, so did the value of the oil Landreth kept in storage, presenting greater difficulty in obtaining loans. A strategy based on the quick, spectacular return was more difficult to use at a time of falling prices.

By contrast to the imagination and daring of the Landreth strategy, the approach developed by Robert R. Penn was cautious and restrained. A more conservative and a more typical independent operator than Landreth, Penn did not make high-priced all-or-nothing gambles. As a result, he never experienced the roller-coaster ups and downs that marked Landreth's career. In approaching oil ventures, Penn was a consummate team player, unlike Landreth, who inclined to the loner's role. Penn developed a business strategy emphasizing diversification of investment and cooperative activity within the oil industry; his extensive acquaintance within the growing Dallas oil and gas communities of the twenties, particularly with representatives of major companies, greatly assisted his business operations.

Oil was a second career for Robert R. Penn. Following his graduation from the University of Texas, where he studied literature and geology, he went to work as a reporter for the *Dallas Morning News*. In a decade he worked up to the post of city editor, making many informal contacts in the Dallas business community as he did so. When oil activity boomed in Corsicana and Mexia in 1921, Penn went to those oil fields to write newspaper features; after several days, however, he became convinced that he could make more money in oil in a week than he could as a newspaperman in a year. Accordingly, he quit his job with the *Dallas Morning News;* he telephoned instructions to his wife, Elizabeth, to sell two house lots they had purchased, borrow as much on their personal property as she could, and bring him the proceeds. The capital she raised enabled Penn to buy leases. He spent $3500 but discovered, to his chagrin, that what he bought had few takers: he later reflected, "I did not know it was possible to lose $3500 as fast as I lost mine." Fortunately, his innately conservative approach to investment saved him, for he had not used the whole of his stake. With what remained, he bought other leases, which he succeeded in selling to the Atlantic Oil Producing Company. This was a fortunate break for Penn, not only because his lease trade was successful but, more important, because it began a close and mutually successful collaboration with Atlantic.[55]

Once launched in the oil business, R. R. Penn entered into a variety of activities. He continued to buy and sell leases and royalties, but he also acquired a large interest in several drilling rigs with members of the W. H. Black family. He worked in a number of exploration partnerships, including those with Truett Cranfill (later active in Cranfill Brothers) and with S. P. Farish, brother of Humble Oil president W. S. Farish. After bringing in several profitable wells in the Mexia-Corsicana area and doing some successful trading in leases and royalties, Penn decided to strike out into a new area. In 1925 he liquidated his interests in a number of partnerships, incorporated the Penn Oil Company, and headed for the Permian Basin.[56]

Penn initially turned his attention to Mitchell County, scene of the first commercial Permian Basin oil discoveries, and bought eighty royalty acres for $20 each. It was as well that his conservative approach to investment kept him from plunging headlong into Mitchell County royalties, for he never realized a return on his $1600 investment. Still, this small loss was soon offset by more profitable ventures. Early in 1926 Penn drilled a well for Atlantic near San Angelo, then the hub of Permian Basin oil activity. H. H. King, a reporter for the *Oil Weekly*, visited the site and wrote an article on Penn's drilling operation, describing both rig and camp as the most modern and up-to-date in the region. Such a glowing endorsement was a welcome asset to Penn's growing drilling contracting operations and enhanced his standing with his most important drilling customers, Atlantic and Humble.[57]

Penn's first major Permian Basin success came in Pecos County. When Penn heard of the tests under way by the Transcontinental and Mid-Kansas oil companies on the Ira Yates ranch, he moved quickly to acquire some royalty acreage in the area being tested. Once he decided what he wanted to acquire, he pursued Ira Yates — to San Angelo, to Wichita, Kansas, and back to Pecos County. Penn made an offer for lease and royalty purchases on nine sections of land only to receive Yates's dampening reply: "I do not care to do so at present." Penn did not give up. He drove out to the Yates ranch in his new Packard touring car for further dickering; finally Yates, who had admiringly eyed the Packard during conversation, agreed to come to terms — if Penn threw in his fancy car as sweetener. Penn agreed without hesitation. It was well worth the bother and expense of a taxi ride to Midland to obtain acreage close to the Transcontinental–Mid-Kansas test, which came in as the discovery well of the giant Yates field shortly after Penn concluded his deal with Yates.[58]

The return from this Pecos County investment was fantastic. Starting with one half of the royalty interest in 320 acres, which he purchased in 1926 for $900, Penn sold royalty acreage to Atlantic, Cent-Texas Oil Company, the Peerless Oil and Gas Company, Imperial Royalty, and Monarch Royalty. In all, royalty trading on only three of Penn's nine sections brought him $163,625.[59]

Following his coup in the Yates field, Penn moved into Upton, Howard, and Winkler counties. Initially, these ventures did not yield great profit. Penn's speculation in an extension of the McCamey field cost about $40,000 in mineral investments alone, and he had recovered only $5000 of this amount by 1931. He fared better in Howard County, where he entered lease and royalty trading and did contract drilling. His greatest gains, however, were made in collaboration with Atlantic, a steady customer for his deals and drilling services. Indeed, Penn virtually performed the work of an exploration department for Atlantic, and in return, Atlantic shared his risks by subsidizing his ventures. The net financial effect of Penn's activity in Upton and Howard counties was the modest enhancement of his working capital; of more consequence, however, was his emergence as a "winner" in oil and gas circles. His track record was good, and he was proving to be a reliably profitable oil finder for both Atlantic and Humble.[60]

Penn's greatest financial gains in 1928 and 1929 came in Crane and Winkler counties. In the former Penn purchased royalty interests, some as small as one acre, in at least ten different sections, and sold most of

them over a two-year period. For the most part he profited from these
transactions. He sold four Crane County royalty acres he purchased from
Pure Oil at a base price of $1000 an acre, for example, to the Monarch
and Imperial royalty companies for $3375 an acre within a year. Simi-
larly, a small holding in Winkler County acquired from T. G. Hendrick
for $87.50 per acre sold at a base price of $1200 an acre several months
after purchase. Forty royalty acres Penn acquired for $31.25 each early
in 1928 sold to R. S. Matthews for $200 each within six months. In
all, Penn's early royalty trading in the Hendrick field was uniformly
profitable.[61]

Even royalty trading in a proven field, however, was not without its
pitfalls. The most obvious danger was the end of flush production. As
production declined, the value of royalty investment followed unless a
sudden rise in the price of oil offset the effect of dwindling production,
and that seldom happened in developed oil fields. In Winkler County
the price of crude oil began to fall in an increasingly glutted crude market,
and so did the return from royalty investment. Penn's return on his
Winkler County investments delineated the obvious strategy for royalty speculators: acquire interests before a field booms and sell them before
production or prices decline.[62] Penn lost money when he held Winkler
County property too long. Thus, on the heels of his early success, he
purchased 100 royalty acres in Winkler County sections 27 and 28 at
a base price of $250, one of the highest prices he ever paid for royalty
acreage. He held this property for two months before he disposed of
75 acres at his original price. Thereafter, he found no buyers for the
remainder; lower crude oil prices and proration of production in the
Hendrick field greatly diminished his property's appeal for investors.
In all, Penn lost $6500 on this acreage.[63]

Penn's Winkler County lease and royalty trading was wrapped up,
for the most part, by early 1929. By that time he had received $125,000
for his investment of $80,000. At that, he retained enough property to
earn at least $4200 from oil produced by Humble and Southern Crude
on his leases in the Hendrick field. Added to production income from
properties in Navarro, Pecos, Howard, and Glasscock counties, Penn's
profits on mineral and lease trading gave him a substantial stake for
future ventures. His drilling operation was profitable as well.[64] By the
standards of his time, Robert R. Penn was well on his way to becoming
one of the most successful intermediate-sized independent operators in
Texas. Unlike Ed Landreth, however, Penn made no financial killing
worthy of the news headlines; he avoided the impulse to place large bets
at long odds.

Though his overall business strategy was more cautious than Ed
Landreth's, during the late twenties Penn did an increasing amount of
that riskiest of oil endeavors, rank wildcatting, in the Permian Basin.

In taking on wildcat ventures, Penn had several advantages. One was his geological training at the University of Texas; he was in a position to understand and use the latest scientific thinking when he considered prospects. Indeed, his geological training probably contributed to his desire to explore a region about which so much remained unknown. Penn's drilling business was another asset, for he could use his own equipment in drilling tests and keep a close control on costs. But the greatest asset to Penn's wildcatting was his habit of sharing out risk in wildcat ventures; he found well-financed partners, often major companies, to assume the greater portion of risk in exploratory ventures. That meant that only a modest share of the return of a good discovery would be his, but it also meant that a dry hole did not spell financial catastrophe. Having major-company participants in his wildcat tests had the additional advantage of heading off the problem of finding a purchaser for remote production. Unlike Ed Landreth, Penn did not worry about pipelines and storage; he let his major-company partners handle the oil he found.

Penn's wildcat ventures in 1929 demonstrate both his approach to wildcatting and his close working relationship with major companies, Atlantic in particular. As the year began he was drilling a wildcat test on the E. G. Bowles ranch in Reeves County to a depth below 5000 feet, which for the time and place was deep indeed. Penn had only a one-sixteenth interest in this venture, in which Amerada had a half-interest; Atlantic took a quarter-interest and Magnolia took three sixteenths. As soon as there was a show of oil, Penn's caution got the better of him; he sold his interest in the well to the Eastland Oil Company and George Lyles for $50,000 cash. At the same time, however, he placed about half the income from this sale in 960 royalty acres near the test. Penn's faith in the area's potential was ultimately justified by oil discoveries, but they were not made until after his death; Bowles No. 1, for all its early promise, did not produce a commercial quantity of oil.[65]

Penn had better luck on a rank wildcat on the Bennett ranch in Ward County, a joint test with Atlantic. The discovery initially produced over 200 barrels of thirty-five-degree-gravity oil, relatively high gravity for Permian Basin shallow production, and Atlantic connected it to its growing pipeline system. Two other ventures in which Atlantic took part, another joint venture in Ward County and a test in Glasscock County, resulted in dry holes. Penn's greatest accomplishment in Permian Basin exploration in 1929 was his discovery of oil in commercially attractive quantities in Ector County. In a sense he followed in independent Josh Cosden's footsteps; Cosden had drilled the county's first oil well in 1927 but did not find commercially viable production. Penn approached Humble with a proposal to drill a test roughly three miles north of Cosden's well on acreage Humble had under lease. He contracted to drill to 3800 feet in exchange for a one-third interest in a block of six sections. Rather than risk substantial funds of his own, Penn then sold half his interest to Atlantic, receiving sufficient funds to pay most, if not all, of the direct costs of the test well. The venture was a major technological success; at about 3700 feet, the drilling crew found low-gravity crude oil flowing at the rate of about 175 barrels a day, but treat-ment of the well raised its potential production to 325 barrels. As an economic success, however, the well was less impressive. Though he had opened a large and prolific field in an area that came to be known as Penwell, after the Penn well, there was little demand for low-gravity crude in a market amply supplied with crude of higher quality. The par-ticipation of Humble and Atlantic guaranteed pipeline connections and sales, but given market conditions, Penn's major-company partners could not share the usual wish of the independent to see available acreage developed rapidly in order to yield additional operating capital. Penn's return on this venture did not become particularly significant until the late thirties; he, personally, never realized it. The discovery well, Kloh No. 1, was pinched back to 100-barrel-a-day production in 1930. With the price of oil at less than 60 cents a barrel, it furnished little new ven-ture capital for Penn.[66]

Following the economic disappointment of his Ector County discovery, Penn attempted to widen his geographical exposure by looking for busi-ness opportunities in other parts of Texas. He made some small invest-ments in leases and royalties in South and East Texas; when the Van field was discovered in 1929, he considered shifting the focus of his activ-ity from the Permian Basin to East Texas. In this instance, his decision to stay in West Texas was shaped by two elements of his business strategy that ordinarily worked for him, caution and cooperation with major com-panies. Penn and his geologist conferred with scientists working for Atlan-tic, Humble, and Magnolia and came away with the opinion that East Texas possibilities might better be discounted. Penn disposed of his only large block of East Texas acreage, in Wood County, barely six months before C. M. "Dad" Joiner's Daisy Bradford No. 3 began the great East Texas oil boom. Once out of East Texas, Penn stayed out.[67]

Penn reacted to increasingly hard times in the oil industry in 1930 and 1931 by reducing the overall scale of his operations and by working ever more closely with major oil companies. He bought fewer leases and royalties, limiting his purchases to areas where he was drilling tests. He successfully sought to increase the amount of contract drilling he did for major companies, and he tied his own exploration ventures squarely to the exploratory aims of Atlantic and Humble. He could see that at a time when major companies were cutting back on crude oil purchases virtually everywhere but East Texas, the only Permian Basin crude likely to find a purchaser was the crude that major purchasers had invested in finding. But with these adjustments in strategy, Penn also realized that there were limits to an individual's ability to deal with national industry problems. He took a leading part in the American Petroleum Institute's campaign to limit oil production and promote oil conservation, becoming chairman of the API's Division of Production. Neither Penn nor anyone else, however, saw a quick solution to the industry's difficulties. Of 1931 Penn remarked, "This . . . has been a year of travail, sorrow, and bitter experience for the entire oil industry."[68]

During the grim course of 1931, Penn took to spending long hours on field locations, giving increased time and attention to field operations. Following one lengthy stay at a test site in Cochran County, Penn telegraphed his wife that he would return to Dallas after a brief break for some hunting. As he set off in his car, his gun accidentally discharged, wounding him fatally. Thus ended the career of one of the most efficient and successful independent oilmen to take part in the opening of the Permian Basin.[69]

As different as the business strategies of Ed Landreth and R. R. Penn were, by 1930 they had one characteristic in common: they did not work as well as they once had. By the end of the decade, the promising conditions of the early twenties that had drawn Landreth, Penn, and many others to the industry — growing world demand for petroleum, fears of petroleum shortages, expectations of higher prices, possibilities for quick profits — had given way to a less supportive business environment in which profits were harder to make. At the beginning of the decade, the growth of demand for petroleum had created tremendous incentive for exploration, and that exploration had been overwhelmingly successful. The Permian Basin was but one of the many oil-producing regions discovered and opened in the twenties. Hungry for reserves, the major companies encouraged independents to explore new regions; they helped independents like R. R. Penn finance ventures, they bought oil independents found, and they snapped up reserves that independents like Ed Landreth developed. Majors and independents cooperated to bring an unprecedented amount of oil to market.

Once that flood of oil glutted the market, however, it changed the relations between major companies and independents. Major companies continued to have an interest in independent exploration, for independents could help them explore acreage leased back when the market had not been as well supplied with oil. Major-company encouragement of independent development and production was another matter. In an oversupplied market, major purchasers were choosier about what oil they bought and where they bought it. Therefore, they cut back purchases of sour heavy crude in the Permian Basin and the Rocky Mountains. They cut back on purchases that involved relatively high transportation costs from regions like the Permian Basin and the Texas Panhandle, as well as from older, less profitable regions like North Texas. They stalled on additional investment in gathering lines and long-distance pipelines; they were in no hurry to connect remote discoveries to market. For independents, these changes in major-company strategy meant that previously reliable purchasers could no longer be counted on to buy enough oil to keep them in business. Under such circumstances, if an independent had a ready buyer, he also had a stronger inducement than ever to produce as much oil as possible, as fast as possible, to make up for real or projected losses. That strategy, multiplied by thousands of independents, kept national markets glutted with oil and kept crude oil prices low.

For most independents, the steady erosion of crude oil prices meant that the most basic business strategy, that of finding oil and selling it for a quick profit, became increasingly difficult to follow. But what individual could meet the challenge of an industry-wide problem? By the end of the twenties, many producers, both majors and independents, were ready to support industry-wide efforts to cut back national production and thus stop prices from falling further. There was no general agreement among producers about how this should be done. If anything was done, it would mean a new development in the petroleum industry: regulation that worked.

3: TRIBULATION AND REGULATION

For American investors, the bleak years of national depression began on the New York Stock Exchange in October 1929. For American oilmen, catastrophe did not occur until a year later, with the discovery of the giant East Texas field. At that, in October 1930 no one could have predicted to what dire straits the East Texas oil field would reduce the American oil industry in a matter of months. As a tidal wave of East Texas production swamped the national crude oil market, prices fell to levels at which production was often unprofitable. East Texas brought oilmen to abandon the hope of the late twenties that the industry could resolve its own problems and regulate itself without outside interference. In a painful, five-year struggle punctuated by violence, oilmen adapted to government regulation. Only desperate times, however, brought a majority of independents to acquiesce in regulation. The passage from freewheeling flush production to proration and regulation was rocky and turbulent.

The problems that the discovery of the East Texas field brought so sharply into focus were not new problems in kind. Any veteran of the oil field, from the president of Humble to the transient roustabout, was familiar with the cycle of flush production: maximally rapid development of properties, wide-open production, production beyond local market demand, and resultant falling prices. This cycle had been characteristic of American oil fields from the earliest Pennsylvania discoveries onward. Once a new field ran through the cycle and production tapered off with declining reservoir pressures, the amount of oil reaching the market decreased and local prices normally increased. Before the scientific prospecting of the twenties, important discoveries had taken place in random fashion, from region to region; they were so spaced in time that periods of strong production alternated with periods of strong demand. The greatest impact of the new fields had been on local rather than national markets.

In the late twenties, however, market problems that had once been of limited duration and essentially local scope became prolonged national problems. The successful wildcatters of the twenties, some of them benefiting from scientific prospecting, brought in field after field, not only in the Permian Basin but also in the Texas Panhandle and Gulf Coast areas, and in Oklahoma, Arkansas, Louisiana, the Rocky Mountains, and California.[1] To domestic discoveries were added new fields in Mexico and Venezuela. Except for a lull in 1924, each year brought the discovery of several giant fields. As oilmen followed the time-honored strategy of producing them as fast as possible, there was never a time from 1926 until World War II when the supply of crude oil did not exceed the demand for it. Ever-larger new discoveries vastly increased reserves of crude oil, and prices declined, undermining the financial position of an increasing number of independents across the country.

The obvious remedy for the producers' distress was a cut in the amount of oil reaching the market. But translating this solution from principle to practice raised many knotty problems. One alternative with considerable appeal to many American independents was cutting imports, either through quotas or through conventional import tariffs. Major companies with Latin American production joined consumer advocates, who wanted crude oil prices to stay low, in opposing import restrictions. During the twenties, these pro-import forces prevailed. But contrary to the persistent arguments of independents, a tariff would not have solved their problem, for the supply of domestic oil on the market would still have exceeded domestic demand. Prevailing low prices were a problem that producers would have to resolve at home.[2]

Of course, if American producers could agree to produce less oil, refiners would soon draw down oil in storage, and prices would rise. But how could they reach such agreement? The nature of petroleum, entrapped in the interconnected pore spaces of reservoir rock, posed special problems for those seeking an equitable way to regulate production. As a well produces, oil moves laterally through porous rock into the well bore. Property lines are no barrier to this underground movement. In United States law, property owners own the minerals beneath the surface of their landholdings, unless the minerals were reserved or conveyed prior to their ownership. According to the American legal principle of the rule of capture, whoever brings petroleum to the surface of the earth owns it. That the petroleum produced from one person's well may once have moved under someone else's land does not alter his ownership of it. Because of this rule, the mineral owner who finds someone is producing oil from property adjoining his own must drill his own wells to prevent his oil from being drained by the neighboring producer. One person's decision to drill fewer wells and produce less oil would only encourage his neighbor to drill more wells for additional production.

In the unlikely event that producers could agree to limit production in a field, they faced the difficult task of devising a production plan satisfactory to all property owners. Should the owner of a large lease always produce more than the owner of a house-lot tract? Should the owner of a well capable of vast production always be allowed to produce more oil than the owner of a more modest well? At that, if producers agreed to limit production with the obvious intention of bringing about a price rise, would they be open to the legal charge of collusion to fix prices? There were no ready answers to these questions, as the mass of literature written about them attests.[3] In any event, even if producers in one field agreed to restrict production in the interest of higher prices, that field would have to be giant indeed—as East Texas was—to affect the national market and national prices.

As producers of the late twenties faced their problem of a glut of oil on the market, it was obvious that changing the situation would not be easy and, under existing law, might be impossible. One indication of the industry's pessimism is the gradual conversion of industry leaders to support of government intervention. By 1927, W. S. Farish, president of Humble, had decided that "the only solution of the trouble of the oil industry is in government control and help. . . . The industry is powerless to help itself."[4] At that time, however, most oilmen found the suggestion of government intervention unpalatable; they had not given up hope that the industry might resolve its problems. For that reason, two schemes to limit production in new Permian Basin fields drew industry attention. So eager were oilmen to see these experiments as answers to national problems that they overlooked the peculiar local conditions that made them relatively successful.

In 1926, independents discovered two giant Permian Basin oil fields, the Yates in Pecos County and the Hendrick in Winkler County. The principal attraction of both fields was the giant wells they contained, wells producing from relatively shallow and easily drilled formations. For independents, such wells had the allure of quick payouts; though it was costly to get equipment and materials to the field, a well that came in for 1000 or more barrels a day, not uncommon in either oil pool, easily met costs. Both fields, however, had the liability of being in regions that were isolated, bleak, and underpopulated even by West Texas standards. Producers in these fields were far from existing pipeline systems and even farther from refineries and markets. The small pipelines that were hastily built soon after oil was discovered were incapable of handling more than a fraction of what these giant fields could produce. Thus, producers in both fields faced marketing problems after only a few months of development. It was roughly twenty miles across shifting sand dunes from the Hendrick field to the Texas and Pacific Railroad, so some Hendrick producers found it economical to build their own pipelines to railroad gathering racks. But the rugged, rocky terrain between the Yates field and the Orient Railroad kept Yates producers from using this stratagem; Humble and the Ohio Oil Company took on the expense of blasting pipelines through rock to take Yates oil, but smaller, independent producers could not fund such projects. That made the small producers dependent on the two pipeline operators, who, in turn, could control levels of field production by pipeline purchase policies.[5]

From the perspective of eventual regulation, the Yates and Hendrick fields differed in one particularly important respect: the number of oil producers in each field. Two large companies, Benedum's Transcontinental Oil and Ohio Oil's subsidiary the Mid-Kansas Oil and Gas Company, together owned 8000 acres, on which the Yates discovery came in; Humble, Gulf, Pure, Marland, and the California Company bought large tracts of acreage in adjoining areas. With large companies bidding for leases, it was difficult for small independents to enter the Yates play. As R. R. Penn learned, Ira Yates was reluctant to lease small tracts, and only Penn's Packard roadster persuaded the rancher to deal with the independent. While some small independents, among them the Mazda, Red Bank, and Savoy oil companies, held leases in Yates, the field was largely the preserve of large integrated companies.[6] As a result, there were not a great number of Yates field producers.

In mid-August 1927, the continuing discovery of enormous wells in the Yates field led W. S. Farish to attempt to achieve a voluntary curtailment of production. He had a strong economic incentive to do so, because Humble had large quantities of oil in storage; Farish knew that the value of that oil would decline if gigantic production in the Yates field and others like it pushed crude oil prices lower. Farish's initial attempt to bring Yates producers together in Fort Worth, however, failed. Among the larger producers, Gulf was unwilling to consider cutting back production because it needed additional feedstock for its refineries. Most large independents expected the immense production of Yates to subside to a manageable level, as production in most oil fields did after a few months of production.[7]

Yates was different. No decline was evident by mid-September, and Farish once again pressed Yates producers to meet, this time with limited success. Gulf, which had just completed an expensive short pipeline to a loading rack on the Orient Railroad, would not agree to cut its production, but other producers, most of them dependent on Humble Pipe Line for a market outlet, accepted a system of pipeline proration in which the individual producer was allowed to produce up to an allotted percentage of pipeline capacity. Allocations were determined initially on the basis of potential well production, a system one observer called "proration in its most primitive form."[8] Transcontinental and Mid-Kansas, for example, could produce an amount of oil roughly two thirds the potential of the whole field; of its 30,000-barrel-a-day pipeline capacity, Humble allotted 22,000 barrels to Transcontinental and Mid-Kansas. That arrangement left only 8000 barrels to be apportioned among all the other producers. The major flaw in the scheme, however, was that it encouraged each producer to increase his pipeline allowable by boosting his potential production. Frenzied drilling broke out in the Yates field. Transcontinental and Mid-Kansas, for example, kept fourteen rigs drilling in an effort to maintain their position. By mid-November the Yates drilling boom had alarmed observers with even a smattering of current engineering knowledge, for some wells were beginning to produce salt water, a phenomenon believed to be a result of overdrilling and taken as an indication of the approaching end of production. The drilling boom, moreover, produced more and more West Texas sour crude oil, which was losing its share of the market to the sweeter crudes from other fields because the latter were cheaper to refine. Still, drilling crews worked around the clock, and roustabouts swarmed over the field, connecting new wells with already full pipelines. By the end of the drilling campaign, the potential production of the Yates field exceeded pipeline capacity tenfold.[9]

As the initial proration plan proved unworkable, Yates producers negotiated another agreement. In January 1928 they adopted a second plan in which a producer's pipeline allowable would be determined by the amount of proven acreage he held within the recognized boundaries of the field. Like the first plan, this arrangement suited Transcontinental and Mid-Kansas, which held roughly two thirds of the field's proven acreage; large companies like Humble and Roxana, holding large tracts, similarly benefited. But Simms Oil, a large independent that had a small tract with vast potential production, lost out with the new scheme. The new plan, moreover, encouraged additional drilling on the perimeter of Yates, as producers sought to prove up their undeveloped leases in order to gain greater allowable production. By mid-1928, both attempts to achieve voluntary cutbacks of production had failed. Simms Oil came forward with a third plan that offered more advantages to independents: production allocations were to be made by dividing up the field into 100-acre production units that would be permitted to produce a proportion of their maximum production potential. Though Yates producers with extensive production gave the plan a skeptical reception, they agreed to try it, and they asked the Texas Railroad Commission to monitor and supervise its operation.[10]

The Simms plan proved to be an arrangement most Yates producers could live with. But like its predecessors, it offered no remedy for the limited capacity of the pipelines in the field. In 1929, when potential production from Yates was nearly 5 million barrels a day, the pipelines could carry only 87,500 barrels; of this amount, large companies had the lion's share. Thus it was difficult for smaller independents working in Yates to produce enough oil to pay their bills, and by 1930, smaller companies like Red Bank had left the field because they could not sell

enough oil to cover production costs. Even Simms, which bought Red
Bank's leases, sold its Yates holdings by the end of this year.[11]

The production curtailment in the Yates field made a highly favorable
impression on industry observers, one of whom termed it "the best form
of proration in the United States today."[12] Much of its appeal lay in its
voluntary nature; producers asked a state agency to supervise regulation after they had reached a general agreement among themselves on
what was to be done. Though the precondition of the plan, inadequate
pipelines, ultimately forced small independents from the field, the plan
nonetheless appeared to be equitable. Best of all, it kept a huge amount
of heavy sour crude from flooding the market and pushing prices down
further. With these advantages in mind, industry observers saw the Yates
plan as a model for voluntary proration, to be reproduced in other fields
and regions. In reality, a modification of the Yates plan was not as successful in the Hendrick field, only one county removed from Yates.

In contrast to the Yates field, the Hendrick field included scores of
five- and ten-acre tracts, easily afforded by small independents. Though
major companies acquired substantial Hendrick field acreage, they were
far outnumbered by independents. As these small fry hastened to cash
in on the Hendrick bonanza, production quickly surpassed the capacity
of the pipelines. In December 1927, when Hendrick production reached
a daily average of 50,000 barrels, the Southern Crude Oil Purchasing
Company, then second only to Humble as a Permian Basin crude oil
purchaser, announced that it would buy no oil not already under contract. This step should have slowed the pace of Hendrick development.
It did not do so, primarily because independents with small Hendrick
tracts continued to drill offset wells to keep owners of adjoining leases
from producing their oil. Two prolific wells on adjoining tracts owned
by the independent partnerships of Cranfill and Reynolds and Collett-
O'Keefe, for example, prompted nearby leaseholders to drill more than
fifty offset wells. As drilling proceeded at a headlong pace, some large
and intermediate independents stored oil, while others invested in pipelines to loading racks on the Texas and Pacific Railroad. These independent pipelines kept market outlets open for small independents despite
Southern Crude's attempt to slow down production development. Prices
for Hendrick crude dropped: by March 1928, posted prices averaged
60 cents a barrel, while spot market prices dipped as low as 10 cents
less.[13] So much oil was on the market that there were few bidders for
it; no prudent purchaser bought and stored oil while prices were steadily falling.

The sharp drop in prices was not, however, the most serious problem
producers faced in the Hendrick field. Late in 1927, some Hendrick wells
were producing increasing quantities of water and diminishing quantities of oil. Though producers first thought the problem was caused by

faulty casing on an abandoned gas well, by February 1928, when nearly half the field's wells were producing significant amounts of water, it was clear that water incursion was widespread. No one knew exactly what caused the problem, no one knew to a certainty how to stop it, and no one knew how much worse it might become. All producers, however, faced the immediate threat of seeing their crude oil displaced by sulphur water in the near future.[14]

The producers' immediate response was the time-honored step of producing as much oil as they could before water reached their various parts of the field, devil take the hindmost. This tactic alarmed major-company engineers; they were convinced that accelerated production would hasten water incursion, which would in turn lower the amount of oil that could be recovered. The engineers believed that aggressive drilling by independents and wanton flaring of gas by all producers were responsible for lower reservoir pressure and water incursion. Though existing engineering technology could not offer conclusive proof of this theory, the engineers' argument provided important justification for cutting back production. As the water problem worsened, the engineers' view gained acceptance among producers, who recognized that it was in their interest to support the basic principle of voluntary regulation.[15] The engineers' theory also moved the Hendrick situation from the sphere of economics to that of conservation; on those terms, it was possible for the Texas Railroad Commission, legally charged with preventing physical waste in oil fields, to intervene.[16]

In February 1928, representatives of the Hendrick field producers began a series of meetings with the railroad commissioners in Fort Worth; in April, the producers' representatives selected a six-man committee to work out a production proration plan for the Hendrick field. The committee, chaired by R. D. Parker of the Railroad Commission, included W. B. Hamilton, head of the oil and gas bureau of the West Texas Chamber of Commerce; major-company representatives W. S. Farish and Underwood Nazro; and three independent representatives. But because the independent representatives included C. F. Kelsey, of the large Independent Oil and Gas Company, and Ed Landreth, who was involved with Roxana in Winkler County, small independents were not given representation proportionate to their numbers in the Hendrick field. Only committee member Tom Cranfill, an intermediate-sized Dallas independent, was a small tract holder whose interests were akin to those of the many small operators. Not surprisingly, in committee meetings Cranfill was often a minority of one.[17]

At the end of April, the committee produced its proration plan. Like the Simms plan in Yates, the Hendrick scheme divided up the field into producing units; these units were of forty acres each, reflecting the smaller size of many holdings. Half the field's total daily production was divided equally among units; the other half was apportioned on the basis of the ratio of each unit's potential production to the total potential production of the field. Within a unit, leaseholders had to share the allowable. The Railroad Commission was to set allowable production for the field as a whole and supervise proration with an advisory committee of field operators. At the end of April 1928, the commission issued its initial order, setting Hendrick production at no more than 150,000 barrels a day, less than one fifth of what it was estimated the field could produce.[18]

Like its Yates counterpart, the Hendrick proration plan was weighted against the small producers in its operation. Within a unit, an operator could produce only his share of the unit's allowable. If he held only a five-acre tract in a unit with four or five other producers, his income was drastically slashed, no matter how prolific his wells were. If he was too small to have substantial production in other fields generating income to keep operations going, Hendrick proration amounted to economic disaster; it ended the handsome profits that elephant wells on small, cheap tracts had guaranteed. The small independent's only recourse was drilling more wells within his unit, thereby increasing its production and gaining additional allowable production for it. As independents responded to the Railroad Commission's first allowable by drilling more wells, they tied up additional amounts of capital with little hope of meeting costs, let alone making a profit on their investments.

Small producers were not the only ones to find Hendrick proration a burden. Companies like Texon Oil and Land that had contracted to deliver large quantities of Hendrick crude to major-company purchasers found it necessary to buy crude they might have produced in order to meet their contracts. Texon, however, was large enough to have substantial production in other places, and like other larger producers in a similar position, it could give proration grudging acceptance.[19] It had not staked its future on profits from Winkler County. Those who had were hard pressed.

After nearly a year of proration, one enthusiastic journalist cited the Hendrick cutback as "definite assurance that the industry can and will eventually solve the problem of over-production."[20] With the field producing at only 6 percent of its estimated potential in March 1929, production was indeed curtailed dramatically. Proration in the Yates and Hendrick fields did keep West Texas crude prices from continued decline, but it did not stabilize national prices because flush fields in Oklahoma and California continued to flood the market with oil. In the long run all of the producers who retained wells in the Hendrick field benefited to some extent from proration, though not as greatly as they expected. After a year engineers claimed that the field's life had been prolonged by 20 to 50 percent through proration. But the conservationists' ostensible aim, that of halting water incursion, was not accomplished. By mid-November 1929, only 6 of the 565 wells produced oil without water. The positive effects of proration on prices and reservoir conservation were more modest than economists and engineers had forecast, a point not lost on disgruntled independents.[21]

The Hendrick plan, while it had originated with operators and was adopted by voluntary agreement, was by no means to the interest and liking of all producers, and those who would not comply with it could not be compelled to do so. Some producers quietly continued to move oil produced in excess of their allowables to railroad loading racks twenty miles away. Others openly thwarted Railroad Commission supervision. In February 1929, for example, the Hendrick field proration umpire alleged that the Bankers Producing Corporation of El Paso, owner of a five-acre Hendrick lease, had run its 4000-barrel-a-day well wide open for a month; the oil company denied that it had run its well to capacity but did not claim that it had stayed within its allowable. Several producers argued that the Railroad Commission lacked the legal power to enforce proration. The Murchison Oil Company of Dallas thus obtained two temporary injunctions against Railroad Commission proration of its wells late in 1929 and produced 5400 barrels of crude a day from its Winkler County properties.[22] The Railroad Commission could admonish producers to comply with regulation, but forcing compliance was beyond its statutory powers.

That some producers chose to violate a plan for regulation that had been drawn up and voluntarily accepted by other producers points up the diversity of opinion and interest among oilmen on the subject of regulation in general and proration in particular. By the time the Hendrick experiment was launched, many major companies favored limiting production in areas producing more oil than they needed. Yet even among major companies there was no uniformity of opinion on regulation, as Gulf's reluctance to see proration in the Yates field demonstrates.[23] Among independents, attitudes toward regulation and limitation of production varied with individual business strategy, business interests, financial position, and perspective on national problems. There was no single "independent" attitude toward regulation. In the Hendrick field, Ed Landreth took a prominent part in advancing regulation of production; he did not wish to see the value of the oil he had in storage decline with falling prices, or the value of his producing properties plummet in the face of water damage to producing formations. His borrow-and-sell-out strategy gave him an interest in Hendrick proration. Similarly, R. R. Penn became an outspoken advocate of regulation and conservation; Penn had seen the value of his Hendrick field royalties fall when the field developed production problems following hectic drilling. Tom Cranfill, by contrast, accepted proration with far less enthusiasm.

The owner of a 15,000-barrel-a-day well on a twenty-acre lease, Cranfill saw proration wipe out the potential profits from his bonanza well.[24] Still, like the majority of Hendrick producers, Cranfill finally cooperated with proration. Only a minority of producers refused to comply with the measure and held rigidly to the strategy of offsetting falling prices by boosting production.

The different reactions to Hendrick proration showed how business interests influenced attitudes toward regulation and also demonstrated that size alone was not a reliable guide to an independent's position on regulation. Though of comparable size, Penn and Cranfill saw Hendrick proration in quite different terms. Small independents like Bankers Producing Corporation resisted proration—but so did the much larger Murchison Oil. By 1930, when production regulation became a Texas political issue, the large Tulsa independent Danciger Oil and Refining, with production in fields throughout Texas, had begun tooth-and-nail opposition to proration, which it carried to the last judicial ditch. Large or small, independents based their positions on regulation on their business strategies and business interests.

Outside the Permian Basin, voluntary agreements to curtail production were far less successful than in either the Yates or the Hendrick field. From autumn, 1926, to summer, 1927, for example, producers in the new Seminole, Oklahoma, field tried and failed to reach agreement on cutting back field production. Though Oklahoma had a regulatory body for oil, the extent of the Corporation Commission's powers had never been subjected to thorough legal testing, and many Oklahoma operators did not feel bound by law to observe its directives. The reception given large independent Tom Slick at a Tulsa meeting in 1929 is indicative of independent opinion; in a discussion of regulation, Slick announced, "No state corporation commission will tell me how to run my business," and was roundly applauded by his fellow producers. When production cutbacks were finally achieved at Seminole, they reflected the natural decline of flush production rather than stringent regulatory control. In 1930 the commission tried issuing a statewide proration order, only to have it immediately challenged in court by a group of independents and the Sinclair Oil Company. As one journalist understated the matter in December 1930, "proration has never had the universal approval of Oklahoma crude oil producers."[25]

Limiting production was just as controversial and difficult in California, and California did not have a regulatory counterpart to the Texas Railroad Commission or the Oklahoma Corporation Commission, a body to which oil producers could resort for help in effecting plans to limit production. In July 1929, California passed a conservation law encouraging voluntary agreements to restrict production, but small independents in Long Beach, Santa Fe Springs, and Playa del Rey, many drilling on town lot sites, ignored it. In February 1930, conservationists attempted to cut back state production to less than 600,000 barrels a day, but once again, many smaller producers made no attempt to limit their production — and no one could make them do so.[26]

The obvious difficulties and limited successes of curtailment of production on a field-by-field and state-by-state basis led the API, in which major companies had the dominant voice, to try to launch a nationwide cutback effort in 1929. It advanced a plan to set production quotas for all oil-producing states; although the API could not secure federal assurance that its scheme would be immune to antitrust prosecution, it urged adherence to its quotas. Accordingly, when the Texas Railroad Commission set allowables for fields whose production it supervised, such as Yates and Hendrick, it took API quotas into account. In 1929, however, the Railroad Commission regulated production in only a handful of fields, so the quotas had relatively little effect on levels of either state or national production. And in California and Louisiana, where there were no regulatory counterparts to the Railroad Commission, there was no effective way to apply the API quotas.[27] So one more attempt at industry self-regulation had scant result.

One other method of self-regulation, control of production through unitized operation of oil fields, had its proponents by the late twenties, but this idea excited great controversy within the industry. Unitization meant the pooling of holdings of all operators in a given field so that the field could be produced as a unit, as if it were in the hands of one owner. One operator, acting for all, would make decisions on drilling and production. Unitization eliminated both uneconomical offset drilling and production beyond immediate market demand; it could be used to ensure reservoir conservation. Despite these advantages, small and intermediate independents generally did not accept unitization because it tended to slow payout and tie up capital for longer periods. Consequently, when the API suggested in 1931 that unitization might help resolve the problems of the industry, the Independent Petroleum Association of Texas responded with strenuous opposition. By that time, however, there had been one widely publicized success in unitization, the Van pool in eastern Texas. This experiment was a success because the Pure Oil Company controlled the bulk of the field and the other leaseholders were major companies supportive of both proration and long-run conservation.[28] It was as hard to generalize from the Van field as it was from Yates and Hendrick to the petroleum industry as a whole. Despite these local successes, the petroleum industry could not solve its national problems.

There was another possibility, that the federal government would enter into oil regulation. Before the East Texas cataclysm that possibility had little appeal for most oilmen. Throughout the twenties federal oil policy rested on the assumptions that the United States had a rapidly dwindling supply of oil, that most of it was wastefully produced, and that it was desirable to meet the increasing needs of the domestic market with imported oil. The federal government, in short, wanted American oil to remain in the ground.[29] With this aim in view, the Hoover administration stopped issuing permits for exploration on federal lands in March 1929, a step that all but shut down activity in the Rocky Mountain district. Then, on June 10, at a federally sponsored conference on oil conservation at Colorado Springs attended by governors of oil-producing states and oilmen, conference chairman Mark Requa suggested the creation of a federal commission to set the total volume of domestic production and allocate it among the states. As if that suggestion were not enough to raise oilmen's hackles, Requa astonished the delegates with a threat of coercive federal action if the industry did not curb overproduction.[30]

Requa's tactless and provocative remarks did more than demolish the chance that the Colorado Springs conference would make any progress toward oil conservation; they so outraged many independents that a number of these delegates met the following day at the Antlers Hotel and organized the Independent Petroleum Association of America (IPAA). This gave independents a vehicle for proclaiming differences with federal bureaucrats and major companies on matters of public policy, and after the Colorado Springs meeting they were increasingly inclined to do so. Many agreed with IPAA president Wirt Franklin, an independent from Ardmore, Oklahoma, who charged that the Colorado Springs conference revealed "in all its hideousness . . . the true intent [of] so-called conservation programs: to shut in domestic production and turn the United States petroleum market over to major companies importing oil from South America."[31] Independent suspicion of federal bureaucrats took firm root at Colorado Springs.

In response to Requa's threat, the newly formed IPAA launched a countercampaign against federal regulation of the oil industry and, especially, for a protective tariff on imported oil. The latter cause proved highly useful in rallying support within the independent sector of the domestic industry. By 1930 even the relatively staid Mid-Continent Oil and Gas Association, prodded by Wirt Franklin and R. R. Penn, joined the IPAA in endorsing a protective tariff. In both 1930 and 1931 the IPAA followed up by sending large delegations of members and friends to Washington to lobby for a duty of $1 a barrel on imported crude.[32] Support for the protective tariff was one matter upon which independents with widely diverging interests could agree.

As the IPAA worked to form an effective national lobbying group, it encouraged formation of independents' organizations on state levels.

Oklahoma independents had organized before the Colorado Springs conference, and the events of 1929 brought independents in Texas and California to organize state independent organizations in February 1930. The Independent Petroleum Association of Texas (IPAT), meeting for the first time in Fort Worth on February 22, 1930, elected feisty Tom Cranfill its president. IPAT's membership was restricted to those operators "being strictly independent of major company connections."[33] Had freedom from major-company connections been taken as excluding any independent who did a substantial part of his business with major companies, IPAT's ranks would have been small indeed. The membership rule, however, served to identify economic interest; it was a conscious separation of approaches toward industry affairs from the policies of major companies. IPAT's meetings not only served to whip up protectionist fervor but also provided independents with a forum in which to air grievances against major companies and the Texas Railroad Commission.

Grievances were not hard to find. Delegates to IPAT's first meeting agreed to oppose proposals to tax natural gas, to fight the enforcement of proration in flush fields, and to launch their own offensive against major companies by pushing for passage of a common purchaser law for pipelines in Texas, legislation similar to that passed in Oklahoma in 1915. After less than a month of intensive lobbying, IPAT members had the satisfaction of seeing the Texas Legislature pass a bill making all firms with crude oil storage facilities and affiliated pipeline systems public utilities. Such oil purchasers had to purchase crude oil ratably, from all producers and without discrimination among oil pools. The act named the Railroad Commission as the agency to regulate and enforce these provisions. To do so, however, the Railroad Commission had to oversee all oil producers and oil pools. It was, in effect, given the task of monitoring statewide pipeline proration. In August 1930, two months after the Common Purchaser Act went into effect, the Railroad Commission issued its first statewide proration order.[34]

Although the Common Purchaser Act of 1930 broadened the Texas Railroad Commission's scope of operations, it failed to clarify the commission's power to enforce regulation. With regard to the commission's powers, moreover, matters were further complicated by legislation of the previous year, the Conservation Act of 1929. Under this statute, the Railroad Commission was clearly given power to intervene to prevent the physical waste of crude oil, but it was equally clearly forbidden to intervene to prevent "economic waste," the production of oil in excess of market demand. The proration indicated by the Common Purchaser Act could easily be construed as contrary to the Conservation Act of 1929. Thus, the commission's statewide proration order was variously challenged, enjoined, and ignored. In the new Darst Creek field, for example, proration was soon a dead issue as operators competed to drill offset wells. In the Panhandle, the Danciger Oil and Refining Company enjoined the Railroad Commission from enforcing proration, arguing that it could not restrict production in the absence of proof that the company was physically wasting oil or gas. During the lengthy legal battles that followed, Danciger ran its wells wide open.[35] Anyone assessing the power of the state to regulate the petroleum industry in Texas in October 1930, then, would not have seen the Texas Railroad Commission as the potential savior of the industry. It lacked both the will and the way. There matters stood when oil was discovered in what would be known as the East Texas field.

On October 3, 1930, Columbus Marion "Dad" Joiner brought in the Daisy Bradford No. 3 in Rusk County, Texas. At a time when the so-called poor boy, the underfinanced operator who drilled for shallow oil with the minimum of resources, was common, Joiner ran the poorest of poor-boy operations. His rig was a dilapidated affair composed of various secondhand parts and worn machinery; the crew fueled its boilers with brushwood and discarded auto tires scavenged from the neighborhood. Joiner's geologist, A. D. "Doc" Lloyd, upon whose recommendation Joiner ventured into the area, was a man whose charitable colleagues thought him eccentric, a trendologist who drew lines between oil fields throughout the nation and saw that they intersected in East Texas. Joiner did not drill exactly where Lloyd wished, for he chose to drill on leases he had obtained from Mrs. Daisy Bradford in return for nothing more than his promise to drill a well. The occasional major-company oil scout who stopped by the Bradford lease chuckled at the makeshift nature of Joiner's operation and the samples from the well, which looked suspiciously like samples from wells in Corsicana. Gossip held that Joiner's third test, which eventually brought in the East Texas field, had been salted from the time it was only 1500 feet deep.[36]

Since it was not easy to take Joiner's test seriously, industry observers were stunned when Joiner actually brought in a promising quantity of oil. The initial major-company reaction, as one eyewitness recalls, was disbelief:

> They dropped that [tester] in there, and, man, here comes gas and oil, gurgling and going on. About that time, here comes the oil, over the derrick, and all the pine trees down-wind from us for several hundred yards were just soaked with oil. . . . It was after dark before I got away. . . . I went in and called my boss in Houston. . . . I got Ryan, head of the [Shell] land department, told him about it, and he says, "Son,

are you sure you know what you're talking about? We've heard
lots of stories about this well."[37]

The oil field Joiner stumbled upon was giant even by world standards.
Some 134,000 acres in extent, it dwarfed the great fields of the twenties, Yates, Seminole, and California's Kettleman Hills. During its first
ten years, the field produced an estimated 1.5 billion barrels of sweet,
high-gravity crude; by 1940 it contained twice the number of oil wells
found in all of California. The average depth of production in the field
was relatively shallow, 3667 feet, and the average thickness of its producing sand was 40 feet. By any standard in the industry, the field was
colossal.[38]

Any field promising an abundance of sweet, high-gravity crude oil
at shallow depths was alluring to an independent, and never more so
than in increasingly difficult times. East Texas, moreover, offered additional attractions. Operating costs could be remarkably low there. The
field's formations were easy to drill; an average well could be completed
in twenty to thirty days, and many were drilled in far less time. There
were no hazardous high-pressure gas strata or troublesome water sands
to penetrate. Ample supplies of cheap lumber meant that an operator
could build wooden derricks, adequate in relatively shallow work, rather
than use more expensive steel derricks. As unemployed workers from
other regions flocked to Rusk and Gregg counties, labor costs fell to rock
bottom. All told, the average well was completed for about $25,000 in
1931; some wells cost as little as $9,000.[39]

Though Joiner found oil, the modest production of Daisy Bradford
No. 3 led most major companies to await the results of other working
tests before they approved large-scale leasing campaigns. Their hesitation left the field open to independents. The most promising acreage
in the area was quickly carved up into small tracts. Some holdings were
exceedingly small; one 15.34-acre tract near Joiner's well, for example,
was subdivided into six separate leases in 1931. Each lease was between
2 and 3 acres in extent, and eleven different individuals and companies
had interests in this property.[40] Even when lease prices jumped to
$1000 and $1500 per acre, the price of a small tract remained within
a small independent's reach. The limited participation of major companies in the field meant that there would not be an immediate drive
for prorated production; prolific wells could be produced to the maximum, for a quick return of investment. Market outlet presented no
problem. Good roads connected the towns within the region, railroads
ran through all but the Joiner area of the field, and the field was not
far from population centers. The field's sweet, high-gravity crude was
particularly attractive to independent refiners, whose relatively primitive
equipment could extract a high proportion of the most salable and

lucrative products from it. Within one year of the discovery, some 35 companies had built sizable refineries in the East Texas field; in addition to these plants, there were about 100 "teakettle" refineries, constructed with steel drums for cooking vats and turning out gasoline and kerosene of "serviceable but questionable quality."[41] All of these features made East Texas an independent oilman's paradise. Not surprisingly, within a few months of Joiner's discovery hundreds of independents left depressed fields in older areas to take their chances in East Texas.

As independents plunged into drilling and producing the new bonanza, they began that familiar cycle of flush production and falling prices. This time, however, the cycle began when prices for high-grade crude were already at 67 cents a barrel, the lowest in many years. By June 2, 1931, the East Texas oil field was producing 350,000 barrels of crude oil daily from over 700 wells, and Humble led major purchasers in announcing a price cut to 37 cents a barrel for top-quality crude. Some buyers stopped posting prices altogether, but on June 20, those who had continued to do so dropped the price to 20 cents a barrel. By this time most sales on the spot market brought 15 cents or less a barrel. Late in June one producer even sold 40,000 barrels of his crude for 2.5 cents a barrel. The collapse of East Texas prices made prices elsewhere tumble; on July 8, 1931, Humble's posted price for top-grade Permian Basin crude dropped to 10 cents a barrel.[42] At these prices, a producer's chances for profit all but vanished. For producers in other parts of the country, the best hope lay in the possibility that the East Texas field would decline rapidly. Yet the volume of East Texas production continued to mount, like a tidal wave from which there was no escape.

The Texas Railroad Commission, having failed to secure compliance with its statewide proration order in 1930, was now reluctant to try to stem the flow in 1931. As David F. Prindle recently pointed out, the elected commissioners were well aware of the political liability of appearing to snuff out the one boom on the state's darkening economic horizon. Before the field was more than a few months old, moreover, some industry observers believed that East Texas was already too complex for the commission to handle and that the field would have to run its own course through boom to bust.[43] But because of the Common Purchaser Act, once pipelines were in place, the commission had to take a regulatory role in the field; it could not remain a spectator as the field developed. Its political position would have been easier if, as in the Permian Basin, producers had agreed on a regulatory plan and then asked for commission help to implement it, but though production mounted steadily in East Texas, they did not do so.

In April 1931, the Railroad Commission made its first move; it set the total allowable in the field at 90,000 barrels of oil per day. The results were not encouraging. Only one month after the order became effective, it was already clear that the commission's order stopped no one who wanted to produce more oil. As in other fields, a number of independents enjoined the commission from enforcing its order and they proceeded to produce as they wished. Plans for production cutbacks advanced by IPAT president Tom Cranfill and J. F. Lucey, a widely respected Dallas oilman, were no more successful. When it was obvious that no voluntary proration agreement could be reached, Texas governor Ross Sterling, a former president of Humble, intervened by calling a special session of the Texas Legislature and charging it with devising effective conservation legislation. The legislature had the alternatives of reworking conservation laws so that the Railroad Commission could enforce them or of keeping existing laws and creating a new, more effective body to regulate oil.[44]

Once the special session was under way, legislators heard testimony from both pro- and antiregulatory forces. The testimony demonstrated that in the summer of 1931, there was still a wide diversity of opinion on limiting East Texas production, and that the contending groups did not line up in a clear-cut majors-versus-independents division. Ed Landreth joined Humble president W. S. Farish in speaking for effective control; Joe Danciger joined Gulf vice president Underwood Nazro in arguing against it.[45] While the legislators deliberated, however, a panel of three federal judges, hearing *Alfred MacMillan* et al. v. *Railroad Commission of Texas*, firmly ruled against the Railroad Commission's exercise of power to prevent anything beyond the physical waste of oil. With the MacMillan decision as a guideline, the legislature passed the Anti-Market Demand Act, a measure that gave the Railroad Commission the power to stop every imaginable variety of physical waste of oil but specifically barred the commission from trying to adjust the supply of oil to market demand. The legislature thus guaranteed that there would be no quick remedy for East Texas problems.[46] Worse yet, the act prohibited statewide proration orders and annulled all prior conservation statutes. That meant that until the commission drafted new orders in line with the Anti-Market Demand Act's narrow guidelines prohibiting physical waste of oil, it could be assumed that East Texas production was not regulated.

With no effective help from either the Railroad Commission or the Texas Legislature, producers in East Texas and elsewhere who favored production limitation once again attempted to promote voluntary cutbacks. During the first weeks of August 1931, a movement for voluntary field shutdown until prices improved spread through the Mid-Continent producing region. On August 14, East Texas leaders of this movement called a mass meeting in support of voluntary shutdown, but much to their chagrin, production increased the next day. That development led some 1500 producers to request Governor Sterling to declare martial law to effect a shutdown. While he deliberated, the problem worsened: on Saturday, August 16, the East Texas field produced more than 1 million barrels of oil. On Sunday, August 17, the governor sent the Texas militia to close down production in the field. It remained closed until September 5; when production resumed, the Railroad Commission's authority was reinforced by martial law.[47]

The shutdown of the field temporarily improved conditions in the crude oil market; without the flood of production from the East Texas field, prices rose from 10 cents to as much as 85 cents a barrel in the region. It was still clear, however, that such control as the commission could exercise in the field was precarious, depending as it did upon martial law rather than acceptance of the commission's authority. Obdurate East Texas producers did not back down. In 1932 the commission issued nineteen successive proration orders, and producers challenged each of them successfully in the courts. It seemed that the commission's hands would be permanently tied by legal tests of its action.[48]

The apparent impotence of the Railroad Commission led many of the independent producers who had been active in the Texas Oil Emergency Committee, a body favoring effective regulation, to push for a new regulatory agency to replace it. Acting in concert with a number of majors, Humble prominent among them, Ed Landreth, Charles Roeser, Roy B. Jones, Frank Zoch, and other independents organized the Texas Oil and Gas Conservation Association (TOGCA) late in 1931. Though the independents most prominent in TOGCA had large or intermediate-sized operations, TOGCA's aim of effective regulation appealed to independents of all sizes outside East Texas because, large or small, independents in other Texas fields could trace their economic problems to what East Texas production did to prices. TOGCA, however, aimed for support from outside the industry as well. Striving for broad-based membership, it published a newsletter, the *Conservationist,* that it distributed to newspapers, public libraries, and chambers of commerce with the aim of building support for effective production regulation. Unlike IPAT, TOGCA was ready to include any and all who would rally to its cause. Moreover, TOGCA's aims were positive. By 1932, IPAT had become an organ of independent resistance — to compulsory unitization plans, to market demand proration, to proration plans based on acreage, and to replacing the ineffective Texas Railroad Commission with a new commission capable of regulating oil and gas. As IPAT and TOGCA took opposing stands on this last issue, independents were pitted against one another in what one journalist called the Texas Free-for-All.[49]

When the Texas Legislature met in January 1933, TOGCA was prepared to push for a new oil and gas regulatory body, a Natural

Resources Commission, whose members would be appointed by the governor. After stormy debate, the bill to create such a commission passed the House of Representatives on April 24. At this stage, however, the TOGCA effort met unexpected disaster. On the evening of April 25, TOGCA leader Charles Roeser and some friends happened to meet a prominent Railroad Commission proponent, Representative Gordon Burns from Huntsville, in an Austin hotel lobby. An exchange of insults exploded into an all-out fracas in which Roeser sustained a black eye and Burns enough injury to require a three-day stay in a hospital. The main casualty of the fray, however, was the proposed Natural Resources Commission. The legislators rose to defend one of their own; they denounced Roeser and his friends, and they killed the TOGCA-supported bill. Seeing a chance to rebuild public support after its near-demise, the Railroad Commission set a new, higher field allowable in East Texas. There were good political grounds for this move, but it resulted in another setback for producers: the price of crude oil fell to half its previous level in most parts of the state and to 10 cents a barrel in East Texas.[50]

The drama of events in East Texas during the early thirties — the headlong drilling boom, the howling confrontations between parties in the struggle over proration, the dynamiting and vigilante justice that surfaced when hot oil producers openly broke the law — obscured the casualties caused by East Texas oil outside the region. Whether or not the owners of prolific East Texas wells could profit from 10-cent-a-barrel oil, producers in older settled fields in other parts of Texas, and in older areas of Oklahoma, Kansas, Wyoming, and California, could not. As prices plummeted in East Texas, national prices followed; not every region experienced 10-cent-a-barrel oil, but prices nonetheless reached unprecedented low levels. Though martial law brought about a partial price recovery, it was clear that in the long run, the precarious fortunes of the entire industry — majors and independents alike — rested with the Texas Railroad Commission, a body with, at best, an uneven record in regulation.

Though the commission could not keep East Texas production off the market, it was much more successful in making its orders stick in older fields in other parts of Texas. In the Permian Basin, allowables were pruned back so severely that majors like Gulf, which had come to let West Texas production play an important part in its refinery supply, were hurt along with small independents.[51] Pinching back production outside East Texas took a deep bite from the income of both independents and majors. In 1931, Gulf and Shell lost $23 million and $27 million respectively, while Amerada, Barnsdall, Sinclair, Continental, Ohio Oil, and Phillips sustained lesser but substantial losses. By 1935 there had been casualties among all sizes of companies within independent ranks.

Two of the most striking were the receiverships of IPAA president Wirt Franklin and the large independent Simms Oil. The prevailing business conditions spawned grim humor:

> The question was asked of an oil producer, "What is the difference between a major oil company and an independent?" His answer was that "The major companies are broke, but the banks don't know it, while the independents do not know they are broke, but the banks do."[52]

As long as the Texas Railroad Commission was powerless to stem the tide of oil from East Texas, there was little hope that conditions would improve. The reality of trying to do business outside East Texas, as much as the turbulent conditions in that field, led many oil producers, independent and major, to support federal regulation.

Within six months of Franklin D. Roosevelt's inauguration, Washington supplied the petroleum industry with a variety of regulatory measures. Most important in the context of control of production was section 9(c) of the National Industrial Recovery Act (NIRA), which prohibited interstate or foreign commerce in oil produced in violation of state regulations, known as hot oil. This section of the NIRA effected a new curtailment of East Texas production, which led, in turn, to rising crude oil prices.[53] In June 1933, API and IPAA representatives met in Chicago to draw up the model of what became the Code of Fair Competition for the Petroleum Industry. The code gave a petroleum administrator the power to suggest production quotas, restrict oil imports, control withdrawals of oil in storage, and fix prices in emergencies. At the time the code was drawn up, Secretary of the Interior Harold Ickes was to fill the post of petroleum administrator. Restriction of imports and control of withdrawals of stored oil had been two objectives of the IPAA; its president, Wirt Franklin, presented the measure as a triumph for the independent oilman and especially for the IPAA. He proudly told IPAA members assembled for their annual banquet in November 1933, "A new day is dawning for the petroleum industry."[54] Had he known how accurate his statement was, he might not have had as much enthusiasm for the future.

That the head of the very organization founded by independents to resist threatened federal regulation should so wholeheartedly plead for and welcome it was a measure of the extremity to which many oilmen saw themselves and their industry reduced. Desperate times seemed to demand strong measures. Indeed, many producers were prepared to support far more sweeping federal control of oil than that mandated by the NIRA. Dozens of leading independents spoke for the Thomas-Disney bill in 1934; that measure proposed to give the Secretary of the Interior the power to prescribe quotas for domestic production, regulate crude production and withdrawals from storage, and control intrastate as well as interstate oil transport. Federal control would thus extend directly to the wellhead. While both the Texas Railroad Commission and IPAT opposed the measure, Wirt Franklin maintained that the Thomas-Disney bill realized goals "for which the independent division of the petroleum industry has long contended." Axtell J. Byles, president of the API, called such federal control "essential not only in the protection of the public interest . . . but to prevent complete chaos and bankruptcy in the industry itself." Speaking for the National Stripper Well Association, H. B. Fell argued that only the federal government could effectively regulate oil. East Texas editor Carl Estes, a former foe of proration and regulation, argued that federal control was necessary if East Texas oil operators, of whom he considered "eighty-five percent . . . plain, unadulterated thieves," were to be brought to law: "I would rather take Harold Ickes, and have State, National, international [government], or Soviet Russia control my country than a band of thieves." Congressmen, less enthusiastic about the Thomas-Disney bill, voted it down.[55]

The struggle for federal regulation intensified in 1935 when the U.S. Supreme Court declared section 9(c) of the NIRA to be invalid. Senator Tom Connally of Texas hurriedly brought in a bill that would permit federal seizure of contraband oil in interstate and foreign commerce over a period of two years. The Connally hot oil bill was rushed through Congress with the approval of most industry groups, IPAT being the most prominent exception. The Connally Act continued to be renewed for two-year periods until 1942, when it became a permanent regulation.[56]

By the end of 1935, the American petroleum industry no longer faced crisis from East Texas oil. Federal agents and a federal tender board reinforced the operation of state-ordered proration in the East Texas field, where production was at last beginning a natural decline. Activity was gradually shifting to other areas — to South Texas, back to the Permian Basin, to new pays in North Texas, and to western Kansas; there were discoveries to be made in new fields, and independents moved on to them. Other changes occurred in East Texas. By 1935, major companies were much stronger there than they had been in 1931, because they had bought out many independents.[57] With a declining field in which there were fewer producers and few remaining areas for exploration, it was far easier to regulate production. East Texas was no longer the nemesis of the domestic oil industry.

Though the East Texas crisis faded away, it had a profound and lasting effect on both industry regulation and business strategies. The federal government had responded to oilmen from both independent and major ranks and had regulated a part of the industry. The practical effect of barring oil produced in excess of state allowables from interstate com-

merce was to bring the federal government into the oil field. The immediate impact of federal regulation on daily oil field operations, however,
was minor. The scope of federal responsibilities was modest, and regulation was widely accepted as necessary to economic survival. On industry
horizons, it was the cloud no larger than a man's hand.

More apparent was the growth of state regulatory power emerging
from the East Texas crisis. The tide had turned in favor of state regulatory
agencies with several court decisions of 1932. In March 1932, the Texas
Court of Civil Appeals upheld the Texas Railroad Commission in one
of its legal battles with Danciger Oil by deciding that limiting production to market demand was a way of heading off physical waste and thus
a legitimate function for the commission. Then, in May, the U.S.
Supreme Court upheld Oklahoma conservation statutes in the Champlin
case, in which limiting production to market demand was once again
seen as prevention of physical waste.[58] These rulings in favor of both
the Texas Railroad Commission's and the Oklahoma Corporation Commission's right to regulate production with respect to market demand
were followed in Texas by passage of the Market Demand Act late in
1932; with this act, the legislature gave the Railroad Commission specific
power to prevent economic waste. In subsequent years, the Railroad
Commission's power to regulate well spacing and to revise regulation
withstood court challenges. Within the oil industry, the gradual acceptance of Railroad Commission authority was eased, as David Prindle
argues, by the political skill of Colonel Ernest Thompson, who came
to head that agency during its crisis. As a result of East Texas, state
regulation of production was upheld in two of the nation's most important oil-producing states.[59]

The expansion of state regulation became practicable because of the
growing recognition within the petroleum industry that some state and
federal regulation of petroleum could be beneficial. This awareness was
not universal. Among independents, there were holdouts like East Texas
producer Jack Blalock, who dug in his heels against federal and state
regulation alike. Moreover, as August Giebelhaus points out in his study
of Sun Oil, even officers of the same company held different opinions
regarding proration and hot oil legislation. Nevertheless, the majority
of oilmen had come to accept regulation by 1935. How far some were
prepared to go was indicated by the comments of Arthur Seeligson, a
San Antonio independent, on the Marland-Capper bill, which proposed
far more sweeping federal control of oil than the New Deal effected:

> Don't let anyone tell you that it is the so-called major com-
> panies who are sponsoring this special oil legislation. . . . Cer-
> tainly 25 cent oil is not hurting them like it is us. It is the
> thousands of honest independent oil producers and the

thousands of landowners in Texas, Kansas, Oklahoma, and
California who are being ruined and are in need of immediate
help. I know what I am talking about because I am one of
them.[60]

As they accepted regulation, however, oilmen of all varieties faced
the need to adjust their business strategies to meet it. For major companies this meant, among other things, recognizing that proration limited
the amount of refinery feedstock that could come from company-owned
reserves. They would continue, as they had done before regulation, to
purchase some of their crude from independents; nature and economic
prudence had always barred producing all their reserves at once. Proration, however, encouraged the majors to broaden their geographical exposure beyond the domestic sphere; many of the majors thus came to supplement domestic production with crude from foreign reserves.

Proration encouraged independents as well to broaden their geographical exposure. Activity in more than one field had long been good strategy
for reducing risk; with proration, producers in Texas, New Mexico, and
Oklahoma had additional incentive to increase the number of fields in
which they had production; then, if the allowable was cut in one field,
the loss might be made up in others. With more limited capital than
the majors, few independents were able to balance losses from proration with overseas ventures; they attempted instead to spread domestic
exposure. In terms of day-to-day business, the greatest effect of proration upon independents was its effect on the rate of return on investment. With low allowables, mandatory shutdown days, and low prices,
even a sizable find might take years rather than months to pay out. That
reality encouraged further cutting of operating costs. Particularly for
smaller independents, the ability to cut costs and corners was the key
to survival.[61]

Was proration, as one author has recently argued, the best thing that
ever happened to independents, "a means to force majors to provide independents with a market" for their oil, ensuring that "the majors would
have to connect their pipelines to every independent producer"? Historical
evidence does not bear out this generalization. Under proration, major
purchasers in Texas told the Railroad Commission what they were prepared to purchase, and the commission set allowables on the basis of
those statements. Major companies continued to prefer to buy crude
from fields near their refineries rather than far from them, and to prefer
to buy sweet, rather than sour, crude. Therefore, the gain realized by
an independent depended largely on the location and quality of his oil.
In the Permian Basin the majors did not purchase as much sour crude
as Railroad Commission allowables permitted, nor did they hurry to
connect new sour crude production to trunk pipelines. Many indepen-

dents in Crockett County found it took years to get pipeline connections to small discoveries made from 1939 to 1941. As late as 1958, after more than a quarter-century of proration, the Railroad Commission denied a request from independent producers that common carriers be required to connect all wells to their lines.[62] In general terms, proration ensured that Texas independent producers would get a share of the market; it did not guarantee that individual producers in all regions could sell their oil.

In the long run, proration did bring an important benefit to independent producers by making prices and production more stable than they had been in the twenties. One journalist reflected, "In the old days, an oil company might have 5000 or 6000 barrels per day production from one or two wells on Saturday and Monday morning have one or two salt water wells instead";[63] in his opinion, by limiting the rate at which wells could be produced, proration headed off such catastrophe. When proration made income from production more predictable, bankers began to take a more favorable view of loans to oilmen and to make loans on production. This enhanced the independents' access to capital; in the decades that followed, bank loans became increasingly important in independent operations.

For oilmen, the crisis accompanying East Texas development forced a break with the industry's past. From optimism that internal industry action would solve the national problem of declining prices, oilmen were driven to realize that East Texas had pushed their industry beyond the remedy of self-help. They accepted regulation in extremity: indeed, many of them fought for it and pleaded for it as an alternative to ruin. But the cost of federal and state aid in maintaining prices was coping with regulation that extended to the wellhead in states like Texas, Oklahoma, and New Mexico. Once new rules were in place, independents adapted to new business conditions resulting from regulation. Inveterate optimists, they could at least hope that the future would bring new opportunities.

4: BEAN JOBS AND FARMOUTS

As the history of regulation indicates, between 1931 and 1935 events in East Texas shaped the future course of the petroleum industry. Yet despite the sensation of East Texas, activity continued on a much-reduced scale in the older regions. Even in the Permian Basin, activity did not cease during the Depression, though at times it came close to doing so. It reached its nadir in the second week of July 1933, when only three wells were completed in the entire region. Of these three wells, only one was a wildcat, and it was dry.[1] The years 1931 to 1933 tested the independents' ability to survive; thereafter, opportunities revived slowly. Not until the outbreak of war was a strong national demand for crude oil reestablished. Even then, in the Permian Basin major-company purchasing policies, along with state and national regulations, limited opportunities. For smaller independents in particular, a large part of business strategy between 1931 and 1945 involved coping with the economic effects of unfavorable market conditions and new regulations. How well an independent could do during this period depended in large measure upon adjustment of his strategy to low prices and extended payout periods.

The profound decline in Permian Basin activity that took place as the great East Texas oil boom got under way took a heavy toll, not only upon the fortunes of individual businessmen who stayed in West Texas but also upon the nascent oil and gas communities of San Angelo and Midland. These business communities had begun to grow with the Permian Basin exploration of the twenties. Though a few local merchants and cattlemen traded in leases and minerals once oil activity was under way, businessmen and companies from outside the Permian Basin took the dominant part in the most costly exploration.

Apart from the major companies, independent firms based in Fort Worth and Dallas were especially active in the Permian Basin. Such Fort Worth firms as the Landreth Production Company, Roeser and Pendleton, and the Eastland Oil Company, and Dallas-based independents like Penn Oil, Cranfill Brothers Oil Company, and Cranfill and Reynolds participated in many new West Texas fields. Nor were all the outsiders from Texas. Among the companies with offices in Midland in 1929 were Fisher and Lowrie, a Denver firm, and the Rector Oil Company, headquartered in New York. Such Oklahoma companies as the Independent Oil and Gas Company, the Delmar Oil Company (a subsidiary of the Indian Territory Illuminating Oil Company), the McMan Oil and Gas Company, and the Marland Oil Company played prominent roles in Permian Basin development. In 1929, the *Texas Oil Directory,* published in San Angelo, listed eighty-two individuals, partnerships, and companies doing business in that town; the previous year there were forty-one entries in the *Midland City Directory* for individuals and firms in the oil business.[2] These two local oil and gas communities, whose development seemed promising in 1929, were casualties of the plunge in regional activity.

By 1932, the extent to which Permian Basin oil activity had subsided was evident in the outward appearance of its new oil towns, with their empty office buildings, untenanted hotels, and abandoned work yards. In Midland, for example, only eighteen of the forty-two petroleum-related firms listed in the 1930 city directory were still doing business in town in 1937. The town's fine new office building, built by Fred T. Hogan, had tenants only on two of its twelve floors during the early thirties. The oilmen who remained in town, both independents and major-company personnel, met for morning coffee in the Hogan Building's drug store; there, as one independent recalled, they would occasionally pass around a flask of bootleg whiskey, drinking to toast those who had work and to commiserate with those who lost it.[3] With oil at 10 cents a barrel, they could offer each other little more than moral support.

For traditional driller independents, those independents who operated on a small scale with one or two of their own drilling rigs, the depressed level of oil activity meant a struggle for survival. Even in good times, these small independents commonly worked with slender resources; whether in West or East Texas, Oklahoma or Arkansas, they relied on the quick returns from flush production in new fields to pay creditors and to generate capital for their next ventures. Without flush production, payouts were slow and staying in business was difficult. Driller independents who were fortunate enough to keep their rigs out of the hands of creditors benefited from the gradual turn to contracting out drilling by the major and large independent companies. The Richmond Drilling Company, for example, weathered the Depression by drilling wells for the Big Lake Oil Company in Reagan County. Other customers were less dependable, as a former Richmond owner, E. E. Reigle, recalled: "See, it was such a Depression that many operators would start a well on a promotion basis, and they were unable to finish it. . . . They ran out of money. So we'd have to go out there and tear down the rig and move it back to our yard there at Texon." Reflecting on the company's business, Reigle concluded, "They just eked out an existence . . .

during that time."[4] At that, Richmond Drilling was far better off than many another driller independent, for it kept its rigs working.

Though many operators ran out of cash, wildcatting and developmental drilling continued during hard times, at very low levels. The specific business situations of individuals, as well as production and reserve needs of major companies, prompted some exploration activity. In a few instances, independents had to continue drilling in order to obtain the return of capital previously invested. Fred Fuhrman, for example, had the mixed fortune of making a significant oil discovery in Andrews County in 1930. Local excitement over his find subsided when it became clear that there was no market for that oil. The nearest pipeline was Humble's, and that company had no need for more sour crude of the sort Fuhrman found. Fuhrman waited four long years before Humble extended its line to his wells. In the meantime, he used his own rig to develop additional production, hoping that it might attract a pipeline connection by a major company.[5]

The Depression did not change the basic reality of the oil business — that a barrel of oil produced is one less barrel in reserve. Thus, the varying reserve positions of majors and independents alike prompted some exploration. Gulf, which produced less of its refinery feedstock than other major companies, sought to develop and build production from Ward and Crane counties. Like Humble, it was particularly interested in looking for deep, high-grade production from Ordovician formations, the sort of production found at Big Lake late in 1928. Gulf and Humble carried on tests for such deep production in Crockett, Pecos, and Crane counties, but during the early thirties they found no bonanza to rival Big Lake. Scientific speculation about deep Ordovician production continued despite disappointing results in exploration. One observer thought, "If all the speculations about the Ordovician of West Texas were laid end to end, they would completely encircle the Permian Basin and there would be enough left over to motivate all the windmills in the enclosed area."[6] The only decisive test was the drill bit, and the hope of finding large reserves of high-grade crude oil in a sour-crude-producing region thus prompted exploration even during hard times.

During the depths of the Depression, between 1931 and 1934, those independents who continued to look for oil found it necessary to pare costs to the bone. Those who did not shrink from wildcatting in areas far from existing production were often able to pick up acreage from ranchers and farmers solely in return for the promise to drill a well. As geologist W. Y. Penn recalled, "In many cases you could go to the landowner and get him to give you a lease if you would drill within a reasonably close distance to him — because all of those old farmers *knew* there was oil under their land." Penn's first test took place in 1934 on a block of 3000 acres in Ward County: "And every bit of it was given to me by the landowners." After the mid-thirties, such openhandedness on the part of West Texas landowners grew increasingly rare. Even so, many landowners, desperate for regular income, continued to be accommodating. Midland geologist John Hills recalled that in acquiring acreage to see a prospect through, "Many times we couldn't afford to put out any cash. We'd just try to make a verbal deal with the landowner and then dash around town and try to find somebody that would drill it and pay for the acreage."[7]

Obtaining leases without having to pay cash for them was not the only way in which independents kept costs low. Much independent exploration during the early thirties was carried on in the poor-boy method used in East Texas by Dad Joiner and many others. The poor-boy operator used dilapidated and makeshift equipment and second- or thirdhand materials. He paid his men wages when he was able, paid them in groceries, or got them to take parts of his deal or some of his acreage in return for their labor. Sometimes he paid them no wages at all but supplied them with only board and shelter. Midland independent Ford Chapman, who worked for such poor-boy operators, recalled that workers called such nonwage employment bean jobs:

> The reason they were called bean jobs, literally beans was what they lived on. I know one fellow, he was getting ready to start a well, and he told me, "Well, I have a hundred-pound sack of beans." . . . In those days you'd get them for 3 or 4 cents a pound, so $3 or $4 would buy a whole sack of beans. Then they'd put up tents . . . or shacks of some kind.[8]

Poor boys never paid for anything if there was a viable alternative; some of them became famous for "borrowing" anything they could carry. Chapman described one borrower:

> I wouldn't call him a thief, but he'd go over to something, if you weren't using it, he'd damn sure get it and put it to work. . . . I set next to him in a cafe one day. I was trying to find out what happened to a swab off a well I was working on, asked him if he'd borrowed it. . . . "Hell, no, I didn't borrow no swab over there. If I'd've knowed it was over there, I'd've got it, but I didn't know . . . that you had one."[9]

A venture undertaken by George Bentley in Ward County in 1934 offers a classic example of a poor-boy operation of the period. Bentley obtained an eighty-acre farmout from the Atlantic Oil Producing Company for a wildcat test. He then brought Aere "Peanuts" Bradford into the deal in return for his labor and use of his cable tool rig. Bentley recruited ten other "et als" because they could provide some of the necessary supplies and equipment. One man acquired a "talking interest," one thirty-second of the working interest, by lending his broken-down truck, which the other partners repaired well enough to haul water to the drill site. Once drilling was under way, Bentley and another partner worked around the clock as tool dressers and water haulers, while Bradford managed the drilling of the well. When they found oil, the partners packed the well by using barbed wire, burlap sacking, red mud, and wheat. The successful outcome of the venture gave the partners both production income and the right to drill another well on the same lease. Atlantic also benefited: at very little cost, the company learned that its adjoining properties were likely to yield substantial production.[10]

There was one important limitation to the poor-boy operation: it was geared to finding shallow oil. Given the ramshackle equipment and junk materials poor boys could afford, drilling below 6000 feet was virtually out of the question. In any event, a deep project, taking a long time to drill, would have been beyond the typical poor boy's economic reach. Poor boys gravitated to specific areas, such as the southern part of the Permian Basin (Ward, Pecos, and Crockett counties), where they picked up farmouts or obtained free acreage. Thus the Pecos Valley, Tyler, and Tippett fields produced oil in commercial quantities at less than 1600 feet; one independent found a number of wells yielding as much as 140 barrels a day at 400 to 500 feet in the Tippett field, but these wells were only barely profitable when their production was sharply limited by Railroad Commission proration. The poor boys, small and often colorful independents, nonetheless survived the worst of the Depression and stayed in business by virtue of finding such cheap, shallow oil.[11]

Not all independents who resorted to poor-boy techniques limited their scope to such modest objectives; opportunity for greater gain was provided by cooperative work with major oil companies. During the Depression decade, major companies and some large independents turned a great number of leases over to small and intermediate independents, reserving a proportion of whatever oil was produced from the property. The urgency behind this common practice was supplied by time deadlines: most of the leases acquired in the Permian Basin during the twenties were valid only for ten years unless production was established. Unless they chose to forfeit the leases and lose the money spent to acquire and study them, the majors had either to drill on the leases or to get someone else to do so. With their own income sharply reduced by the depressed demand for petroleum products, the majors had great need of the independents.[12] While independents would often initiate bargaining for farmouts, major companies would also approach independents with farmout offers: as E. E. Reigle explained, "They'd say, 'We'll give you this 160 [acres], and you drill a well on it. We'll also give you . . . dry-hole money.' This was your well, your acreage, see, but it was proving up a whole bunch of their stuff."[13]

Through farmouts, even relatively small independents could take part in exploration in an area in which lease costs were high. In the Andrews, Gaines, and Yoakum county area the small independents working farmouts in 1936 included Midland-based W. T. Walsh, Harry Adams, and E. M. "Big Foot" Wahlenmaier, whose shoe size was famous in oil circles. Wahlenmaier's farmout came from the Midland partnership of York and Harper, which originally obtained a dozen 160-acre tracts from Humble. When independents obtained generous farmouts from major companies, they could raise capital for tests by farming out a portion of what they had to other independents. When they could combine farmouts with sales of acreage and cash contributions in the form of dry- or bottom-hole money, they could readily participate in even an expensive area. In the mid-thirties, Permian Basin independents found major companies ready to do business on such terms. One example of independent success in obtaining major-company help may be seen in a Gaines County venture conducted by Ed Landreth in 1936; having recovered from his earlier reversals, Landreth was able to get help from no less than twelve companies, of which Humble and Gulf were the most substantial participants.[14]

With farmouts and cash from major companies, the independents of the thirties could take on ventures without much up-front capital and without extensive promotion outside the industry. As E. E. Reigle explained:

> We drilled a lot of wildcat wells, but we didn't try to sell you an interest or the druggist an interest, or anyone like that. We went in there and maybe someone promoted us, selling us a lease or something in the area. . . . Anyway, we would drill the well, and then maybe sell off acreage to Shell or Atlantic. Or where we couldn't sell them anything, we'd probably go in there and drill a well offsetting them, and then Atlantic would give us $10,000 dry-hole money, Shell give us $5000 dry-hole money. You know, that was enough to meet bare expenses. We could drill the well . . . once in a while you'd make something. But that's the way we did it. . . . We didn't sell interests in the well; we didn't do any promoting, things like that.[15]

In short, the independents of the thirties developed ways of doing business in times when cash and investors were in relatively short supply.

Farmouts offered attractive opportunities to those who wanted to begin independent careers. W. D. Noel, for example, was a supervisor in a gasoline plant run by Gulf when he decided to go independent in 1940: "I finally realized . . . I would probably never get to be president of Gulf."

He and a partner borrowed $10,000 to buy a cable tool rig and go into business, and they found a farmout from Shell.

> The lease that we obtained from Shell as a farmout was an offset to production. We thought we were probably on the very edge of the field. Turned out that the field went about three miles further. . . . We were almost in the middle of the field. We were able to drill the wells very cheaply. . . . I started out as a tool dresser. We worked twelve-hour tours, worked every day, and I dressed tools until we drilled five wells. And I pumped the wells, kept the books, produced the oil, and made all the reports.

Noel and his partner were able to keep their costs low not only by his doing this work but also by using secondhand materials: "I did buy new pump jacks that were on Bethlehem Steel's obsolete list. . . . They cost about $500. But we could buy tubing and rods for 20 cents a foot, . . . secondhand tanks for about $200, two-inch line pipe for 5 or 6 cents a foot, secondhand casing for 50 to 60 cents a foot." Even on such economical terms, a price of 64 cents a barrel for their oil and an average monthly allowable production per well of 400 barrels meant that Noel and his partner made little more than $200 a month profit per well. It took them three years and another successful farmout to obtain enough income from production to finance substantial ventures.[16]

Farmouts, of course, were not the same as outright gifts of acreage, and they carried with them conditions independents had to meet. Major companies ordinarily retained an interest in whatever oil and gas might eventually be discovered on farmed-out leases. For example, in 1935 Humble farmed out 320 acres to the Falcon Oil Company in what it thought might prove to be an extension of the Winkler County Keystone Field; it kept a one-sixteenth interest in production over 500 barrels a day and reserved all mineral rights on production below 4500 feet. When major companies farmed out acreage in order to meet lease deadlines, they often imposed tight time schedules on the independent, who took over the obligation of doing the drilling that would hold the leases. Many farmouts also included an obligation to carry on continuous drilling in the event production was established; for an independent with slim resources, having to drill a new well before the first had returned much of his investment could mean running out of money.[17]

One independent who did not have to worry about finding enough cash to follow through on farmout obligations was Fort Worth newspaper publisher Amon Carter, and he became one of the largest and most successful independents in Texas during the late thirties. At the time he became active in Permian Basin exploration, Carter had been an investor in wildcatting for more than a decade; he had been one of Roy West-brook's backers in the Hendrick field discovery in 1926. As he increasingly found oil more exciting than publishing, Carter organized his own firm, the Crafton Oil Company. In 1935 Crafton Oil and W. A. Moncrief, a Fort Worth independent, had the unusual fortune of obtaining a 1440-acre farmout on proven acreage in the Keystone field. Though the company granting the farmout, Pure Oil, did retain a reversionary working interest of fifty percent, the independents could scarcely have found a lower-risk venture, and it was highly profitable.[18]

Two years later Carter received another low-risk farmout on expiring leases owned by Continental Oil in northern Gaines county, in what would become the giant Wasson field. In return for spudding in four tests, Carter obtained a half-interest in six sections of land and an option to purchase acreage from Continental in six additional sections. The test, Carter-Continental Wasson No. 1, was successful, producing 294 barrels of 34.4-degree gravity oil and 4000 Mcf (thousand cubic feet) of natural gas per day. Soon afterward, Carter extended production in the field by three miles on another Continental farmout; this test brought in a well with a potential flow of more than 2000 barrels per day. Still later in 1937, Carter extended the Harper field in Ector County with a 608-barrel well on another farmout. His successes continued through the end of the decade. In 1940 he discovered the second and third producing horizons in the Wasson field when he followed the advice of his geologists and deepened two wells in the center of his lease block. Similarly, he reentered his Winkler County leases and found deeper production.[19] For Amon Carter, farmouts offered high-return, relatively low-risk opportunities.

Another Fort Worth operator to profit from farmouts was Sid Richardson, a paragon of the Texas good-ol'-boy oilman. With equal ease, he negotiated for leases while drinking buttermilk with Baptist ranchers and traded properties with fellow oilmen while downing more potent beverages. Though a shrewd businessman, Richardson liked to convey the impression that he was just plain folks. "Luck," he once remarked, "helped me every day of my life. And I'd rather be lucky than smart 'cause a lot of smart people ain't eatin' regular."[20] Despite this self-effacing observation, Richardson's success had far less to do with luck than with a canny ability to seize and exploit the peculiar opportunities of time and place — in this instance of Winkler County in the mid-thirties — and to do a lot with a little bit of money. Sid Richardon's success was not just luck.

In 1932, Sid Richardson was an independent of the traditional driller-promoter variety. He had made several small fortunes in developing and trading properties and lost them down dry holes. He had, however, managed to hold on to producing properties in Ward County that yielded a modest income. Richardson stretched that income as far as possible. He used secondhand equipment; like many a poor-boy operator, what he could not buy on credit, he borrowed. When other operators paid workers twice a month, Richardson paid once a month; sometimes he paid workers in groceries he obtained on credit. For all this, he got along well with his hands, kidding them and cadging sandwiches from their lunch boxes at the rig.[21]

In raising capital, Richardson augmented production income by borrowing on any asset a lender would accept as security for a loan. The daughter of a rancher from whom he leased many eventually productive acres noted, "My abstracts are full of liens against Sid Richardson." By the mid-thirties, however, Richardson had succeeded in interesting banks and other large lenders in his ventures. This development was in large part a result of proration; with regulated production and stable prices, banks and other lenders began to look more favorably on settled production as security for loans. Because proration was strictly followed in the pipeline-short Permian Basin, Richardson was able to obtain loans from First National Bank of Dallas on his production. He was also able to attract private lenders like prominent publisher Charles E. Marsh. As the scale of his operations grew and Richardson moved in the intermediate rank of independents, he found that his financial needs took him to banks in Chicago, Boston, and New York. Like their smaller Texas counterparts, these banks viewed oil as less speculative after statewide control of production was assured by the Texas Railroad Commission.[22] Richardson thus tailored his strategy to take advantage of new conditions.

On the basis of his earlier success in Ward County, Richardson negotiated a 240-acre farmout from Gulf, Skelly, Tidal, and the owners of minerals under other Winkler County leases. He improved this holding by gaining an additional contribution of acreage from Shell, with the right to purchase additional leases from companies leasing acreage from the Keystone Cattle Company and the J. B. Walton ranch. After reaching these agreements, Richardson marshaled the resources for his test well. Like most independents, he relied on his suppliers to provide credit, which was customarily extended for ninety days, with mechanics' liens on equipment taken as security. With a small stake of his own, and even more borrowed from others, Richardson drilled his well. It came in for 250 barrels a day; with a well completed by Gulf a week earlier, this discovery of a new productive sand opened the way for extensive development in the prolific Keystone field. The discovery well completed, Richardson exercised his options on acreage and acquired additional leases, accumulating twenty-one separate leases in the field.[23] Generous farmouts, shrewd dealing, and adequate financial backing, as well as the luck he was fond of citing, put Sid Richardson on the high road of success. By the end of 1940, Sid Richardson had 33 producing wells in the Keystone field, 7 in the Slaughter field, 38 in the South Ward field, and 47 in the Scarborough field. With more than 120 wells in three contiguous counties, Sid Richardson had put bean jobs far behind him.[24]

As major companies scrambled to hold acreage by meeting lease deadlines, other independents were able to follow Richardson's example on a more modest scale. In the discovery of production in the central Permian Basin, independents benefited not only from major-company investment in leases but also from expensive scientific work the majors had done earlier. The surface features of the central Permian Basin, an area including Andrews, Gaines, Yoakum, Hockley, and Cochran counties, as well as portions of Lea County, New Mexico, offered little information to geologists. There was much promise, however, in the data generated by the geophysicists who worked for Amerada, a large independent, and the major companies. Small and intermediate independents were priced out of the new science. In 1937, for example, the services of a reflection seismograph crew in the central Permian Basin cost roughly $9000 a month, while a torsion balance crew cost about $4000 a month.[25] These branches of exploration technology were thus beyond the reach of most independents.

The current stage of development of geophysics also limited its use by independents. The instruments and techniques available in the mid-thirties proved to be relatively reliable in locating large geological structures; for large companies with funds to invest in extensive lease inventories, they were valuable aids in reducing risks. Most small independents, however, worked one prospect at a time, and their leases were usually too small to be tested economically by the new geophysical methods. Even for intermediate independents, who might be able to assemble suitably large blocks of leases, the time required by geophysical testing was a drawback. Most crews worked during the summer and fall, when the weather was most favorable; data were processed during the winter and spring. While majors and large independents used this time for planning and implementation of other programs, small and intermediate independents found that the lead time extended their payouts beyond what they could accept. For these reasons, relatively few independents were able to take direct advantage of the most advanced prospecting techniques of the mid-thirties. But when major companies farmed out acreage on which their geophysical data showed promise, independent operators benefited from major-company science. Nor were they the only independents to gain.

Major-company interest in any area usually drove land prices up, making it harder for independent prospectors to acquire leases for themselves. The majors were well aware of the inflationary effect of their acquisitions, and this awareness provided opportunities for independent land-men, who often bought leases on assignment by the majors. The land-man signed the leases in his own name, paid the agreed-upon bonus, and then turned the leases over to the major or large independent in return for repayment of the purchase price plus a commission based on the number of acres involved in the transaction. In this way, during the thirties, Midlanders W. A. Yeager and Paul Davis, both former employees of major companies, were able to go into business as brokers of leases and minerals. Like other brokers, they were also able to pur-chase leases and minerals for themselves because they were well informed about shifts in leasing activity.[26]

Knowing where the action would move became particularly advan-tageous as the pace of activity quickened in the central Permian Basin during the mid-thirties. The first portent of hectic times was a well Humble drilled in 1934 on 20,000 acres of Andrews County leases that were to expire in 1936. That test brought in the rich Means field. A few months later and about forty-two miles to the northwest, in Yoakum County, C. J. Davidson and the Honolulu Oil Company brought in a discovery well on a 5100-acre lease farmed out by the Texas-Pacific Coal and Oil Company. This test provided strong reinforcement for seismic evidence of a trend running north from Andrews County. Major companies, as well as old drillers who knew how to lay a ruler on a county map, took a keen interest in this part of the Permian Basin, and lease prices on available land soared, rapidly becoming too expensive for most independents. But since major companies had an even stronger reason to hold on to their acreage, independents readily found farmouts.[27]

By 1940, oil activity in the Permian Basin had gone through another cycle of revival and decline. In 1937, one sign of revival in the indepen-dent sector of the petroleum industry was the reappearance of the small-scale promoter, a breed of independent whose operations suffered when the Depression decimated the ranks of small investors. Dad Joiner, for example, having survived his legal problems in East Texas, surfaced in Winkler County, where he picked up a lease on a section of land near existing production. Thereafter, like Roy Westbrook a decade earlier, he sold off small tracts within his lease, thus realizing a profit without drilling a well. Roy Westbrook himself undertook new Permian Basin ventures. These old-fashioned promoters still operated on the basis of popular notions of trendology rather than sophisticated science, and with the revival of oil activity, they were once again able to find small investors.[28]

The renewal of regional oil activity also permitted those oil and gas communities whose progress had been cut short in the early thirties to grow again. As the focus of regional activity shifted northward, Midland grew at a faster rate than its rival, San Angelo. By 1940, Humble's area headquarters had been located in Midland for eight years; Gulf, Shell, Stanolind, Continental, and Sinclair-Prairie were among the major companies that also had offices there. Better times drew some local ranchers to try their luck in oil. Holt Jowell and Roland L. "Buck" York, for example, took up trading in leases and minerals and later went on to become oil operators. For the most part, however, the community grew as outsiders opened offices in Midland and local major-company employees decided to go into business for themselves. Among independent firms from out of state were Barnsdall, Amerada, and Anderson-Pritchard, all from Oklahoma, and Forest Oil and Sloan and Zook from Pennsylvania. Several driller independents relocated in Midland from out of state, among them Joe L. Crump of Oklahoma; most oil field service businesses, however, located in Odessa, which was centrally positioned in the most active part of the region. A few oilmen moved to Midland from other towns in the area, among them T. N. Sloan; John and Prentiss Moore, landman and geologist respectively, moved there from San Angelo.[29]

As market conditions improved and area drilling activity increased in the latter half of the thirties, the Permian Basin oil and gas community in Midland also grew because scientists and landmen employed by major companies were tempted to go independent. Sometimes these professionals went independent on the basis of individual perception that the time was ripe for such a step; thus, scientific professionals O. C. Harper and George T. Abell decided to go into business for themselves. Others took the step after corporate management changes, mergers, and acquisitions left them in vulnerable positions or out of work. When the Sinclair takeover of Prairie Oil and Gas properties led to a consolidation of operations and a reduction of Permian Basin staff in the mid-thirties, for example, W. A. Yeager, a landman, and Edward Armstrong, a geologist, left Sinclair-Prairie and set up a partnership. Similarly, when geologist J. C. Williamson found himself increasingly at odds with the local management of Phillips, he decided to go into business on his own.[30]

Though the former company employees often went independent with relatively little capital, their past employment gave them significant advantages in business. Having worked for major companies in a management center like Midland, they had usually had a chance to become acquainted with independents in town and with employees of other companies. That exposure gave them potential business associates. Their previous employment had also familiarized them with major-company procedures, an advantage when approaching those companies with prospects or requests for farmouts. Among new independents, the geologists had a special advantage because they had often worked prospects that had been rejected by the major company but might be practical for a small independent. Both geologists and landmen, moreover, had become familiar with arenas of major-company activity, giving them access to the most promising areas. This specific knowledge, together with experience gained on major-company payrolls, was often the new independents' main asset.

Because geologists and landmen outnumbered engineers on major-company payrolls before the forties, they were most numerous among the ex-employee independents. The partnership of the geologist and the landman was an especially common and workable combination. Ordinarily the geologist worked up a geological prospect for which his landman partner acquired leases; they would then try to sell the package to a major or a larger independent that would undertake drilling. Thus the partnership combined scientific talent and business savvy. With a landman partner, the geologist had both ideas and land; with a geologist partner, the landman had the greater likelihood both of buying desirable leases and of enhancing their sales appeal with geological data and interpretations. Typically, once the partners were launched in business, they retained a working interest or an overriding royalty interest in their prospects, and they purchased mineral and royalty interests in the vicinity of the leases they sold.

One of the best-known and most successful of such partnerships in the Midland oil and gas community of the thirties was that of York and Harper. O. C. "Kip" Harper, a native of Chicago, had worked as a geologist for Gulf in the Permian Basin until 1927 when he decided to become an independent consultant. A brilliant geologist, Harper eventually was responsible for the discovery of nine oil fields; he supplied the geological data that led to Amon Carter's spectacular wildcat success in what became the Wasson field. Harper went into partnership with Buck York in the early thirties. By contrast to Harper, the sober scientist, York is remembered as one of the most unusual and colorful independents ever to work in West Texas. A rancher, York had worked in a county clerk's office, where he learned one of the basic skills of a landman, that of tracing titles. The other essential skill, the ability to talk readily with landowners, York enjoyed by virtue of his background and personality; as Tom Sloan, son of T. N. Sloan, observed, "Buck York could buy a lease from anybody." A large, tall man, York was a natural prankster with a broad streak of generosity. On one occasion he is said to have looked out a hotel window in El Paso and noticed people in a park below; deciding that they looked hungry, he called room service and ordered sandwiches and drinks for everyone in the park. Midland folklore holds that he once bought a Cadillac in Fort Worth and had its cost charged to his hotel bill: when the new desk clerk, unfamiliar with York's wealth, called up to his room and asked, "Well, sir, can you tell me who you are with?" York is said to have turned from the phone and asked, "Hey, honey, what's your name?" Stories of this kind have been told about countless oilmen, and York was not above telling them on himself because he understood the value of a high profile within the oil and gas community. When opportunity could depend on being known and remembered, Buck York was not the sort of man anyone was likely to ignore or forget.[31]

York and Harper's first major commercial success was the discovery of the Foster field in Ector County. As in earlier ventures, Harper's geology was innovative and departed from prevailing opinion about the area. When it came time to sell this prospect, Harper took special care to do up meticulous maps and diagrams, for he knew that buyers would not be easy to convince. The partners traveled to Fort Worth and met with representatives of a major company to talk over the prospect. Then, as William Y. Penn, who knew both men, recalled it:

> They got in, and Kip gave his spiel and pulled out all these beautiful colored cross-sections and the maps he'd drawn up, and along about the end of Kip's presentation, Buck says to him, "Kip, could I see you out in the hall for a minute?" So they stepped out in the hall, and Buck says, "Kip, goddamn, if it's that good, let's keep it ourselves!" And they did. And it's the one that made 'em. They borrowed money, they did everything but steal that first well down, and that was the thing that made 'em.

By 1940, the field was producing about 19,000 barrels of oil a day.[32]

As the number of independent scientific consultants, landmen, traders, and operators at work in Midland grew in the late thirties, the investment base of this oil and gas community broadened. It became possible, on a modest scale, to generate prospects, sell deals, drill wells, and operate producing wells with the resources of the business community. By this time, the town's two banks, the First National Bank of Midland and the Midland National Bank, were making small short-term loans to independents with tangible assets to offer as collateral. Then as now, the banks did not provide loans for wildcatting, but their increased willingness to treat local oilmen like conventional personal and commercial borrowers served to multiply the funds available to them within the community. That in turn encouraged further growth of the local oil and gas community and fostered the proliferation of local business and investment circles.[33]

Despite spectacular regional finds and a high overall level of petroleum activity, both the prosperity and the growth of the Midland oil and gas community were constrained by prevailing market conditions and regulation. The chief barriers to local growth in the late thirties and early for-

ties were low crude oil prices and the general reluctance of major purchasers to buy large amounts of sour crude when sweet crude could readily be found elsewhere. The revival of oil activity, not only in the Permian Basin but in western Kansas and South and Southwest Texas as
well, added great quantities of oil to the Mid-Continent market, assur-
ing that supply would keep pace with rising national demand for gasoline
and petroleum products. In 1937, geophysical prospecting brought in
large southern Illinois fields, shallow production in close proximity to
refineries and major markets. Production from Illinois flooded the market
and depressed the price of crude oil. From 1936 to 1938, national crude
prices averaged $1.13 per barrel, but they dipped to $1.02 in 1939 and
1940 as increasing amounts of Illinois oil reached the market. Unlike
Texas and Oklahoma, Illinois had no state regulatory commission for
petroleum, and Illinois producers fiercely resisted efforts at control of
production.[34]

That major crude oil purchasers had attractive alternatives to Permian Basin crude was evident in regional prices. Even before Illinois
oil flooded the market, the top prices posted for Permian Basin crude
were well below the national average. In 1937, for example, posted prices
in West Texas ranged from 78 cents to $1.08 per barrel. The following
year, prices dropped an average of 13 cents, and major purchasers posted
prices ranging from 53 cents to 95 cents a barrel. Only some Rocky
Mountain and heavy Pacific Coast crudes sold for less. When an inves-
tigative committee of the Texas Legislature looked into the marked difference in prices between West and East Texas crude oil in 1937, major-
company spokesmen defended lower prices for West Texas crude oil on
the grounds that it was less profitable than East Texas crude to transport
and refine. In addition to damaging pipelines and refinery equipment
with its corrosive sulphur content, purchasers argued, West Texas crude
yielded smaller quantities of gasoline and other profitable products than
other crudes.[35]

Major Permian Basin purchasers continued to keep the lid on production by pipeline proration where their lines extended and by delay-
ing the construction of new lines. Nowhere was this policy more obvious than in the giant Wasson and Seminole fields, where producers
had to wait until 1940 for pipelines capable of handling as much as the
allowable production, which was low. To that time, most oil was hauled
from these fields by tank truck at high cost. Producers had a long
wait for low-cost transport, and when they received it, their runs were
prorated by purchasers. When the Railroad Commission raised the
Wasson field allowable in 1940, in response to new well completions,
Humble cut back runs from all wells by 25 percent. Sinclair-Prairie,
Cities Services, and Tidewater customarily took only 50 to 65 percent
of well allowables for their pipelines serving other West Texas fields.

In 1943 one journalist summed up West Texas' past and present by remarking, "Nature give it the handicap of being on the end of the line"; and what nature initiated, crude oil purchasers perpetuated.[36]

As conditions in the Permian Basin demonstrate, the passing of the East Texas crisis and the gradual improvement of petroleum prices in the late thirties did not mean that the economic problems of independents were past. Nor was proration, where it existed, an unmixed blessing. It worked to keep prices stable, but at a cost to the producer. For example, the Texas Railroad Commission, using market demand to determine regional and field allowable production, placed stringent limitations on Permian Basin production. In 1939, it responded to the flood of Illinois crude reaching the national market by trimming Texas production. It cut the allowable of most West Texas fields by 20 percent, but in the Pecos Valley field, where small independents were numerous and active, it cut production back 75 percent. In addition to lowering allowables, the commission also held production down by ordering statewide field-shutdown days; in 1939, there were 119 such days. Particularly for producers in older fields, this regulation slowed return on investment and retarded activity.[37]

At the same time that independents contended with low prices and extended payout periods, they faced steadily rising costs. While drillers like Peanuts Bradford continued to work on shoestring budgets, the days of hiring men on bean jobs and receiving free land from farmers and ranchers had come to an end by the late thirties. As the search for oil took prospectors to ever-greater depths — 6000 to 10,000 feet by the early forties — drilling became more time-consuming and expensive. In some places, drilling to new depths meant encountering types of formations, such as heaving shale on the Gulf Coast and hard chert in the Permian Basin, that posed difficult and costly drilling problems. In the Permian Basin, as in other areas, operating required increasing amounts of capital. In 1932, for example, the average cost of a well was $12,000; by 1938, that figure had reached $25,000. A half-dozen years later, the cost of drilling to 4000 or 5000 feet averaged $35,000.[38] By present-day standards, such costs seem amazingly low, but to the independent of four decades ago, financing his tests through farmouts and dry-hole money, they presented an increasing economic challenge.

Given the nature of the economic problems facing most independents at the beginning of World War II, it was reasonable to expect that war would bring new prosperity by increasing the demand for petroleum. But war, far from relieving independents' problems, aggravated them in some regions; prosperity was not universal.

American oil producers experienced the first adverse effect of European conflict in 1939, when the outbreak of war disrupted European petroleum markets. Within the first year of European warfare, American petroleum exports to Europe fell 23 percent. Texas producers, in particular, were hurt by the loss of French and Italian markets for heavy crude oil. As the supply of this oil far exceeded the demand early in 1940, the Texas Railroad Commission reacted by increasing the number of statewide field-shutdown days and cutting back allowables 20 percent. The cutbacks led one imaginative Texas independent, Jerome McLester of Graham, to seek his own overseas outlet for production: he cabled an offer to Winston Churchill of 50,000 barrels of his crude oil for the Allies if they would both talk the Railroad Commission into letting him produce it and pay its transport cost.[39] Most independents, however, resigned themselves to tighter constriction of their production.

Much worse was to come. The greater part of the Texas crude oil that reached East Coast refineries was carried from the Gulf Coast by tanker, so maintenance of that transport system was of great importance, not only to shippers and refiners but to the national defense as well. Yet before it entered the war, the United States lent Great Britain fifty tankers from this system. The consequence of the loan was clear in 1942, when enemy submarine attacks on the remainder of the fleet caused serious disruption in the movement of oil from Texas ports. Responding to the tanker shortage and consequent pressure on Gulf Coast storage facilities, major purchasers cut back shipments of oil to the Gulf Coast. Permian Basin producers were especially affected by this cutback, since most Permian Basin pipelines fed trunk lines to the Gulf Coast. By November 1942, West Texas daily production was 100,000 barrels below what it had been a year earlier, and the area was producing less than 60 percent of its potential. While producers in Illinois, Oklahoma, and Kansas benefited from accelerated demand for oil to supply Midwestern trunk lines and refineries, Permian Basin producers were worse off than ever. Their lot did not greatly improve until the last year of the war, when the completion of the Big Inch and Little Inch pipelines provided an efficient alternative to tankers supplying the East Coast.[40]

While wartime dislocations of transportation and marketing created particular problems for Texas independents, all independents faced difficulties from the lengthened payouts that resulted from federal regulation. In May 1941, President Roosevelt created the Office of Petroleum Coordinator for National Defense, which in 1942 became the Petroleum Adminstration for War (PAW). At the head of this agency Roosevelt placed Harold Ickes, who thereby obtained much of the regulatory power over the petroleum industry he had sought for almost a decade. A believer in conventional notions of petroleum conservation, Ickes initially used his new power to achieve the objective of federal policy of the twenties and thirties: keeping American oil in the ground. Ickes lost no time in putting a lid on uncontrolled production in Illinois and California; his office took over the Bureau of Mines' practice of suggesting maximum allowables and, where there were no state regulatory agencies, imposed those allowables upon production. In states with regulatory bodies, Ickes's allowables did not have absolute force, but for the most part state agencies like the Texas Railroad Commission set production levels close to the amounts suggested in Washington.[41]

Though Ickes consulted industry advisers, PAW regulation suffered from lack of familiarity with the realities of oil field operations. Blanket regulations, issued to apply to the whole nation, emerged as neither efficient nor equitable. Order M-68, for example, applied a forty-acre spacing rule to all United States oil fields, without regard for the variability of geological formations. Similarly, it defined a wildcat well as one that was a minimum of two miles from production, even though the complex geology of some regions meant that bona fide wildcats could be much closer to existing production. To obtain a waiver to Order M-68, it was necessary to dig through an avalanche of red tape. Major companies and larger independents with scientists on the payroll could present expert arguments for granting exceptions where the rules were particularly unworkable, but few small independents had the resources to conduct such campaigns.[42]

The PAW's power to enforce Order M-68 and other regulations lay primarily in its control, through recommendations to the War Production Board (WPB), over operators' access to materials that defense needs placed in short supply. Wartime needs for metals cut into the supply of raw material for such oil field necessities as pipe, steel for rig building, and machinery. To obtain controlled materials, operators had to deal with a formidable quantity of paperwork. One oilman who wished to obtain 700 pounds of arc-welding electrodes claimed that he had to fill out 199 priority forms, each three pages long and requiring the seal and signature of a notary. Large companies, both independent and major, were at less disadvantage than small operators, for most large companies had materials in inventory on which they could draw while waiting for Washington to process forms. Smaller operators turned to used equipment dealers and the black market; if price was no object, they could readily find what they needed.[43] Even with these expedients, shortages and red tape combined to slow the pace of oil field activity and raise costs for independents.

Doing business during the war was complicated by shortages of manpower as well. Enlistments and conscription took a toll not only on the oil field labor force but also on the ranks of scientists and other professionals. The impact was evident in local oil and gas communities. In Midland, for example, nearly 40 percent of the independent oilmen and consultants listed in the city directory in 1941 were absent from that listing in 1945. Of this missing segment of the community, the largest number were those who had gone into business for themselves after 1935. Some old-timers, among them Fred Fuhrman and Fred Turner, remained in business during the war. The more recent consultant partnerships like Lloyd and Penn, and Yeager and Armstrong, were busier than ever. Indeed, the few scientific professionals who worked as independent consultants during the war had all the business they could handle.[44] But war caused the oil and gas community to contract in size, despite the national wartime need for petroleum.

The effect of wartime regulation upon the American petroleum industry was indeed striking. Though crude oil production reached a record level, in 1944 the amount of new oil discovered dropped to the lowest level in a decade; wildcatting, drilling, and additions to reserves all dropped sharply. Regulation and constricted market outlets forced West Texas and New Mexico independents to cut down their activity. As W. D. Noel recalled:

> We had a lot of wells shut in, the capacity shut in. And the manpower and the steel and the industrial equipment needed in drilling oil wells was needed in the war effort. . . . During this period of time the only priority that we had was keeping the wells that we had producing. . . . We did sell one of our leases during that time; I think we would have had trouble servicing our debt had we not done that, because allowables were so restricted. We did no drilling at all from the early part of '43 . . . until after the war was over."[45]

Larger independents than Noel kept drilling, but regulatory red tape and wartime shortages greatly impeded their business. How great a slowdown war meant for independents may be gauged from the operations of Texas's largest drilling contractor of the early forties, Carl B. King. King had been active in the Permian Basin during the late thirties, and during the war he continued to drill wells similar to those he had drilled earlier, in fields with which he was thoroughly familiar. Before 1941, King drilled eight wells in the North Cowden field in Ector County, taking an average time of five weeks per well; during the war, each of six wells he drilled in the same field, to approximately the same depth, took an average of thirteen weeks to complete. A large and efficient contractor, working in a familiar area with the most modern equipment, King took more than twice as long to get work done in wartime as in peace.[46] To the independent, such wartime delays meant not only that drilling was more expensive but also that the time between investment and payout was ever longer.

Lengthening of payout time was an important cause of the drop in wildcatting, drilling, and additions to reserves. In wartime, independents faced a longer wait for the return of their capital and, hence, a longer wait between projects; the number of new ventures they could fund under such circumstances declined. Had Washington let demand for petroleum determine prices, the constrictions of income caused by delays would have been offset to some extent by higher prices. But that was precisely what government officials did not do. Instead, the Office of Price Administration (OPA) set a ceiling on oil prices at the October 1941 level. There they remained until the war was over. By 1943 the developing cost-price squeeze in the petroleum industry brought even Harold Ickes to join the IPAA in lobbying for higher crude oil price ceilings. The OPA obdurately turned their pleas aside.[47]

By 1945 the oilmen who survived the national cataclysms of depression and war had adjusted to a business environment quite different from the twenties. Low prices and regulation of production changed basic ground rules; the unrestrained flush production that sustained many independents was now, for the majority of producers, a thing of the past. Those who coped with 50-cent-a-barrel oil and twelve shutdown days a month, however, had reason to be optimistic as the World War ended. Though wartime dislocation and regulation had created some formidable barriers to profit making, market conditions in 1945 were much better than in 1933. Wartime improvements in pipeline systems made it easier for producers to sell the oil they produced. All that seemed to stand in the way of a new era of prosperity was federal price regulation. Surely that would go the way of blackout curtains, and the future would be brighter.

5: A TIME TO GROW

For independent oilmen, the decade after World War II was prosperous beyond expectation. Unprecedented demand for petroleum led to the highest prices for crude oil since the early twenties, and these higher prices, in turn, spurred a record level of exploration and development. There was only one unpromising feature in this otherwise happy picture, and that was the rapidly mounting cost of finding new oil. Though domestic prices for both crude oil and natural gas reached levels that would have seemed fantastic to operators during the thirties, costs of operation rose much faster than prices. For both independents and major companies, the ever-higher cost of finding new oil had a profound effect upon strategies and operations.

Much to independent producers' chagrin, burdensome federal regulation did not vanish soon after V-J Day. Though the Petroleum Administration for War began to disband its operations a few months after Japan's surrender, it was not officially terminated until May 1946. That sharpest thorn in the oilman's side, the Office of Price Administration, continued as active as ever, and as reluctant as ever to permit increases in petroleum prices. Not until April 1946 did the OPA concede a 10-cent across-the-board increase in crude oil prices, a concession it justified by acknowledging that independent producers were not equaling even the modest rate of return they had enjoyed between 1936 and 1939. So niggardly did the OPA's action seem to independents that it prompted Texas operators to unite that same month to found the Texas Independent Producers and Royalty Owners' Association (TIPRO). The association's first president, H. J. "Jack" Porter, a forceful Houston independent, announced that the group's main objective was "to get out from under the OPA." When the OPA's control of petroleum prices finally terminated on June 30, 1946, TIPRO shifted its lobbying activities to include a wider variety of issues, and it continued to be active on both national and state levels.[1]

Not only did prices stay frozen far longer than oilmen expected but shortages of materials also continued to hold back operations long after the war was over. Structural steel, casing, drill pipe, tubing, pipe fittings, clutches, chain belts, and electrical equipment were in especially short supply; all steel products were hard to find because they were in demand by other domestic industries and by postwar reconstruction programs in Europe. In the face of strong demand for steel, the United Steel Workers union pressed for higher wages. When management refused, workers struck mills, foundries, and shops. The consequences were soon evident in the oil field. By 1947 materials shortages had become so critical that TIPRO pressed for a congressional investigation of them; Jack Porter charged that the major companies and the federal government were largely responsible for the situation. The majors, he claimed, had stockpiled tubing and pipe for shipment abroad, to use in the development of their foreign concessions. The federal government, for its part, used the scarcity of goods to retard the recovery of the domestic industry, with the intention, according to Porter, of using resultant oil shortages to justify regulated domestic crude prices and stepped-up imports. TIPRO called for action from both Congress and the petroleum industry; it asked for a federal ban on export of scarce tubular goods and a pooling of stockpiled items in short supply for allocation on a priority basis.[2] Neither proposal came to anything. Congress ignored the call for an export ban, and industry members continued to stockpile the materials they could get. Shortages of steel goods gradually eased as immediate postwar needs were met, but the high level of activity in the petroleum industry kept the field equipment high-priced and subject to spot shortages.

Steel goods were not the only oil field materials in short supply. So pressing were the postwar needs of so many industries that unpredicted shortages developed in materials that oilmen had obtained with less difficulty during wartime. Cement, for example, was in great demand for road and building construction. Field operations in regions like West Texas slowed down as operators waited for deliveries. Ever-deeper drilling, moreover, required larger quantities of cement per well; a deep well to formations below 10,000 feet took 12,000 or more sacks of cement to complete.[3] Thus, in well completion, as in other oil field operations, essential items were increasingly scarce and expensive.

If most oilmen did not foresee the postwar problems with materials shortages, even the most seasoned of industry observers were unprepared for the massive and sustained demand for petroleum that came with peace. Humble president H. C. Wiess, for example, thought the first year of peace would bring a contraction of demand for oil and gasoline, which would in turn bring falling prices and cuts in production of crude oil. But as often happens, reality confounded the experts: gasoline consumption rose rapidly after the end of rationing, and new patterns of consumption greatly enhanced demand for other petroleum products. Perhaps most important was the marked increase in the use of fuel oil at the expense of coal, a development encouraged by postwar strikes by the United Mine Workers. While demand for fuel oil skyrocketed, even natural gas, previously a virtual by-product of oil exploration and long without a large national market, enjoyed burgeoning demand after the war, both as a fuel and as the source of a growing number of products. By 1949, for the first time in the nation's history, consumption of oil and gas outstripped that of all other energy sources, including coal.[4]

The postwar demand for oil and gas was so great that during 1946 and 1947, the petroleum industry barely met consumer needs. Demand rose 11.2 percent in the first three months of 1947 alone, and there were localized fuel oil shortages in the East and Midwest. By autumn, 1947, the national supply of oil seemed so far below demand that the Texas Railroad Commission ordered no field-shutdown days, the first time that had happened in eight years. This extraordinary demand was met in part with imported crude oil, and in 1948, despite peak domestic production, the United States became a net importer of oil. Though many spokesmen for independent interests were dismayed by this development, rank-and-file independents did not rally to oppose it.[5] Finding oil, rather than political lobbying, had their full attention, and as long as business was booming, imports did not threaten them.

As demand surged, petroleum prices rose to heights unequaled in almost three decades, beginning as soon as OPA controls ceased. The posted price of a barrel of intermediate-gravity West Texas crude, for example, frozen at 92 cents during World War II, jumped to $1.27 in July 1946, rose another 10 cents before the year's end, and went to $1.62 in March 1947, to $1.82 in October, and to $2.32 in December 1947. The last price increase, of 50 cents a barrel, was unprecedented; major companies resisted it, giving in only when the lesser majors and independent refiners threatened to seize the lion's share of new connections.[6]

Strong national demand and resulting higher prices prompted a tremendous burst of exploration and development. Independents moved quickly to drill locations left untouched because of wartime regulation, shortages, delays, and low prices; they completed a record number of wells in 1947 and 1948, and exploratory drilling reached all-time high levels. High prices encouraged wildcatting even in areas like the Rocky Mountain district and off the coasts of Texas and Louisiana, where operators faced exceptionally steep costs. In older fields, independents prospected for new and deeper pays. As a result of this frenzied activity, record-breaking additions were made to American petroleum reserves.[7]

In the Permian Basin, the years following World War II were years of all-out boom, both because of high petroleum prices and because the completion of wartime pipeline projects meant a tremendous enlargement of the region's outlet for oil and gas. By 1948 major pipeline arteries connected regional oil fields not only with Gulf Coast and Oklahoma refineries but with West Coast markets as well. Refiners from outside Texas, particularly those from the fuel-short Midwest, moved in to compete with Gulf Coast purchasers. Competition grew so strenuous that purchasers began to offer producers novel inducements to sign contracts. Apart from price bonuses, some offered casing and other scarce tubular goods; one purchaser created an oil loan department to advance working capital to individual firms for drilling, in return for purchase rights. Though buyers were most eager for lighter sweet crudes, even heavy sour crude found a ready market when the U.S. Navy entered into purchase programs with Gulf Coast refiners for massive quantities of fuel oil to replenish the stores it had used up during the war. By 1947, a barrel of heavy West Texas crude sold for $2, a price beyond the wildest dreams of a Permian Basin producer two decades earlier.[8]

Purchasers were eager to make contracts in the Permian Basin not only because they knew it was capable of great production but also because, by the postwar years, an increasing volume of the region's production was high-gravity sweet crude oil, the sort of crude oil most profitable to refine. Prospectors had sought this desirable oil since the deep Big Lake discoveries of the late twenties. For the most part, it came from formations below 4000 feet, most particularly from the Devonian and Ellenburger formations. The discovery of high-grade crude below the Permian formations encouraged deep tests in both new areas and old fields; it also led to reinvestigation of areas where prospecting had been unsuccessful in the twenties and thirties.[9]

Prospectors were also increasingly inclined to seek oil in new places, applying new geological theories. At a time of strong demand and high prices, the risks of wildcatting and experimentation were more easily afforded by independents; with higher income, they could be more venturesome. Prospectors' interest turned to a long-neglected area, the eastern part of the Permian Basin, where the Midland Basin and the reef structures near the Permian Basin's edge offered new opportunities to test geological theories. Independents made the first breakthrough in this area in 1947; Plymouth Oil–Slick and Urschel's Alford No. 1, the discovery well of the Benedum field in eastern Upton County, brought in commercial production from the Ellenburger formation at about 12,000 feet. The strike, which railroad commissioner Ernest Thompson declared to be the most important Texas discovery of the year, was first thought to herald a giant, East Texas–sized field. Such hopes were far too optimistic, but the oil found in the Benedum field did prompt geologists to speculate that there might be much more oil at greater depths in the Midland Basin than they had thought. The practical drawback to such speculation was the expense of testing it: the cost of drilling to 11,000 or 12,000 feet ran as high as $300,000, a daunting amount to most independents. Major companies were thus predominant in the initial search for oil in the Midland Basin, and their scientists were so intent on finding deep oil that it was more than a year after the Benedum field discovery before they realized that there might be desirable production at shallower depths than 12,000 feet.[10] In the meantime, a series of discoveries in the Scurry County area took the limelight away from the Midland Basin, capturing the attention of scientists, prospectors, and promoters alike, for they outlined a new oil trend on the eastern edge of the Permian Basin. The trend, an arc-shaped series of Pennsylvanian reef formations capable of yielding an enormous quantity of oil, extended through Scurry County to Kent, Borden, and Howard counties; oil-producing formations could generally be tapped at depths of 6000 to 7000 feet.

Prospecting in the trend was highly attractive to independents, particularly because landholding patterns favored independents and lease brokers. Unlike other parts of the Permian Basin, where large ranches predominated, much of the land in central Scurry County was divided into 80- to 320-acre farms. As Joseph I. O'Neill, Jr., who had just begun lease trading, put it, "Thank God there were small tracts. . . . If you'd been dealing with one or two large ranchers, there would have been no place for an independent." It was O'Neill's good fortune that he and John Castleman, his partner, had acquired about 1500 Scurry County acres before the discovery of oil in the Canyon Reef formation. As one Midland oilman recalled,

> Scurry County was sort of the graveyard of counties up here. So [Castleman and O'Neill] went up there and bought a whole bunch of leases. They tried to sell the things. They were buying them for $5 an acre; you could buy any lease in Scurry County for $5 an acre. And they called me up at Cities Service, and I'm sure they did every other landman, and wanted to sell those leases for $25 an acre. I said, "We're not interested in anything. We weren't interested in [them] at $5 an acre, we surely wouldn't be at $25." And they were stuck with them, with the leases, and of course they found that production.

In O'Neill's words, "Lightning struck, and we hit within the first year." Other new brokers, among them Midlander William D. Kennedy, secured smaller Scurry County tracts; in some instances, leases as small as an acre traded hands, often being picked up by small independents.[11]

Though Standard of Texas made the great Canyon Reef discovery, independents were especially important in defining the limits of production. Much as in the northern and central Permian Basin in the thirties, independents established the boundaries of the giant Canyon Reef field by following productive geological formations into neighboring counties. The excitement surrounding the opening of the giant field made it easy to find risk capital even outside the oil industry. W. A. Moncrief, for example, found Hollywood celebrities Bob Hope and Bing Crosby ready to invest in a Scurry County project with him in 1949, a venture that brought in good production. By 1951, production in Scurry County encompassed an area of roughly seventy-five square miles; 1650 Canyon Reef wells produced 3.5 million barrels of sweet, high-gravity crude during the month of January 1951 alone. The eastern part of the Permian Basin seemed like an oil prospector's dream come true.[12]

Activity in Scurry and contiguous counties provided tremendous stimulus for growth to the Midland oil and gas community. Between 1946 and 1951 the number of independents and major oil companies doing business in Midland climbed from 135 to 363, an increase of more than 160 percent. Many of the new entrants were already engaged in business elsewhere and set up district or divisional offices in town. J. S. Abercrombie of Houston, Rowan Drilling of Fort Worth, and the Lion Oil Company, an integrated Arkansas company, opened offices in Midland for the first time, though they had long been active elsewhere. The early success of some Midland independents — Castleman and O'Neill, for example — also encouraged local businessmen to try their luck at oil; among them were a local Chevrolet dealer, a former rancher, a gasoline distributor, and a dentist who had married into a local oil family.[13]

Midland banks became increasingly active in oil and gas lending, to the point that fully one quarter of the loans of the First National Bank of Midland and a comparable proportion of those of the Midland National Bank were extended to oilmen. Both banks developed specialized professional staffs of geologists and engineers, and they set up departments for oil and gas loans during the boom period. Most of the loans available locally were still relatively small. The banks provided funds mainly to solve the perennial cash flow problems of independents. Many independents had good properties but lacked the funds to tide them over between the time that drilling, service, and supply companies required payment, often as long as ninety days after delivery, and the accumulation of the requisite income from production. Much like conventional commercial loans, most of these loans were given on the basis of "balance sheet" evaluations of assets, liabilities, and cash flow. Only gradually did the local banks include analysis of scientific data on reserves as a component of loan decisions.[14]

Even with the growing number of local investors and the increasing willingness of local banks to expand their commitment, independents based in the Permian Basin still had to find most of their funds for exploration projects elsewhere. Movie stars and other tax-motivated investors provided large quantities of risk capital for independents. Some of the new independents, especially those from other parts of the country, specialized in placing "foreign" capital from Eastern and Midwestern investors. In fact, the raising and placement of capital from nonproducing regions became the specialty of one group of newcomers, who were usually tagged the Ivy Leaguers. Some of them, notably George H. W. Bush and Earle M. Craig, Jr., both Yale alumni, were literally Ivy Leaguers. Others, such as John and Hugh Liedtke, were identified with the group because they had been educated at Eastern schools and raised funds through financial connections in Ohio, Pennsylvania, New York, and other Northern states. The Ivy Leaguers and non–Ivy Leaguers alike looked outside the local business community when they needed large loans for development projects. Midland independents obtained loans from Dallas and Houston banks, but they took extensive projects to Chicago and New York for funding. In the process they developed close ties to larger banks, among them the Continental Illinois Bank and Trust of Chicago and the Chase Manhattan Bank of New York. These ties facilitated the partial integration of the local oil and gas community into the broader national business community. Though local circles firmed up during the fifties as the newcomers found their niches and local associates, the development of stronger links to other regions and to nationally important banks both provided necessary funds during the great boom of the late forties and early fifties and kept opportunities open for the Ivy Leaguers and other newcomers.[15]

By the end of June 1950, when the Permian Basin was the most active drilling area in the world, there was a wide range of business opportunity, not only for oil operators but for drilling contractors, well service companies, and other oil field enterprises. By 1950, the Permian Basin was an alluring area for investments in oil. Not only did a high level of wildcatting take place in the region after the war, but that wildcatting was remarkably successful. While few discoveries as spectacular as the Canyon Reef emerged, of 245 West Texas wildcats drilled in 1948, 63, or 25.7 percent, were productive, a strikingly successful record when the nationwide wildcatting success rate was but half as good. The combination of record amounts of exploration with extensive development produced a prodigious quantity of oil. By August 1950, the Permian Basin produced roughly 1 million barrels of oil a day: its production capacity was comparable to that of Venezuela, then second only to the United States in world production.[16] The region had achieved an awesome importance in the American petroleum industry.

In the hectic prosperity that followed World War II, it was easy to overlook signs that the postwar golden age might be short. Yet by 1950, problems that would plague independent operators for the next three decades were visible, if not as obtrusive as they would become. One problem, production in excess of market demand, was certainly not novel. After 1948, the postwar demand for oil tapered off; supply caught up with demand, and prices slid downward in many areas. In Texas, the Railroad Commission responded to declining prices by cutting back allowables. The seller's market in oil ended, and in its place were the more familiar ebbs and flows of demand in response to short-term conditions.[17]

Far more foreboding than prices, however, were signs that increased regulation, at both state and federal levels, would make operations ever more complicated and expensive. It is ironic that much of the controversy over regulation that followed World War II concerned not oil but gas, for so long of secondary importance in the petroleum industry in general and certainly to Permian Basin independents in particular. The growing market for natural gas that developed during the war, however, brought both the Texas Railroad Commission and the Federal Power Commission to intervene in matters relating to gas production; the Railroad Commission asserted itself in the name of conservation, and the FPC on behalf of a growing number of consumers in nonproducing states. With differing objectives, the two regulatory agencies often emerged with conflicting policies; oilmen were caught in the middle.

Reacting in part to the postwar upturn in the market for natural gas and its products, the Texas Railroad Commission turned its attention to conservation of gas produced coincidentally with oil. As engineers learned more about oil reservoirs, they came to value gas as a prime agent in recovering oil: the more one conserved an oil reservoir's gas, the greater the recovery of oil one could expect from the reservoir. But conserving gas was easier to talk about than to practice.

For an operator, the great barrier to conserving casinghead gas, as all gas produced with oil was commonly termed, was finding a way to use it without losing money. There were two major problems: casinghead gas varied at the wellhead in pressure and amount, and field-shutdown days shut in both oil and the gas produced with it. For these reasons, large gas purchasers were not eager to acquire casinghead gas as it came from the wellhead. They needed large, dependable supplies of gas at constant pressures to fill their pipelines. As a result, most of the casinghead gas that got used was used in or near the oil fields. Some operators used it for fuel in operations. Others sold gas to local carbon black plants, if there were such facilities. The few large and intermediate operators willing to reach unitization agreements and invest substantial sums in equipment and expertise used casinghead gas to restore pressure in oil reservoirs. More commonly, operators looked to local gasoline plants, which processed liquids from gas and sold or disposed of the residue, to take casinghead gas off their hands.[18]

If gasoline plants capable of processing all of the gas produced with oil had been located in all oil fields, there would be no reason for operators to flare off casinghead gas; this ideal situation would have met Railroad Commission conservation objectives during the late forties. But while gasoline plants solved conservation problems, they presented their own economic difficulties. In addition to the postwar shortages of construction materials, there was also the unavoidable reality of high construction costs of gasoline plants and gathering lines. Few small and intermediate independents could afford to invest in them; they lacked both capital and the incentive to raise it because the rate of return on investments in gasoline plants was unusually low, certainly much lower than the return on other investments in oil. Gasoline plants also were economical only in large fields with many wells. In small, underdeveloped, and isolated fields, operators often had no alternative but to flare gas produced with oil. Moreover, in the few small fields with installations, the facilities often lacked the capacity to process all of the gas produced. For these reasons, economics frequently dictated a course at odds with conservation.[19]

Despite these economic problems, in 1947 the Texas Railroad Commission ordered well shutdowns where it found operators flaring large quantities of casinghead gas.[20] Its first target was the Seeligson field, in Jim Wells and Kleberg counties, where it required that all oil or gas be put to use that conformed to its conservation orders. The Seeligson order marked the first shot in a series of legal battles over gas conservation from which the commission emerged triumphant; like it or not, oil operators would have to live with the commission's new policy. By the end of 1948, eighty-two projects utilizing casinghead gas had been completed in Texas and forty-three more were under way. Investment in such projects, however, was undertaken almost exclusively by major companies and large independents, often acting cooperatively. In the West Texas Slaughter field, for example, Stanolind, Texaco, Magnolia, and Honolulu constructed a large plant as a joint venture; Phillips operated plants in the Goldsmith and McElroy fields, while Shell built an installation in the TXL field. When the average well's daily output of casinghead gas sold for only 90 cents, the small independent was in no position to finance such projects: he had to depend on larger companies to supply an outlet for his gas. The alternative was a shutdown of his wells by the Railroad Commission.[21]

When the Railroad Commission embarked upon its crusade to end the widespread waste of gas, it argued that higher gas prices would eventually help meet the cost of conservation. On the issue of prices, however, commission goals ultimately clashed with the rate-setting policies of the Federal Power Commission. This body, created by the Natural Gas Act of 1938, had as its primary function the regulation of interstate commerce in natural gas, a role modeled on that of the Interstate Commerce Commission. Though the Natural Gas Act originally forbade FPC intervention in production and gathering of gas in the field, by the end of the war the FPC had enlarged its scope over over transmission and gathering. When the U.S. Supreme Court directed the FPC to control the price of gas sold by producers to interstate operating companies in 1954, the FPC gained control of gas in the field. It sought, as in past years, to keep those prices low. For producers, this sequence of events had two important consequences. First, federal control of the interstate market kept interstate prices lower than those prevailing on intrastate markets. Second, producers therefore found the intrastate market increasingly attractive in marketing their gas. As more gas found its way to the intrastate market, the price of casinghead gas stayed low.[22]

At the same time that operators of all sizes faced increased regulation, they also encountered higher operating costs across the board, in all segments of the industry. Many of these increases were specific extensions of postwar inflation. During a three-year period between 1948 and 1951, average wages rose in the oil industry by as much as 36 percent; costs of casing, tubing, and drill pipe rose 24 to 30 percent. But there were also conditions peculiar to the oil industry that contributed to higher costs. Drilling for deeper and deeper oil raised costs of exploration and development dramatically. It cost three times as much to drill to 10,000 feet as to 7000 feet; it could cost ten times as much to drill to 14,000 feet as to 7000 feet, a phenomenon explained by problems with hard formations, high temperatures, extreme pressures, and equipment limitations at great depths. The greater cost of deeper drilling, however, was not necessarily matched by greater returns. With a few exceptions, the Scurry County bonanza being among the most important, postwar prospectors found smaller fields and thinner pays. The result of these developments was an ever-higher cost of finding oil to replace oil produced. According to one estimate, by 1947 it cost six times as much to find a barrel of oil as it had in 1935. It was clear to operators that costs were rising faster than prices and attractive returns were hard to get.[23]

Small independent drilling contractors were among those hardest hit by soaring costs. While the great demand for rigs in the postwar exploration boom provided encouragement to enter contract drilling, rising costs pinched contractors' profits. In the Permian Basin between 1941 and 1947, the drilling contractor's cost of labor rose 37 percent, his equipment expenses 31 to 49 percent. During the same period, his revenue per foot drilled dropped 2 percent. Contractors were able to offset costs to some extent through more efficient operation. Improved equipment and technology enabled them to drill 25 percent faster in 1947 than they had in 1941. It was challenging, however, for a drilling contractor to make a sizable profit, even with greater efficiency and a sharp eye to holding down costs.

To meet the challenge, some contractors applied new strategies to meet local conditions. In the Midland Basin during the late forties, drilling contractors commonly agreed to drill to 8000 or 9000 feet on a footage basis, at $10 per foot, and then proceeded with deeper, slower drilling on a day-rate basis, thus shifting the higher cost of slow work to the operator. The drilling crew would race through the hole drilled on footage as fast as they could, to reach the level at which they would drill on a day-rate basis. Though this approach increased the drillers' revenue, it had a disadvantage for operators: in their haste, the crew occasionally drilled through and missed productive horizons at shallower depths. Even with such local stratagems, however, it was increasingly difficult for contractors to show a profit. A similar situation existed in geophysical services, where, between 1940 and 1954, wages doubled and other operating costs rose by 40 percent.[24] While crude prices rose, they did not keep pace with costs, especially during the Korean War, when prices were frozen. Though the cost-price gap is difficult to establish precisely for a single region, the situation in the Permian Basin seems to have reflected national trends. According to one estimate, in 1956 a barrel of oil cost all U.S. producers an average of $3.16 to replace, though the average price of a barrel was only $2.78.[25]

Like all interesting figures, after the maxim of one scholar, these are probably unreliable; they should be used only with caution as indications of the profitability of oil production in the mid-fifties. Most of the oil sold at $2.78 on average was actually discovered and produced at a figure below the sale price of it. Despite claims of the shriller spokesmen for the industry, oilmen simply were not losing 38 cents on every barrel of oil produced. What they were losing, however — the financial incentive to replace the reserves they were depleting — was of greater consequence than short-term profit.

But rising costs caused no mass defection from the ranks of the independent oilmen. The most pervasive response to the cost-price squeeze was the promotion of greater efficiency in the field. Producers of all sizes gave more attention to the recovery of the maximum amount of oil from their properties. Doing so gave new importance to understanding the behavior of reservoirs; it made reservoir engineers indispensable to a well-run production operation. Looking to maximum recovery also gave new impetus to workovers of declining wells. Though workovers seldom brought a spectacular increase in production, the average cost of workovers in West Texas almost never exceeded $5000 before 1952; the return on this investment was slow, but production could be sustained at less cost than drilling new wells.[26]

As the cost of finding new oil rose, it became more attractive for all operators to produce oil someone else had found. It became increasingly profitable both to buy reserves and to invest in secondary recovery projects. The latter strategy served to sustain production from older fields in which reservoir pressure had been depleted, often to the point at which production costs exceeded revenue. By injecting water or gas into these formations, operators stimulated stronger production. In the early fifties, operators had returned to the old oil fields of eastern Kansas and northeastern Oklahoma to undertake waterflood projects. In the Permian Basin, major companies experimented with secondary recovery in Ward and Winkler counties during the forties. During the following decade, a growing number of large and intermediate independents took part in secondary recovery projects, especially in Scurry and Ward counties.[27]

Engineering expertise was of paramount importance to successful secondary recovery projects, so waterfloods and other work fell more often to the newer independents, the scientists and technicians, rather than to the traditional drillers and promoters, who commonly lacked the expertise necessary to the completion and management of these technical operations. The new importance of secondary recovery did not generally mean greater opportunities for the traditional small independents, because the financial terms of such projects rarely permitted rapid payout. Like the purchase of production, secondary recovery projects tied up capital for extended periods. On the other hand, the scientists and the financiers who specialized in purchases and recovery work began to receive enthusiastic responses to such projects from bankers familiar with oil loans. As technological progress permitted engineers to make more exact determinations of reservoir characteristics and capacity, production loans became less risky.[28]

The expanding importance of secondary recovery projects also reinforced the case made by majors and large independents for unitization and control of production. In conducting such secondary projects as waterflooding, it was necessary to place all leases in the oil pool in the hands of one operator. What had been anathema for most independents during the twenties and thirties, when it had been seen as a device permitting major companies to restrict production at will, gained acceptance when maximum return on larger investments was at stake. These changes in attitudes found legislative expression in Texas in 1949, when a measure was passed permitting unit development under voluntary agreements. Unitization in the interest of repressuring reservoirs and obtaining higher production came into use not only in fields where flush production had vanished decades before but also in relatively new fields, like those in Scurry County, where operators wished to ensure continued high rates of recovery.[29]

The challenge of rising costs was a powerful incentive to change strategies and attitudes. Small independents were slowest to abandon traditional expectations and methods; highly local opportunities often enabled them to continue to use older approaches in small-scale ventures. But the greatest Permian Basin oil play of the fifties, that of Spraberry Trend, made it clear that successful independent strategy of the future would be tailored to using new science and technology and to working with state and federal regulation. In Spraberry, many traditional independents and promoters who rushed into projects without regard for their geological and economic complications were badly burned.

Compared to that in Scurry County, Spraberry activity got off the ground slowly. A large independent, the Seaboard Oil Company, made the first Spraberry discovery in 1943, but it did not establish commercial production until January 1949, when its well, Lee No. 2-D, flowed 319 barrels per day after being shot with nitroglycerin. During February 1949, Arthur "Tex" Harvey, an East Texas wildcatter, found oil in the same formation, some sixty-five miles to the south of Seaboard's well. Later in the month the Hunt interests of Dallas discovered Spraberry oil to the north, in Borden County. These three discoveries were overshadowed by the more sensational discoveries in Scurry County until 1950, when the limits of most of the Canyon Reef reservoirs were clearly defined.[30]

In 1950 a sequence of discoveries stimulated new interest in the Spraberry Trend. On January 8, Humble plugged back an Ellenburger test, Pembrook No. 1, in northeast Upton County, to bring in Spraberry production at about 7000 feet. Then, on March 6, a group of independents including the Fryer Drilling Company of Dallas, James H. Snowden of Roswell, New Mexico, and Ted Weiner, who had drilled many Permian Basin tests in the forties, shot their well, Andrew Fasken No. 1, with nitroglycerin and brought in flowing production of 69.5 barrels of high-gravity oil per day, from a depth close to that of the Humble well. This well, about nine miles north of the Tex-Harvey pool, had been drilled, plugged, and abandoned by Seaboard and Standard of Texas in 1945; Fryer obtained a farmout to deepen it and sold parts of the deal to the other independents. Later in the year Spraberry production came in as a new pay in the Benedum field; Humble found Spraberry production between the Tex-Harvey and Pembrook pools, in southwestern Midland County; and operators made two additional Spraberry discoveries in central and north central Dawson County. As the extent of the trend was defined by these discoveries, a tremendous drilling boom was under way by 1951.[31]

Both the size of the trend and speculators' expectations of it were enormous. Feverish wildcat drilling during 1951 further established the trend's dimensions as roughly 150 miles from north to south and over 50 miles from east to west, running through ten West Texas counties. Some optimistic geologists estimated that its ultimate extension would encompass an area equal in size to the state of Connecticut, with recoverable reserves of more than 10 billion barrels of sweet crude oil and an unknown quantity of natural gas. Even more cautious observers expected the trend's productive area to be four times larger than the East Texas field; potential production was thought to be at least as great as that of northeastern Oklahoma or the Central Kansas Uplift. Few observers doubted that another major boom was in the making. Landmen and royalty traders plunged into purchases scattered through ten counties in a campaign that soon equaled the frenzied trading in Scurry County two years earlier. Indeed, it looked as if Spraberry would be a grand version of Scurry County, East Texas, and Hendrick all combined.[32]

Small independents, promoters, and speculators, meanwhile, flocked to Midland, the nearest town with adequate lodgings and office facilities, and set up local offices from which they could oversee the Spraberry action. As the available office space was inadequate to meet the sudden demand, small companies with close working relationships commonly shared what work space they could find. Thus some of the most active Los Angeles and Fort Worth developers of the Tex-Harvey area shared a single room at Midland's run-down Crawford Hotel, from which they ran their local operations.[33] It is one of the many paradoxes of the Spraberry story that these "outsiders," operators whose main base of operations lay outside the Permian Basin, were the initial "insiders," those most active in the trend's development.

For a short time it seemed like the Spraberry promoters could not lose: nearly every well drilled brought in production. As one observer remarked in 1951, "It has now come to the point where it is difficult to determine just what constitutes a wildcat in the area." The near-certainty of getting oil made it easy to find eager Spraberry investors, whose numbers included celebrities like Don Ameche. Better yet, from the promoter's point of view, it took relatively little money to complete a producing well in the Spraberry; production was comparatively shallow, drilling relatively quick, and costs usually ran between $100,000 and $125,000. At the federally frozen price of $2.58 a barrel for Spraberry crude, a well could be expected to pay out when it produced 50,000 barrels of oil. Considering that the Spraberry was conservatively estimated to hold at least 1000 to 3000 barrels of recoverable oil per acre, that alone would have made the trend attractive to investors. Prevailing estimates of the trend's potential, however, were anything but conservative; they reached as much as ten times the 3000-barrel-per-acre figure.[34]

The more flamboyant Spraberry promoters did not rely on economics alone in approaching potential investors but developed a combined appeal of money and sex. As E. E. Reigle recalled, some Los Angeles promoters imported a bevy of Hollywood beauties to the oil field for promotional pictures: "They had a whole bunch of models come out to the rig, every one of 'em nude. They had them working the tongs and the brake and all that, every one of 'em nude. I suppose they sold a lot of interests in [the well]".[35] The pictures surely marked an imaginative departure from the timeworn photo of a wild gusher.

While Spraberry promoters had little trouble finding investors, local Midland oilmen did not rush to buy into their deals. Small and intermediate independents in Midland tended to approach the Spraberry with caution. Some local geologists, like William Y. Penn and George Gibson, were skeptical that Spraberry production would return the rewards its enthusiasts expected. J. C. Williamson recalled: "Every time I'd get enthusiastic about the Spraberry, I'd look at a core: it would look so bad that I'd lose interest." Another Midland operator, Earle M. Craig, Jr., recalled that his partner, who had studied banking in college, refused to enter Spraberry because he thought it "uneconomic."[36] So while independents outpaced major companies in exploring the trend, local Midland operators and investors were outnumbered by their counterparts from other places. Though time would prove the local skeptics right, the outsiders who were the trend's avid promoters plunged into development at top speed.

The general course of the Spraberry Trend's development is clearly illustrated by the history of the Tex-Harvey field within it. Independents predominated among leaseholders in this area, and among those who got in on the ground floor were Harry B. Lake, the Wilshire Oil Company, Joed Rosenthal, Ted Weiner, the El Tee Oil Company, and the Texas Crude Company, all holding choice leases. During late 1950 and 1951, development of their properties proceeded at a brisk pace; operators planned more than 500 wells on conventional forty-acre spacing, over an area covering roughly thirty sections of ranchland. Harry B. Lake raised funds for 4 wells, Joed Rosenthal for 5, and El Tee for 16. During the early months of trend development, those who invested with these operators had good reason for optimism: initial production was encouragingly strong. Harry B. Lake's Floyd Estate No. 1, for example, flowed nearly 40,000 barrels of oil in its first sixteen months; even under proration, the well produced 2303 barrels of oil during May 1951. The discovery well in the field paid out in about fifteen months; it was then reworked to produce 74 barrels of oil per day from another pay zone.[37]

Such healthy production sustained the heady expectations of vast profits for Tex-Harvey operators and investors.

After a few months of rapid development, however, expert analyses of data from a growing number of wells provided increasing support for the pessimists. Many a Spraberry well declined quickly from its impressive initial production and had to be pumped to secure even a scant amount of oil. This turn of events stumped many of the experts; the trend had some puzzling characteristics they were at a loss to explain. On October 19, 1951, more than 650 oilmen met at Midland High School to listen to the most knowledgeable geologists and engineers discuss unusual aspects of the trend. The scientists could not agree on fairly basic observations — whether the formation was sandstone or siltstone, for example — nor did they agree on the origins of the oil in the trend; some claimed that it came from sand, while others argued that it originated from shale deposits. Still other scientists asserted that the oil actually migrated through the myriad of minute vertical fractures that seemed to permeate the formation. The final theory was the most easily defended because the irregular fracturing had been encountered by drillers in all areas of current activity.

As additional data accumulated, it became clear that the high expectations of production from the Spraberry trend would have to be significantly revised. The irregular vertical fractures of the formation presented formidable problems for reservoir engineers. The Spraberry sand itself, moreover, was exceptionally tight; operators resorted to shooting and the more recently developed technique of hydrofracturing to stimulate production. There was no evidence of gas cap or water drives; gas-oil ratios varied from 300 to 1 to 1000 to 1 in different parts of the trend. Given such widely varying conditions, there were almost as many different drilling and completion techniques as there were operators on the trend. Small wonder, then, that William J. Murray, Jr., of the Texas Railroad Commission decided that no one "could even hazard a guess as to reservoir performance or proper conservation techniques." As a journalist concluded two months later, in the Spraberry "practically every well differs from its neighbor."[38]

While experts argued over the Spraberry's potential and how it might be realized, by the end of 1951, there was no denying that wells in the trend were not living up to their early promise. Where some forecasters had estimated 10,000 to 20,000 barrels of reserves per acre, as production data accumulated, predictions for recovery plummeted to 400 to 800 barrels per acre, depending on the thickness of the Spraberry section opening to the well bore. In practical terms, this change meant a well at the top of the range would still fall short of repaying drilling and operating costs. By 1952 it was clear that the operators in the Tex-Harvey field, far from getting rich, would be lucky to break even.[39]

Major companies responded to the chilling realities of economics in the Tex-Harvey field and other parts of the trend by cutting costs. The least complex tactic involved freeing themselves of the common lease obligation to drill one well per 40 acres. Magnolia led the way, pressing the Railroad Commission for mandatory 80-acre spacing. To justify the request, the company cited the wartime shortage of steel and tubular goods; drilling fewer wells would save goods in short supply. This argument had great appeal to other operators who had had trouble meeting lease offset requirements as a result of wartime shortages. Many independents and landowners, however, opposed mandatory wider spacing. Wider spacing meant that oilmen would not be able to make as full a utilization of leases as they had intended and that landowners would not see as many revenue-producing oil wells on their land. But even the most stubborn of independents came to support the argument for wider spacing in Spraberry by the end of 1952. By that time, various engineering and economic studies had demonstrated that even the best wells were unlikely to return a profit of much more than 4 percent a year, hardly an inducement to invest additional capital in closer wells. One author argued: "The return is so low that the area may be considered marginal from the standpoint of capital invested as well as from the number of barrels of oil secured per ton of steel recommended." So bleak did economic prospects for the trend appear that some operators even pushed for a 160-acre spacing rule. After fifty-three Spraberry operators made supportive applications to the Railroad Commission, it finally confirmed the 80-acre rule, permitting both 40-acre and 160-acre spacing on petition.[40]

During 1952, production data continued to fill out a discouraging profile of Spraberry performance. With the sharp drop of the pressure of the natural gas present in the formation, production in many parts of the trend went into precipitous decline. Those operators with enough financing to do so often resorted to hydrofracturing, in effect making it easier for oil to flow through the tight formation, but this step did not reverse the decline of production for long. Resorting to methods that had been relatively effective in the East Texas field, engineers shut in wells in an attempt to build up bottom-hole gas pressure. This experiment failed too. No easy solution was found to the Spraberry production problems. In three brief years the whole trend went from "America's giant oil field" to its local designation as the world's largest unrecoverable oil reserve.[41]

The Los Angeles and Fort Worth independents in Tex-Harvey were hit particularly hard by internal production declines. Production on Harry B. Lake's four leases, for example, fell more than 80 per cent during 1952. After an eight-month shut-in during 1953, his leases rebounded to less than half their low point of 1952. Even this production did not last long. The wells declined steadily during 1954, went out of production officially in 1955, and were plugged and abandoned in 1956. El Tee, with sixteen wells, was hit with even heavier losses. Its production fell from about 27,000 barrels during March 1952 to 3604 barrels one year later. During 1954, El Tee was permitted to produce 5500 barrels per well, but its wells had declined to the point that the company's total production was less than one fifth that amount. One year later ten of the El Tee wells were out of production, and the company was pumping about one barrel of oil per day per well. Some operators, such as Joed Rosenthal, simply plugged and abandoned their Tex-Harvey wells in 1955. Their properties never reached the initially high levels of Harry B. Lake's Floyd Estate No. 1; they had not paid out during five years, and there was little incentive to invest in production experiments on wells that were commercial failures.[42] By June 1955, about one quarter of all Tex-Harvey wells had been plugged and abandoned. The insiders, first on the scene, lost money, in part because the geological peculiarities of the trend were not understood until their funds were committed. Contrary to the conventional wisdom of wildcatting, in Spraberry getting in early meant coping with unforeseen difficulties rather than reaping bonanza profits—yet Spraberry had seemed as close to a sure thing as the oil industry ever encounters.

Declining production, changed spacing regulations, and nationally frozen prices were not the only hazards to the early birds' profits in the trend, for Spraberry operators also ran afoul of Railroad Commission regulation. The commission's intervention in the trend was totally consistent with its current policies in other sections of the state, but it was not expected by the operators. As in other regulatory matters, regulation did not affect the economic interests of small and large operators in the same way.

By 1950, the Texas Railroad Commission's regulation of oil production according to market demand was accepted by most operators as the best available means of stabilizing prices in the crude oil market. The commission determined the maximum efficient rate of recovery (MER) of Texas oil fields, set allowables per well in those fields, and designated the number of production days per month, all with an eye to what purchasers intended to buy. Thus, in 1950, the Railroad Commission regulated production of Spraberry oil by setting top limits on well production. It cut production from Harry B. Lake's J. H. Floyd No. 1, for example, from 242 barrels per day to 121 barrels, with twenty-one production days allowed per month; it cut back Magnolia's H. F. Timmerman No. 1 from 425 to 121 barrels, and Humble's T. O. Midkiff by 40 percent, to 121 barrels. All three wells were thus allowed the same production per day and per month, seemingly an equitable arrangement.

As might be expected, however, the cutback affected Lake far more than the majors, because he lacked production and reserves in quantity in other fields. The loss of 121 barrels of production per day finally meant the difference between profit and loss, as it did not for the major companies. Similarly, the change to 80- or 160-acre spacing in 1952, ostensibly to free operators from unnecessary drilling while materials were in short supply, was generally more acceptable to the majors and large independents than to small operators. Magnolia, with extensive acreage, could cut its long-range Spraberry development costs with 80-acre spacing, but the change left Harry B. Lake with at least one 80-acre lease on which he had drilled only one well and on which he could not promote another thereafter. In the end, he could not make the fullest use of his investment in the lease.[43] Regulatory policies that treated all operators alike simply did not affect all operators in the same way. The same conclusion is unavoidable in looking at the commission's ban on the wasteful flaring of casinghead gas.

No one could deny that flaring gas was widespread in the Spraberry Trend. At the height of the activity, Midland residents could see what appeared to be sunrise on the eastern horizon shortly after sunset; aircraft pilots found that burning gas and lights on oil rigs illuminated hundreds of square miles of otherwise empty ranchland. But there were formidable barriers to the conservation of gas in the trend. One was its very size. Production was spread over hundreds of square miles; the cost of gathering lines to collect gas from every well would be staggering. During the opening years of Spraberry production, moreover, tubular goods were scarce in the oil field. While, as one operator recalled, "you could always get what you were willing to pay the price for," the price of sufficient pipe to complete gathering systems was even higher than usual. Certainly the price of gas, kept low on the interstate market by the Federal Power Commission, could not justify such gathering systems. Indeed, the most a Spraberry operator could hope to sell his gas for was 90 cents to $1.50 per day per well, if he found a buyer. Given Railroad Commission regulations, the operator could produce gas only fifteen to twenty-one days a month. At this rate, a single length of pipe would cost as much as several months' revenue from the sale of gas — if it could be sold: gas companies, alarmed at the growing power of the FPC, hesitated to sign new contracts in 1953. Along with economics, the particular geology of the trend tended to discourage conservation. The flow of oil was so irregular and unpredictable that the operator who invested in conservation could not be certain just where the gas he was conserving originated — or whose gas his neighbor was wasting.[44]

Despite these problems, some wells were connected to gathering systems. El Paso Natural Gas had entered the area as a purchaser in

1949, when the first discoveries in the southern part of the trend were made; by 1953, 468 wells supplied casinghead gas to gasoline plants, whose residue gas was sold to El Paso Natural. Indeed, Arthur "Tex" Harvey had invested about $5.5 million in a system that used all of the casinghead gas his wells produced; this effort to meet Railroad Commission directives cost him $65,000 a month in interest payments alone. In 1952 El Paso Natural decided to expand its purchases in Spraberry from 60 million cubic feet per day to 300 million cubic feet. To do so, it had to secure permission from the FPC, which moved at a snail's pace to consider the application. Hearings on the request were not completed until April 1953, and a final answer was delayed for another year.[45]

While Washington officials dallied, the Texas Railroad Commission grew ever more restive at the conspicuous waste of gas. On April 1, 1953, it issued an order shutting down all wells in the trend, those connected to gathering systems as well as those that were not, until arrangements to prevent further waste were complete. The decision to shut in all wells marked a departure from previous regulation of gas production, but it was designed to meet three important peculiarities of the situation: the amount of gas flared was great — an estimated 220 million cubic feet daily; a huge processing system was necessary and it could not be completed quickly; and the trend's geological characteristics permitted oil to migrate irregularly over great distances. The last was why all wells were shut down; if some remained in production, they would drain oil from those properties that were closed. Thus, the 468 wells that wasted no gas were shut down along with the more than 1800 wells whose gas was flared.

There was something in the commission's order to anger all operators, large and small. Those who had complied with conservation practices objected because they were treated the same way as those who had not. The latter group defended its noncompliance by referring to the FPC's actions and policies. It came as no surprise when the Railroad Commission was faced with a host of lawsuits, from such independents as Tex Harvey, Ted Weiner, and Rowan Oil as well as larger firms like Phillips and Republic Natural Gas. The opposition won the day when the Texas courts ruled against the commission. At the district court level, the commission was enjoined from shutting down wells that were connected to gas gathering systems; the State Supreme Court held that the commission could not shut down wells with the aim of protecting correlative rights, that is, protecting property owners whose wells were shut in from loss. The court required that the commission return to a regulatory scheme consistent with the usual scope of its powers. Accordingly, in June 1953, the Railroad Commission decided to minimize gas waste by cutting back oil production and set a limit of ten producing days a month for the Spraberry.[46]

All operators in the trend lost money during the shutdown, but for large operators the loss was more easily borne than for the small independents. The income Tex Harvey lost during the shutdown, for example, could not be balanced by income from a wide range of other fields or downstream sources, as it could be for major companies. Similarly, for the Blackwood and Nichols Company, whose March 1953 production from fourteen wells was 53,776 barrels, the drop to a total of 223 barrels between April and September meant more than bookkeeping problems. By the end of 1953, small independents in the trend were barely afloat; their income was diminished by natural production declines, and the shutdown had interrupted it for months. Even the shutdown was not the final blow. After production resumed, many operators found that their wells could not be revived to more than a fraction of pre-shutdown output. Joed Rosenthal's Hugh Dixon No. 1-9, for example, which had a daily allowable of 17 barrels, produced only 145 barrels in all of 1954; his M. H. O'Daniel had a 44-barrel allowable, but no production was reported during the same year.[47] For small independents like Rosenthal there was little alternative to plugging and abandoning wells. In a parody of the old-time cattlemen's laments over the saline Pecos River, oilmen dubbed the Spraberry Trend the graveyard of the oilman's hopes.

If Spraberry offers graphic illustration of both general and local problems affecting independents, its history after 1953 provides examples of how some operators successfully adapted to its unusual and discouraging conditions. Prominent among the successful operators were those who were in a position to exploit technological progress to increase production. Improved fracturing techniques later enhanced oil recovery; improved drilling muds and more efficient casing programs cut the cost of wells by one quarter. In all, later entrants realized greater gains because of improved drilling and completion techniques, both of which lowered costs.[48]

After 1954, most operators who held scanty production in the trend sold their leases to those whose production was more substantial, providing the latter with opportunities to lower their fixed production costs by spreading them over a greater number of leases. Once properties changed hands, operators often reworked them by plugging back to the shallower Clear Fork formation, whose production had been overlooked during the height of the Spraberry fever. The most sustained "nursing" of the Spraberry Trend, however, involved the application of newer and more costly production technology in waterflooding. In this endeavor, the larger integrated oil companies dominated activity, for a number of reasons. The rising replacement costs of reserves tended to affect them somewhat more than independents, for their overhead costs in exploration tended to run higher than those of independents. The extensive scientific data majors used in their own exploration projects, for example, were costly to get and to interpret, and that expense gave the majors an incentive to try to offset mounting exploration costs by making thorough use of data gathered and by producing known reserves more economically. In the Spraberry Trend, the scientific data the majors had gathered while drilling wells were indispensable to enhancing production after oil was found, and the majors had the scientific staff ready to put those data to use. By contrast, many small independents active in Spraberry were more interested in promotion than in science, and they lacked the assets to take on projects with high initial costs and slow payouts.[49]

While producers tried every device they could to wring oil and profits from areas like the stubborn Spraberry Trend, there was an economical alternative to coping with the increasingly complex problems of domestic oil operation, that of finding and developing oil fields overseas and importing production and products. When the cost of producing a barrel of American oil averaged 70 cents in 1948, the cost of producing a barrel of Saudi Arabian oil averaged only 20 cents, according to one estimate. Overseas operators, moreover, did not have to shape their business operations around proration, shutdown days, or production cutbacks; they did not have to make heavy investments to avoid wasting casinghead gas. Even after the cost of transport, terminal fees, and tariffs, Saudi oil could be sold at a profit for $2.81 a barrel on the U.S. East Coast. Middle East prospecting after World War II brought in incredibly rich oil fields; domestic discoveries during the same period, though numerous, were for the most part unspectacular. By 1954, the average new Saudi well could be expected to produce for twenty or thirty years.[50] For those well enough supplied with capital to embark on foreign ventures, the economics of shifting oil investment from domestic to foreign arenas was undeniably appealing; for major companies, it was sound business.

Though most independents were barred by lack of capital from extensive foreign activity, in 1947 a group of independent companies founded the American Independent Oil Company to pursue Middle East ventures; in later years well-financed independents like the Hunt brothers and Armand Hammer gained fame as international moguls.[51] But the majority of independents had neither the means nor the desire to embark upon grand foreign ventures. With reason, they saw the development of foreign production and steadily rising imports as major threats to their economic well-being. Accordingly, both the IPAA and TIPRO carried on a vigorous campaign against imports during the late forties and fifties. The campaign shifted into high gear in 1949, when postwar demand for petroleum slackened and state regulatory bodies cut back allowables. TIPRO blamed the cutbacks on the growing part of the domestic market taken by imports. Both TIPRO and the IPAA argued for an increase in the oil tariff from 24 cents to $1.08 per barrel to keep the tariff at the same percentage of the price per barrel as in 1934, when the oil tariff rate was established. Together, TIPRO and the IPAA lobbied against imports in Washington; the IPAA proposed that legislation akin to the Connally Hot Oil Act be devised to keep imports from rising when domestic demand was down.[52] These efforts, like those that independents directed against the FPC, had only limited success.

As independents talked of greater danger from imports, some of them tried to unite the various industry interest groups to campaign against imported oil. In December 1954, for example, representatives of the IPAA, TIPRO, the Panhandle Producers and Royalty Owners' Association, the North Texas Oil and Gas Association, the West Central Texas Oil and Gas Association, and the East Texas Oil Association met in Fort Worth to try to organize a lobbying effort. They agreed that attempts at voluntary agreement to limit imports had not worked. As one journalist remarked, those who were used "to calling a spade a spade and then digging a slush pit with it" tended to look to politics rather than industrial cooperation for salvation. Independent Jack Porter, then Republican national committeeman for Texas, bluntly pointed out that "in the natural and necessary pursuit of maximum profits," importers were not about to reduce imports at the expense of their stockholders. "Importers," Porter told his colleagues, "are not doing anything I wouldn't do or you wouldn't do in their place." Thus, to Porter, the independent's only practical course on imports ran through politics: "There are more of us than of them, and if we work together we can get the job done."[53]

As practical as Porter's insight was, he overlooked several matters of great importance to the independents' crusade against imports. The first was that independent oilmen were not yet sufficiently attuned to national politics to put the necessary muscle behind Washington lobbying. Only 150 members of the six independent groups had left the oil field long enough to attend the Fort Worth meeting; the troops had not responded to the rallying cry. In expecting them to do so, Porter and the other leaders of the Fort Worth meeting were ahead of their time.

The second matter Porter overlooked was the handicap of the oilman's public image of profligate wealth, a liability in seeking government action on tariffs, imports, the FPC's control of gas prices, or virtually any other issue relating to petroleum economics. Major companies had tried various public relations campaigns to improve the public image of the oil industry from the late forties onward, but the results of this effort were not encouraging. TIPRO recognized the problem of public relations in oil in August 1953 and offered its members some homespun advice:

> Let's soft-pedal the headlines, fellas. Be conservative in your statements to the newspapers, your friends, and your associates. If you have famous partners, keep it to yourself. You and they will both benefit. Try to get good publicity for yourself and your industry. If you get drunk and land in the Los Angeles pokey, tell them you raise beets or something. Forget the word "oil" for a change. Above all, do not brag to your friends that the depletion allowance allows you to get rich while they pay all their money to the Government. We all know that isn't so, but a few keep telling that.to kinfolks.[54]

Such recommendations could do little to expunge the public's image of the flamboyant, swaggering oilman, arrogant with unseemly and undeserved profits, an image deeply ingrained in folklore and a great liability to lobbying in Washington. This image was reinforced by the well-known ability of politically active oilmen, such as Jack Porter, to raise funds with relative ease by appealing to other independents; their donations to political candidates were often large, and they were not restricted by the provisions of the Corrupt Practices Act that barred corporate contributions to campaigns. Independents could pack considerable clout on occasion, but widespread publicity on this matter was a liability in Washington.

Third, and most important, Porter underestimated the political ability and influence of the importers and their allies. True, there were more independent companies and operators than there were major-company importers. But the major companies were not the only parties with a stake in low-priced imports: American consumers were the obvious short-run beneficiaries of low-cost foreign oil. They far outnumbered Jack Porter and his friends. For the independents to campaign against imports was a David-against-Goliath sort of encounter, and in this instance, the independents lacked a sling. They could not, as Porter had hoped, "get the job done."

While independents did not persuade Congress to stem imports, in Texas TIPRO succeeded in rallying the Texas Railroad Commission to its cause. In July 1954, Commissioner Ernest Thompson asked all major companies to cut back imports because domestic productive capacity had grown beyond demand. His request prompted a facts-of-life reply from Robert G. Dunlop, the president of the Sun Oil Company. Dunlop told Thompson that thanks to Railroad Commission cutbacks in Texas crude production, Sun had had to buy oil it could have produced from its Texas properties, with a resultant loss of $3.5 million in 1953; Sun intended to import more, not less, oil.[55]

Undaunted, Thompson resumed his campaign six months later by persuading his colleagues on the commission to agree to a quarter-million-barrel hike in the monthly allowable to discourage imports: "If stocks pile up," Thompson argued, "maybe importers will take heed." The following year the commission balked at purchasers' suggestions for cutting back allowable production, again on the ground that cuts would be accompanied by increased imports.[56] But apart from the anti-import publicity it could generate, the Texas Railroad Commission had no power to protect those who did not import from those who did.

With the exception of a short break during the Suez crisis, cheap foreign oil continued to reach American markets in increasing volume. In 1955, when total demand for oil rose 7.6 percent over the previous year, imports increased by 17.2 percent. When domestic demand fell in 1957 and 1958, Texas allowable production was cut in half, but imports continued to rise. The attempts made by IPAA, TIPRO, and other groups of independents to restrict imports came to little.[57]

In the longer term, however, the fight over imports effected important changes. It brought increasing numbers of small and intermediate independents into partisan politics as candidates and contributors, a development that worked to the great advantage of the Republican party. Of equal importance, failure to win the day on imports led large and intermediate independents to adopt new strategies to meet the undeniable reality of cheap foreign crude oil. For the smaller independents, especially those who launched careers during the postwar boom, possibilities were more limited. As always, they could dispose of their properties at depressed prices; retrench to match their operations to dwindling revenues; and, as investors outside the industry turned to other opportunities, seek support within the sizable postwar community of small and intermediate independents. In this last regard, independents benefited from the recent prosperous years. To an extent unparalleled during earlier slack times, the strength and adaptive capacity of local oil and gas communities sustained both activity and independents during the downturn that began during the late fifties and lasted more than a decade.

6: SURVIVAL OF
THE FITTEST

By 1958 the long span of postwar prosperity for independent oilmen had ended. No single event comparable to the East Texas cataclysm brought the boom to an end; there was no drama in the downturn. But it was nonetheless evident during the late fifties and sixties that it was harder for the independent to make profits, and that successful business required an increasing number of adjustments to redistributive politics and federal regulation. A growing number of independents responded to this situation with greater involvement in partisan politics. For the most part, independents assumed a defensive political posture; they saw themselves as frontline defenders of private enterprise from challenge by a hostile coalition of economic and political interests. Political activity may have eased their frustrations with discouraging business conditions, but it did not change the increasingly bleak industry outlook for independents, particularly those of small and intermediate size. In contrast to the buoyant optimism of the postwar boom, many independents came to see their economic future in the light of Darwinian struggle. Houston independent Michel T. Halbouty summed up the new perspective: "As in nature, the principle of survival of the fittest will prevail."[1]

The worsening economic outlook for independents lent both credibility and urgency to the view that, as a group, independents were under economic siege. Rising costs, a permanent fact of business life during the postwar period, continued to be a problem in slack times because petroleum prices did not rise correspondingly. According to industry surveys, drilling expenses increased by nearly two thirds between 1959 and 1972; in one year alone, 1969, the cost of drilling and completing a well rose nearly 9 percent. A good part of this general rise reflected increases in the cost of all goods and services in the national economy as a whole, but the failure of industry revenues to keep pace with rising costs created the economic dilemma that petroleum industry observers termed a cost-price squeeze.[2]

During most of the period between the late fifties and the early seventies, domestic crude oil prices were kept low by a worldwide abundance of oil. It continued to be cheaper to find and produce crude oil in the

Middle East than to find and produce it at home. By the late fifties, exploration and development overseas had resulted in the production of increasing quantities of Middle Eastern oil for the world market. The supply of this oil was occasionally disrupted by political upheaval, as in 1967 and 1970, but the risk of disruption of supply did not halt a growing American dependence on foreign oil. And though the Eisenhower administration finally set mandatory quotas on imports of crude oil and finished products in April 1959, the quotas did not stop the erosion of the domestic producers' position. When demand expanded in the late sixties, domestic producers failed to benefit because additional imports were allowed to flow into the domestic market.

It was clear to most observers that the well-being of domestic producers depended more on Middle Eastern politics than on domestic demand. In 1967, during the Arab-Israeli war, for example, Phillips launched a modest price hike of 5 to 7 cents a barrel among major purchasers. Similarly, in 1970, after cutbacks in Libyan production and terrorist damage to the Trans-Arabian pipeline, domestic crude prices rose an average of 25 cents a barrel. By this time prices had been relatively stationary for so long that even a modest rise seemed spectacular. As Midland independent Dean Wolf said, "I can remember the price of oil going up a dime a barrel, and everybody said, 'Whee!' like this was going to be the greatest thing. From $2.95 to $3.05, and everybody was so excited they could hardly stand it."[3] There were few such occasions for glee during slack times.

While American consumers enjoyed the benefits of low petroleum prices, independents struggled to pay their bills. Their lot was particularly difficult in Texas, for the Railroad Commission reacted to price pressure from cheap imports by cutting back allowable production. It reduced the number of producing days to nine a month in June 1959; a year later it cut producing days to eight a month, a level that held throughout most of 1961 and into 1962. In addition to restricting the number of days on which producers could run their wells, the commission also set low limits on the maximum daily rate of production for individual wells. What these controls meant to individual operators may be illustrated by the history of four shallow wells developed by an intermediate-sized Midland independent, Fred Turner, Jr., in the Noelke (Queen) field in Crockett County. Two of the wells had average potentials of 75 and 80 barrels a day; the remaining pair were rated at 2152 and 1959 barrels. Turner's total potential production from the lease was 4266 barrels per day, but the commission allowed him only 40 barrels per day per well, leaving him with a total of 160 barrels, only 3.8 percent of estimated potential production, that he could produce and sell. During an eight-day producing month, Turner's four wells could produce a total of only 1280 barrels, about 1 percent of their actual monthly potential. Production limitation reduced Turner's potential annual return from these properties from an estimated $1,559,415 to $15,590. An oil find that might have been a financial bonanza, furnishing additional funds for exploration, did little more than meet the daily costs of operating the property. Turner could expect to wait until well into the twenty-first century to recoup his initial investment. It is not surprising that under such circumstances, successful independents found little incentive for wildcatting. As Midland independent Payton Anderson wryly put it, "Even with good production . . . you wouldn't get rich overnight."[4]

The economic plight of independents of all sizes was clearly reflected in the number of property sales from the mid-fifties to 1973. Though properties had always changed hands when operators raised cash for other ventures, disposed of marginal properties, paid debts, or liquidated estates, the economic problems of the domestic industry prompted a rush of sales. During the mid-fifties and early sixties, there were nearly 700 mergers and major property acquisitions in the domestic petroleum industry. Edward L. Kennedy of Lehman Brothers, a leading New York investment banking firm, observed that even the larger independent production companies had joined the rush to sell, as fifteen of thirty-one such companies listed on the New York Stock Exchange in 1952 had either sold out or gone out of business by 1962. Of the remainder, eight had either integrated or gone international. During 1961 alone, there were more than a dozen big deals, including the sale of Honolulu Oil to Tidewater and Pan American; the purchase of Union Texas Natural Gas by Allied Chemical; the sale of Republic Natural Gas to Mobil; and the sales of Monterey Oil to Humble, of Argo to Atlantic, and of Plymouth to Ohio Oil. The buying binge continued during 1963, when $1.3 billion changed hands during the first ten months of the year; among the important acquisitions of this time were those of the Lion Oil Company and the Mound Oil Company by Monsanto. The following year saw more big sales, with Sinclair's purchase of the Texas Gulf Producing Company for more than a quarter of a billion dollars at the top of the list. During 1964 and 1965 there were sixty-four and seventy-nine major sellouts, respectively. There was no slowdown in the shift of reserves ownership until 1966, when higher interest rates and higher taxes diminished the capital available for large acquisitions. Still, even in the later sixties, occasional sales made the news, as when the R. J. Reynolds Company obtained major production in the Middle East by buying Aminoil.[5]

Though not all sales were made by independents in financial distress, there is good reason to think the high volume of sales reflected a thinning of the ranks of independent oilmen. In 1969, after more than a decade of slow times, Michel T. Halbouty estimated that the number of American independents had dropped from more than 42,000 in the mid-fifties to less than 10,000. If Halbouty's estimate of the number of independents at work in the mid-fifties was high, it was nonetheless true that slack times took their toll. In 1961, for example, the IPAA reported 404 membership cancellations resulting from bankruptcy or liquidation in the past five years. In the same year, TIPRO, whose membership peaked at roughly 7000 in 1957, found that its numbers had dropped to around 6500; it told the press that many dropouts said they could no longer afford to pay even modest dues. In 1964, the Department of the Interior offered a more conservative estimate of the decline in independent ranks, some 4 percent since the late fifties. Industry observers could not agree on the number of independents who ceased work, but it was clear that numerous independents either chose to liquidate or cut back their enterprises or were forced by circumstances to do so.[6]

As independent ranks thinned after the mid-fifties, the Midland oil and gas community experienced another pronounced decline. In all, the number of independents doing business in Midland fell by about one quarter between 1951 and 1969. Apart from those headquartered elsewhere who closed local offices, such as Tex Harvey and J. S. Abercrombie, some firms ceased to do business because their owners died or because they were acquired by other companies through merger or purchase. About half the independents or independent firms missing from the Midland community by 1969 apparently had gone out of business altogether. Most of them were lease brokers, a predictable development because slower activity meant the acquisition of fewer leases; majors and independents alike concentrated on developing leases already in their inventories rather than incur additional expense through further acquisitions. The next-largest group of those missing from industry and city directories in 1969 were relatively small independents, those independents who never made the headlines of the oil and gas pages of the *Midland Reporter-Telegram*. They made no significant discoveries, and as a consequence, they lacked sufficient income from production to tide them over slack times. As had been true during the decline of the early thirties, drilling contractors went out of business as the rig count plummeted; oil brokers moved on because purchase commitments of prorated oil were narrowly defined by long-term contracts and Railroad Commission regulation, leaving little room for trading.[7]

Those independents who remained and those who entered the industry as independents during slack times pursued a wide variety of strategies. Some of them confronted the problems of cheap foreign crude and expensive domestic exploration by undertaking limited operations in foreign countries. Among the intermediate-sized Midland independents, C&K Petroleum, John J. Redfern, Jr., and Robert Leibrock all set up offices in Calgary, Alberta, during the sixties and established links with both

Levi Smith (left), the president of the Big Lake Oil Company, and Michael L. Benedum (right), one of America's most successful independents. *San Angelo Standard-Times.*

Chester R. Bunker, printer, promoter, and president of the World Oil Company in a late-twenties photo. Abell-Hanger Foundation Collection, Permian Basin Petroleum Museum.

Robert R. Penn, an oil man and team player—in this instance, on the Dallas Wildcats—at the golf tournament held during the API convention in Dallas in 1929. Mrs. J.H. Penson.

Ford Chapman, who worked on bean jobs during the Depression, was a young drilling contractor when this photograph was taken, in 1938. Ford Chapman Collection, Permian Basin Petroleum Museum.

W. D. "Bill" Noel (center) poor-boying #3 Rogers with a Fort Worth Spudder Model D in 1942. Ollie Williams (left) and Dutch Kovar (right). W. D. Noel.

Ed Landreth (center) with L. H. True of Mobil (left) and Arthur Seeligson (right), a San Antonio independent, at a social gathering in the fifties. William A. Landreth.

Ed Landreth's rigs and storage tanks on "the strip." Jack Nolan Collection, Permian Basin Petroleum Museum, Library Hall of Fame.

Sid W. Richardson, the man who was lucky and smart, in a late-fifties photo. Sid W. Richardson Foundation.

Oil men and regulators socialize at the Wilshire Oil Company's dinner party in Austin in 1949. (Left to right) M. A. Machris and Frank W. Lake, both of Wilshire; General Ernest O. Thompson, a Texas Railroad Commissioner; and Judge Olin Culberson, the chairman of the Railroad Commission. Frank W. Lake Collection, Permian Basin Petroleum Museum.

Adobe Petroleum Corporation officers M. D. Rogers (left), the senior vice president of operations, and B. J. Pevehouse, the president and chairman of the board. *Midland Reporter-Telegram.*

R. O. "Jack" Major explaining the position of MGF Corporation in 1982.
Midland Reporter-Telegram.

John G. Redfern, Jr., the founder of the Flag-Refern Oil
Company. *Midland Reporter-Telegram.*

Canadian and American geologists and operators in Canada. The principal lure of Canada was the vast undeveloped Crown domain, in which modest investments could still lease extensive holdings; in Canada, independents did not face the competition from major oil companies that barred entry into most foreign areas. C&K Petroleum thus leased over a million acres of Crown lands in the Northwest Territories and on Hudson Bay in anticipation of discoveries by larger operators like the Hunt interests, which also owned vast Crown tracts and invested in test drilling during the sixties. With luck, the Hunts would prove up the acreage, and C&K would sell some of its holdings to realize quick returns on its original investment; it would then develop its remaining acreage, thereby building reserves and acquiring cash to fund further development.[8]

The search for reserves also led independents into new domestic plays. Action developed in Alabama, Florida, and Mississippi, initially because leases were relatively inexpensive and later because the return from oil finds in these areas, where production was not stringently prorated, was more attractive than in the Permian Basin and other mature oil provinces. Among Midland independents, Mallard Petroleum, a venture of Charles Marsh II and Robert Leibrock, developed substantial production in this new area. Other independents looked to Kansas and the Rocky Mountain region. Opportunities appeared in western Kansas during the late fifties as major companies virtually abandoned the area to independents after exploiting the large structural traps in the area. By 1970, two thirds of the wells drilled in this part of Kansas were wildcats, with independents drilling 98 percent of them. Among the Midland independents who entered Kansas activity was W. H. Gilmore, Jr., who formed a partnership with his brother in 1959 and developed low-cost properties in Kansas during the sixties. The Gilmores used income from a family-owned gasoline plant to sustain them in the first years of business. The search for attractive prospects also led them to Colorado, where a number of Midland operators had either moved or opened branch offices in order to participate in activity in the Powder River Basin of Wyoming and Montana and the Williston Basin of North Dakota and Montana. These places were attractive to small and intermediate independents because it was possible to keep costs low enough to realize gain from prospects the majors considered marginal.[9]

Within the Permian Basin, independents continued to find opportunities through traditional approaches, new plays, and the application of science and technology to recovery projects. The latter-day poor-boy operators continued to engage in small-scale and highly localized projects, the kind that had attracted their precursors. They reduced costs by drilling in relatively easy-to-drill formations, by drilling for oil at shallow depths, and by providing for themselves many of the services that major companies and larger independents ordinarily contracted out. Thus, Don W. Dittman of Fort Stockton continued to drill with the cable tools he inherited from his father, drawing on a barnful of used equipment and what might be termed intuitive geology. Dittman took his son into the business, giving him the job of tending to the electrical work and any chores that involved climbing a ladder; Dittman performed all other jobs, from driller to pumper. Operating on a somewhat larger scale, W. W. West, a Midland geologist, built a small independent operation in which he concentrated upon the search for shallow oil in Runnels County. West did his own land work and geology; he bought one small rotary rig and hired local farmers and ranch hands to work on it, drilling in areas comparatively free from expensive drilling and production problems. The uncommon thrift of operators like Dittman and West allowed them to beat the cost-price squeeze and to stay in business when most advantages seemed to lie with major companies.[10] While more complicated operations drowned in red ink, such small independents weathered slow times with the cost-cutting approach.

Such small-scale and localized operations did not appeal to the more conventionally ambitious small and intermediate independents. For the oilman who wished to do more than survive with a modest income, exploration for natural gas seemed to present the likeliest opportunity for fortune. The areas in which prospecting for gas seemed especially attractive included California, where proximity to rapidly growing markets favored exploration; southern Louisiana; and the Anadarko Basin in Oklahoma and Permian Basin in Texas, where the size of discoveries and reserves could offset both rising costs and low prices. Within the Permian Basin, the Delaware Basin, an area 100 miles long and 150 miles wide lying to the west of the Central Basin Platform, became the principal target of majors and independents looking for gas in deep Ellenburger formations.[11]

They found that deep gas, in a sequence of important discoveries: the Puckett field in the Val Verde Basin in 1952, the Toyah field in the Delaware Basin in 1954, and the Brown-Bassett field in the Val Verde Basin in 1957. The majors' tests went to record depths and formidable expense; they revealed that not only was there gas in the Delaware and Val Verde basins but there was gas in staggering quantities. In parts of the Brown-Bassett field, for example, the producing formation was over 1000 feet thick; in the Gomez field of Pecos County, discovered in 1963, some gas/condensate wells drew from over 1400 feet of gross pay section, and field reserves were estimated at nearly 400,000 Mcf per acre. Many fields yielded gas from more than one formation; the Coyanosa field in Pecos County, for example, produced from seven zones.[12] Even federal price ceilings could not eliminate the profitability of producing that much gas.

The extraordinary size of the reserves uncovered in the Delaware and Val Verde basins made them the liveliest exploratory arenas in the Permian Basin during the sixties. They were areas, however, in which only those with ample capital resources could compete. Costs, especially in wildcatting, were particularly high, for drilling was deep, technologically sophisticated, and dangerous. It was also slow, as a rule, because of the special hazards of moving through high-pressure gas formations. Despite these drawbacks, better-financed independents did take part in Delaware Basin exploration. One notably successful test was completed in 1965 by Jake L. Hamon, an intermediate-sized Dallas independent; with one major company, Shell, and ten other independent firms and individuals participating in the wildcat adventure, Hamon's Waples-Platter No. 1 opened the Hamon field in Reeves County. The discovery well took 579 days to drill, tapped pay between 20,470 and 21,070 feet, cost $2.75 million, and had a potential of 36.8 million cubic feet per day. Hamon's development wells took less time to drill, but they nonetheless cost about $1.75 million each.[13]

As Hamon's discovery demonstrates, successful exploration for deep gas incurred both high exploratory expenses and heavy development costs. No one could expect to poor-boy such exploration. A blowout or a deep fishing job to retrieve equipment lost in the hole, moreover, could present staggering unexpected expenses. Anyone with a working interest in such a project had to be prepared to meet costs far higher than the original estimated amount of his share of drilling a wildcat test. As one veteran Midland independent remarked, "You can lose your —— ing shirt in gas."[14]

Although the vast amounts of capital at the major companies' disposal gave them an advantage in exploration for Delaware Basin gas, the business methods of independents gave them their own operational advantages in this type of prospecting. In particular, the independents' more flexible, less bureaucratic approach to decision making led some of them to successful and imaginative use of the most up-to-date technology. On Jake Hamon's Waples-Platter No. 1, which set a world record for depth, the operator responded quickly to suggestions from the research departments of service companies for solutions to unusual drilling problems, experimenting in some instances with new and unproven products. The well was completed, for example, with a unique 211,000-gallon acid stimulation treatment designed by one service company. With a similar openness to innovative technology, Midland independent William Roden adopted an imaginative deep-drilling technique advanced by engineer Robert Crittenden; Crittenden's strategy of drilling high-pressure formations with relatively lightweight mud, rather than the heavy mud favored by major companies, proved successful in preventing damage to producing formations. Willingness to experiment with innovative technology enabled some independents to obtain better production and avoid expensive problems, a great asset when the financial advantages lay with the majors and large independents.[15]

For those small independents who were not able to operate on the scale of Jake Hamon, there were less expensive places to prospect than the deepest parts of the Delaware Basin. The Morrow sands in southeastern New Mexico yielded gas at shallower depths, between 8000 and 15,000 feet, though not as much of it as finds farther south. On the other side of the Permian Basin, in Crockett County, independents found commercial gas production in the relatively shallow Canyon sand, at roughly 6500 feet.

The exploratory strategy pursued by one of the first groups to look for this Crockett County gas, a combination including the Houston firm of Johnson and Lindley, Delta Drilling of Tyler, and Pauley Petroleum of Los Angeles, illustrates not only flexible operational methods and reliance on technological innovation but an aggressive approach to marketing production as well. These independents entered the Crockett County area near Ozona, where gas had first been discovered in 1939, looking for Ellenburger oil production. They assumed that shallower gas production, spurned by earlier prospectors, would not be large enough to cover the costs of drilling with conventional technology and based their economic planning on the relatively new technique of air drilling. Using this method, they drilled so rapidly, and at such low cost, that they could exploit Canyon sand gas production to profit. After two successful gas wells, they acquired 40,000 acres in the area and drilled eleven stepouts. They then developed extensive engineering data demonstrating the economic attractiveness of the reservoir. Using those data, they persuaded Northern Natural Gas to purchase their production — no mean feat at a time when neither producers nor purchasers knew what the final effect of FPC regulation would be.[16]

These examples of independent activity in exploration for natural gas in the sixties demonstrate both changing exploration objectives and increased sensitivity to the potential of technology for cutting costs. Growing awareness of technology among the oil industry's smaller businessmen did not develop overnight. It was less an immediate response to the business climate than the result of greater access to advanced technology and scientific data. Forty years ealier, innovative technology and science had generally been the preserve of the major companies. Their dominant role in drilling and service technology, however, eroded after they took to contracting out drilling and oil field service in the thirties. As the new independent drilling and service firms developed technological innovations, they offered them to all purchasers, major and independent alike. By the sixties, any independent with funds could purchase services from Halliburton, Schlumberger, and other companies that would be as up-to-date as what Gulf or Shell could obtain. A similar change took place in the provision and interpretation of scientific data, largely the preserve of the scientific staffs of the major companies during the twenties and thirties. By the late forties, independent information services did a thriving business; independent subscribers to such services could be as well supplied with data on an area covered by the service as major companies. While majors continued to support large scientific staffs, independents could hire geological and engineering consultants to interpret data. By the sixties, what had once been the preeminent domain of the major companies was readily available to all.[17]

At the same time that technological innovation and scientific information were more readily available to independents, their need for technology and science grew. This growing demand was partly a response to difficult business conditions during slow times, for it made sense to use all possible means to cut risks when profit margins were slim. But the growth in demand for improved engineering and geological services also reflected the steady influx of men with scientific training and expertise into independent ranks. The rising number of such independents led one industry observer to predict that "by 1970, the independent segment will be populated almost entirely by producers with technical background." Reflecting the movement of scientists into independent oil, technical journals like the *Petroleum Engineer* and the *Journal of Petroleum Technology* began to feature articles like "Bank Loans on Oil and Gas Production," "Some Guides to Proper Loan Selection in Petroleum Production Financing," and "Bank Financing of Secondary Recovery Projects," catering to readers who had passed the stage at which their most important decision was the selection of the right mud to circulate in a hole.[18]

As independent oilmen, geologists and engineers faced quite different challenges during the slow sixties. The adverse effect of the cost-price squeeze upon income for exploration posed a difficult question to the geologist: where would he find the money to continue to test his ideas? Selling or financing a prospect, especially if the geologist was a relative newcomer to independent business, often meant hours spent pounding the pavement and calling on potential investors. As one Midland independent who became a consulting geologist in the late fifties said, "I've knocked on every door in this town at one time."[19] Many less determined newcomers did not survive. A sour staple of Midland humor in the early sixties ran, "Which company has the greatest number of geologists on its payroll? Sears and Roebuck." A financially secure geologist was said to be one whose wife held a teaching certificate.

In contrast to geologists, engineers found that slack times brought attractive opportunities. Tight profit margins made engineering training essential to exploration and production. In exploration, for example, an operator trying to make intelligent decisions about the potential profitability of stepouts from existing production was as interested in what an engineer could tell him about reservoir performance as in what a geologist would tell him about underground formations. Given high costs, low prices, and short allowables, the independent had to know whether a discovery well would be likely to produce profitably over a reasonable period, a calculation for which the engineer's advice was necessary. When the independent turned to his banker for an oil loan, offering reserves as collateral, an engineer entered the exploration process in yet another capacity, for he advised the banker. In strategies that emphasized production rather than exploration, engineers were indispensable. As the rising cost of finding new oil put a premium on getting the maximum production from oil reservoirs, workovers to stimulate production on older properties became economically attractive; profitable workovers required well-planned engineering programs. The producer's wish to receive maximal production from existing oil reservoirs also made secondary recovery attractive; effective secondary recovery programs were based on sophisticated reservoir engineering.[20] At every turn, prevailing economic conditions seemed to indicate that the engineer was the expert most likely to produce profits.

As independents, the engineers were best prepared to develop business strategies appropriate for slow times. Their approach to finding and producing oil was shaped by their practical experience and their inclination to keep economic considerations uppermost in mind. In exploration, for example, the engineers were less likely to pursue rank wildcat prospects — to look for oil in completely untried areas — than the geologists or old-fashioned driller independents. Engineers tended to prefer low geological risk, even if it brought a relatively slow return. Robert Leibrock, who turned from work as an engineering consultant to exploration, described his firm's strategy in the late fifties: "Because of our engineering background, we were primarily interested in extension-type deals, extending oil fields. We didn't feel that as engineers we had the expertise to jump out and do a lot of rank wildcatting."[21] Another petroleum engineer who became an independent in the fifties, John L. Cox, called himself a close-in operator: "I'll follow the wildcatter and pay higher prices and royalty, but I just don't like to lose money. I expect to make money on every well I drill." Such caution, Cox acknowledged, would not generally mean "fancy returns," but if costs were kept low, he and his investors could expect to do well: "There may not be a big return, but they can expect to make a profit on every well."[22]

For the petroleum engineers who became independents, efficient operation was of greater importance than geological speculation. The desire to make a profit, if only a small one, on every hole was a strong brake on the temptation to enter rank wildcat ventures that could lead to either vast wealth or total loss. As geologist William H. Thams put it:

> Engineers don't handle dry holes very well. They're not dreamers. They don't see anything romantic about putting a bunch of circles on a map. The geologist will get starry-eyed and all visionary about 50 million barrels and stuff like that. The engineer doesn't think that way.[23]

The history of Wood, McShane, and Thams, an independent firm of Midland and Monahans, Texas, offers a good illustration of strategy keyed to the narrower opportunities of slow times. The first of the three partners to go independent, engineer B. Oliver Wood, had supervised local waterflood projects for a Monahans independent in the early fifties. In 1958, he and some partners bought a small drilling rig from veteran poor-boy operator Peanuts Bradford and began to do contract drilling in their area. The income from drilling permitted Wood to establish his own independent consulting firm in 1959, in which he was joined by engineer Joe McShane; several years later William H. Thams became the third member of the general partnership. Wood, McShane, and Thams looked for ventures in which they could make full use of their combined specializations, particularly projects that involved enhanced recovery from known reservoirs. In pursuing such ventures, they limited the geographical range of their operations to a relatively small part of the Permian Basin where subsurface conditions were familiar to them; they set up Wood and McShane, Inc., to manage field operations. They hired secretarial help, pumpers, and occasional services from landmen but did all their own geological and engineering work.[24]

During the early years of the partnership, stripper and potential waterflood properties were readily available in the Permian Basin, and Wood, McShane, and Thams devised imaginative strategies to acquire properties with a minimum outlay of capital. In one instance, they acquired a property to waterflood in return for buying the used equipment on the lease; they then turned to limited partners for operating capital. Such strategy was necessary when they started out, for they had not yet established either sufficient production or a credit rating that might persuade bankers to lend them capital adequate for ventures. The partners found that Humble, Sun, and other major companies were receptive to proposals to take over waterflood projects that had not produced well. The independents then designed new production systems for these properties. By keeping capital requirements low and overhead costs to the minimum, they profited from properties the majors could not manage without loss.[25]

The projects Wood, McShane, and Thams took on not only put their specializations to efficient use but also involved relatively low-risk ventures. Low risk, of course, was not the same as no risk: the amount of oil a project would recover was never entirely predictable, and unforeseen problems like water channeling through a formation could ruin a waterflood project. Payout on secondary recovery projects, moreover, was slow. It could take as long as two years to bring a property up to profitable production; as Thams reflected, "You've got to have a patient banker." Even a successful project would not yield vast production; even a successful project would decline within a few years.[26] Still, with its emphasis on economy, the business strategy developed by Wood, McShane, and Thams—essentially an engineer's strategy—was well suited to slow times.

Such dollar-wise strategies were applied in the Permian Basin and other mature oil-producing regions in part because bankers were both patient and increasingly receptive to loan requests for recovery programs. They usually granted loans after the operation of pilot projects supplied the technical data necessary to predict production and to project cash flow. The terms of these loans were comparable to those of loans secured by production; they were for periods of five years or less, and they were repaid with a percentage of gross revenues that would permit the operator to cover his expenses, with the balance of his income applied to repayment of principal and interest. Because operating problems could diminish income, lenders paid particular heed to the technical training and experience of borrowers. Experience with major companies, work for other independents, and a successful track record on their own all counted for the independents who applied for funds.[27]

It has often been observed that oilmen around the world tend to favor production investments when prices are low. The paramount reason for this preference is that low prices make it more difficult for independents to finance maintenance of reserves through high-risk exploration activities; low prices mean lower income from the sale of oil and gas. Therefore the adverse economic conditions during the sixties encouraged buying production and discouraged exploration; they also led independents to financial stratagems that were novel to their sector of the industry.

Among the traditional means of raising capital that independents continued to employ were the familiar approaches of finding owners of sizable leases who were willing to contribute acreage—and dry- or bottom-hole money—to prove up their holdings. In fact, because major companies found it uneconomical to engage in widespread exploratory drilling in the United States, independents found it somewhat easier than in the early fifties to obtain farmouts from most majors. They continued to raise funds from "et als," participants in joint ventures in specific geological prospects. Seeking to spread risks by participating in a wide variety of projects, oilmen had long participated in each other's ventures, but with the decline in income from producing properties in the sixties, insiders had less money to invest. To find participants for joint ventures, independents turned increasingly to investors outside the industry, typically doctors and other high-income professionals who lacked the experience and the time to manage the funds their practices generated. The tax advantages of participating in joint ventures, taken with the occasionally realized hopes of hefty return on investment, were durable inducements to put money in oil.

During slack times, bank financing became increasingly important in independent financial strategy. In Midland, the First National Bank and the Midland National Bank continued to provide short-term loans for small independents. Intermediate independents with good balance sheets and larger loan requirements went to Dallas, Fort Worth, or Chicago; of the larger banks, the Continental Illinois Bank and Trust Company of Chicago had the reputation of being the most experienced in oil matters and the most receptive to an independent's needs. By the mid-sixties, Continental Illinois had made so many oil loans in the Permian Basin that it evaluated regional properties offered as collateral with personnel and production data available in-house; this enabled the bank to act particularly promptly on loan requests, which enhanced demand for its funds.[28]

At the same time that an increasing number of independents turned to bankers for loans to buy producing properties, a creative approach to such purchases emerged in the ABC transaction, which brought special tax advantages. Though not specifically allowed by either tax law or legal precedent, the ABC transaction became standard practice by the end of the fifties.

In the ABC transaction, A sold his oil and gas properties to B for a cash down payment and payments from future production from the properties. At this point in the deal, B held title to the properties, but they were encumbered by his obligation to A (and by future royalty payments). B would receive enough income to pay operating costs, but his profits would be made only after his obligations to A were paid. A, in turn, would receive regular income, but no more than if he had retained the properties. His assets would still be tied up in the properties. This situation was altered by C, who purchased the oil payment from A, ordinarily borrowing money from a bank to do so. With this, A had cash from B and C, B owned and operated encumbered properties, and C had borrowed money in the properties.

In all phases of this transaction, tough bargaining between the principals determined their relative gains, but special provisions of tax law and regulation made the ABC deal potentially profitable for all parties. A took advantage of two provisions of tax law. The first permitted him to pay only capital gains taxes on the proceeds of the deal. The rate of this tax was lower than the one that applied to income. A, moreover, was often selling his properties to obtain cash to apply against past losses, to lower his tax payments. Independent oilmen, like all businessmen, were permitted to carry net losses forward from one tax year to the next, but only for three years. Thus, when an oil operator found himself in the third year of a carryover period, he might sell properties in order to realize a greater net return of capital; he would offset the immediate gain from the sale with the accumulated losses of previous years. In this circumstance, the tax system encouraged A to sell.

The ABC transaction also promised tax advantages to B and C. Though B acquired properties, he would pay no taxes on the income from them, for it was pledged to C. The final party, C, received the benefit of the depletion allowance, and he was able to reduce his tax obligations because his payments to the bank often absorbed the remaining income from the properties, so he paid no tax on the revenue they generated. With all the tax advantages offered to purchasers of properties by the ABC transaction, the tax system increased the volume of property trading in slow times.[29]

Whatever the tax appeal of selling properties, for independents who aimed to increase their scale of operations, such a step had obvious liabilities. Disposing of good properties meant not only losing production income available for future ventures but also reducing the potential collateral on which bank loans might be made. At that, the role of the banker was necessarily limited by the conservative banking practice of lending not more than half the discounted future value of properties, which meant that as a means of raising capital for business growth, bank loans had a limited utility. These financial realities led independents, particularly those who wished to increase their scope of operations, to try other strategies for raising money. One of them was that of "going public," of issuing shares of ownership in their companies. B. J. "Joe" Pevehouse and his associates, for example, needed additional capital to develop oil and gas fields they discovered beneath nearly 19,000 acres of leases in the Permian Basin. In Pevehouse's experience, "it simply took public money . . . to finance the company. So we went public because we could grow faster. We didn't have the cash flow at that time to drill as fast as we wanted to." By selling $4.5 million in stock in 1970, Pevehouse's Adobe Oil Corporation acquired the capital that supplemented its production income and financed the development of its properties.[30]

During the same period, other Midland independents followed a similar course and created publicly owned companies. Pomeroy Smith and his associates formed the Coquina Oil Corporation; Toby Hilliard,

Tom Brown, Deane Stoltz, Jack Major, Fred Chambers, and Bill Kennedy all raised capital by selling shares in their new companies. For these independents, going public was crucial for growth. As Bill Kennedy, cofounder of C&K Petroleum, observed, cash flow simply did not generate sufficient capital for new ventures: "We were having a hard time coming up with the money." With public money C&K's organization grew from 35 employees in 1969 to nearly 200 in 1981, when Chambers and Kennedy sold their stock to Alaska Interstate Corporation of Houston.[31]

When profits on the sale of oil and gas did not generate enough cash for exploration and development, going public had an obvious advantage, because needed cash could be raised by the sale of assets to new stockholders. But as most heads of new public companies learned, there were some disadvantages to public status. Before they could sell stock, they had to meet the legal requirements of the Securities and Exchange Commission (SEC). Thereafter, they faced the continually demanding task of dealing with stockholders. To some independents, the public relations work essential to the success of a public corporation was good reason not to resort to this method of obtaining funds; even for natural salesmen, it presented a distraction from the business's most important work, that of exploration and production. Independents as a group were not unanimous on the desirability of going public; only a minority chose to create public companies.[32]

One alternative to offering shares in a public corporation was offering shares in a public drilling fund. Selling interests in a package of drillable prospects provided a secure supply of exploration capital, funds to sustain activity over an extended period, as opposed to funds raised for the traditional single-prospect joint venture. This greater supply of risk capital, in turn, permitted the independent to increase his scale of operations in more areas and over a greater number of prospects, thereby limiting the proportion of his own capital at risk in any single venture. Investors shared this same advantage of spreading risk; they also obtained somewhat fuller and more uniform disclosure of operating and financial information than was usual in syndication. As limited partners, the investors in drilling programs, like shareholders in any corporation, enjoyed limited liability. Of even greater benefit to them, the tax rules permitted the general partner to pass special tax advantages along to the limited partners. These advantages included the depletion allowance on produced minerals, the depreciation of fixed assets, and the possibility of writing off operating and other expenses against taxable income.[33]

The most substantial inducement to invest in drilling programs, however, was the tax-oriented investor's ability to charge "intangible drilling costs" against taxable income, a practice that had become common since 1939 and had been specifically approved in the Internal Revenue

Code of 1954. In application, the practice involved charging all of the investments in drilling a well (other than leasehold costs that had no salvage value) as business expenses in a single tax year. Intangible drilling costs, usually more than three fourths of the expense of drilling the average well, included payments to drilling and service contractors. Virtually any expense that did not produce a salvageable asset could be credited as an intangible drilling cost, or IDC. Because nearly all dry-hole costs fell into the IDC category, the investor could receive tax benefits from IDCs though the venture he invested in was unproductive. The ability to count the IDCs as expenses in the year they were incurred, rather than considering them as capital investments to be depreciated over a number of years, provided high-income investors with a considerable shelter for income. In practice, half or more of the dollars placed in a program by an upper-bracket investor were dollars otherwise paid in taxes. Thus the investor who placed what amounted to 30- to 50-cent dollars in a drilling program could accept a relatively high risk of commercial failure in such programs. In other words, the tax code effectively directed assets of wealthy Americans into the high-risk end of the oil business, into ventures that would otherwise have been nearly impossible to finance. Investors could hope that drilling programs would be successful in returning profit, but the preferential tax treatment afforded by the IDC allowance would at least take a good bit of the pain out of failure.[34]

For independents who were eager to expand their operations, willing to wait months for federal clearance of their programs, and able to pay high legal fees to attorneys, public programs offered the possibility of new and larger quantities of risk capital in slack times. The first oil program was offered by the Tulsa firm of Blackwood and Nichols in 1950 for a modest $3.5 million. Only a few companies, among them Apache, Austral, and McCulloch, tried to mount large programs, and they sold them to relatively few investors. Selling costs, moreover, were high, and large institutional investors were inclined to be wary of the new and unfamiliar approach to fund-raising. These early programs tended to be conservative, mixing exploration ventures with production purchases. Though investors seem to have preferred such restraint, these drilling programs lacked the excitement and glamour of the greater gambles in wildcatting. They were salable, but only to limited numbers of the more cautious investors. Unfortunately, it is one of the durable maxims of oil that truly cautious investors do not place their money in the upstream sectors of the petroleum industry.[35]

Selling investors on public programs was the task of a supersalesman, and one appeared in John M. King. Described in print as "a storybook example of the go-getting American Entrepreneur," King was also the paradigm of a big-time independent oilman. Starting out as a small-time investor in oil ventures while in the Illinois legislature, he entered the industry as an operator in 1960, when he formed King Resources in Denver. The company made modest profits in geological services and exploration until the mid-sixties, when King tapped a larger financial market by establishing the Colorado Corporation. Beginning in 1966, he sold two large funds, Imperial American and Royal Resources, to tens of thousands of investors. Emulating the well-known success of mutual funds in attracting small investors, King permitted buyers to pay for shares on the installment plan. He hired astronauts Walter Schirra and Frank Borman as executives, thus building a favorable image of his corporations with the general public and boosting sales.

King raised public money on a scale without precedent in the independent sector of the petroleum industry. His successful approach amounted to a skillful blend of psychology, business acumen, and snake oil. Like all successful promoters, he appealed strongly to the self-interest of both his buyers and their brokers. Buyers were given the expectation of princely returns on their tax-favored investments; King encouraged such expectations by offering a type of investment that combined commonsense notions of risk spreading with uncritical belief in the economy of scale of a large program. Brokers peddled King's funds to a growing market, reaping substantial commissions for their effort. With King's mounting success, the sale of drilling funds of all sorts soared, from $61.4 million in 1965 to $694.1 million in 1968 and more than $1.6 billion in 1969. As the *Oil and Gas Journal* observed, the funds were "a financing phenomenon that's sweeping the investment world like a prairie fire."[36]

In 1969, more than 120 drilling funds were offered to the public, many of them by firms with little experience in managing and selling funds. Inexperience in sales showed when many funds fell far short of their goals; one Houston firm sold less than 5 percent of its $12 million offering that year. Questions about the experience and propriety of fund operations became increasingly common; investors fell out with operators and voiced their complaints in the courts and to the press. John King's star nonetheless continued to rise. The success of his Colorado Corporation sustained King Resources, which received about one quarter of its revenue as the exclusive operator for the funds of King's other company. With a guaranteed income from one fund organization booming his operations, King went on to make a similar arrangement with the Natural Resources Fund of Bernard Kornfeld's company, Investor Overseas Services. This relationship also boosted King Resources, which received more than one third of its revenue from IOS. By 1969, John M. King was flying high, traveling in corporation jets to the watering holes of the rich and famous, hobnobbing with former presidents, and cultivating

Republican leaders with large campaign contributions. He was, as *Time* put it, "the image of an archetypical wheeler-dealer."[37]

His image, as much as anything else, was King's undoing, because it drew scrutiny and criticism to his ventures. Some oilmen, as well as some investment counselors, questioned the propriety of selling interests in oil and gas ventures to small investors who could not cut their risk by making full use of tax advantages. Other critics attacked the tight relationship between King's funds, the Colorado Corporation, and King Resources; the connection seemed to guarantee benefits to everybody but those participating in the funds. By the middle of 1970, economic recession and rumors about the stability of King's operations had put a dent in the sales chart at the Colorado Corporation. Sales, income, and profits were down, as an inevitable result, at King Resources. Worse yet, Bernie Kornfeld's operation was out of cash and near collapse.[38]

Hoping to shore up IOS by restructuring its debt, King drew more headlines by pledging to bail out the company. Observers noted that success would bring King control of Kornfeld's flagging financial empire. When July 1970 passed and King had not succeeded in rescuing IOS, the financial community asked increasingly pointed questions about the stability of King's empire. In August the Ohio state treasurer demanded payment of a questionable loan from the state, and other creditors began to press for settlement of past-due accounts. Within days King Resources stock, selling for $34 a share in 1969, fell to $4.87 a share. By the end of the month, the press reported King's "abdication" from leadership of his enterprises: his financial empire, built on promotion, drilling funds, and borrowed money, collapsed.[39]

King's fall in 1970 left many unanswered questions about the proper management of drilling and development funds, and it prompted action from both the federal government and fund operators. In response to a directive from Congress in 1969, the Securities and Exchange Commission began work on a bill to offer additional protection to investors. In the same year, some of the principal public fund companies began to consider self-regulation through a trade association. Their efforts produced the Oil Investment Institute, a group of about a dozen companies, which established standards for disclosure and investor eligibility. The institute cooperated with the IPAA and the SEC in drafting new regulations for fund operators. That cooperation worked to the interest of most fund operators, for the legislation that emerged from it was directed at regulation of large funds selling to small, relatively unsophisticated investors. It exempted from regulation the smaller fund operators, as well as those funds selling primarily to investors within the petroleum industry.[40]

By the time Congress acted, the drilling fund movement was in retreat. Sales were below the 1969 level in 1972 and 1973, though more than

131 programs were offered. One fund leader, Petro-Lewis of Denver, stopped selling drilling fund partnerships in mid-1973. J. A. Lewis, founder and head of the company, summarized the observations of many independents in his explanation: Petro-Lewis had become too dependent on fund money, altering both the operations and performance of the company. Funds were expensive to sell and manage; administrative costs finally outweighed the general partner's advantages. More important for an exploration firm, Petro-Lewis, like many other fund companies, was unable to generate enough premium-quality geological prospects to sustain a high level of performance. Lewis found that during the final quarter of every year, the taxable dollars that had to be spent were "chasing" deals and drilling rigs, lowering the quality of the former and raising rates for the latter.[41] In this respect, public funds were, at best, a mixed blessing.

These disadvantages of public funds kept all but a relatively small number of independents from offering limited partnerships through drilling funds. High selling and management costs, taken with the year-end scramble to place fund money, had little appeal for established independents. As one successful independent commented, "Almost invariably, the quality of the prospects diminishes. You don't end up with prospects across the board that measure up to your original expectations or to those prospects you had in hand initially. But once you have raised the money, you are compelled to spend it."[42]

Still, several growing Midland independent firms entered the fund business, among them MGF Oil Corporation and C&K Petroleum. MGF started offering public funds in 1970, when it sold limited partnerships directly to individual investors who had participated in previous drilling ventures. Thereafter, the MGF program expanded to include new investors, some of them abroad, but its sales base did not broaden greatly. According to Jack Major, cofounder and head of the firm, the company looked for greater capital resources in order to increase MGF's scale of activity and thereby spread the risks inherent in exploration. MGF, in short, looked for greater exposure. Fund money enabled the firm to cut back on borrowing as interest rates rose and to expand into the Rocky Mountain area and other producing regions outside the Permian Basin.[43] With these company objectives, fund offerings were an asset to growth.

Like MGF, C&K Petroleum joined the Oil Investment Institute, but its experience with drilling programs offered to the public was briefer and somewhat less fruitful than MGF's. C&K's number of limited partners did not reach the number required for SEC registration until 1979. Before that, it had raised relatively small sums: $1.1 million in 1970, $2.7 million in 1971, and $5 million in 1972. With this capital, C&K gradually doubled its level of exploration, acquiring mineral leases and working interests in ventures in the Rockies, Canada, Australia, Turkey, and the Norwegian sector of the North Sea. Thus, like MGF, the firm increased its exposure in areas outside the Permian Basin. Unlike most independents, C&K also ventured with other partners into costly off-shore operations, occasionally as an operator but usually as an investor. C&K had a variable and reasonably typical success with the wider exposure it gained from offering public funds. In 1972, four of its twelve onshore exploratory wells were commercially productive; in 1973, the firm enjoyed considerable success at offshore exploration, as five of its nine offshore wildcats were productive. As C&K pursued a strategy directed toward growth, however, many other independents were content to steer clear of public offerings; to some the fate of John King may have indicated that it was safer to stay small when prices stayed low.[44]

In most of these growth strategies, small and intermediate independents adapted to economic opportunities and to specific conditions created by federal tax legislation. Though they were respondents rather than initiators with regard to the former, they were active participants in the determination of the tax, import, and regulatory policies of the federal government. During slack times, the political struggles over tax-related issues and legislation drew independents of all sizes into the organized political programs of trade associations and political parties. By the end of the era, it seemed to many oilmen that politics had become at least as important as technology and finance and that these elements of the oil business were inextricably intertwined.

For Permian Basin oilmen, the most immediate regulations, those of the Texas Railroad Commission, had been accepted as necessary if inconvenient. They did not accord the same measure of acceptance to the Federal Power Commission during the sixties. The FPC, ordered by the U.S. Supreme Court in 1954 to regulate interstate natural gas prices at the wellhead, floundered along in what one spokesman for independents aptly termed chronic adminstrative chaos: despite the Supreme Court's order to regulate, the FPC had no clear scheme in hand for carrying out that mandate. It soon found it could not review each individual sale contract for gas; its backlog of contracts for review rolled up to the thousands. In the meantime, in the absence of any general regulatory plan from the FPC, gas purchasers hesitated to make long-term purchase commitments. Their hesitation made it more difficult for producers to find purchasers and harder still for prospectors to finance exploration; in the face of indecision and inefficiency at the FPC, a discovery might not yield income for an indeterminate time, a daunting possiblity for lenders and borrowers alike. In 1960 the FPC decided that some more general approach to price regulation was imperative. It opted for an "area wide" scheme for setting prices. The first area it chose to work with was the source of 10 percent of the nation's gas, the Permian Basin.[45]

With a voracious appetite for data surpassing even that of Dickens's Thomas Gradgrind, the FPC staff began to gather information from gas producers. Proceedings stretched over three and a half years, hearings took 250 days, and some 30,000 pages of testimony transcript were recorded. In October 1963, the FPC sent out a 428-page questionnaire, weighing over ten pounds, to be completed in quadruplicate by 114 of the nation's gas producers; industry observers estimated that it would cost each producer an average of $85,000 to complete it.[46] Nobody could accuse the FPC of failing to assemble information. How it used it, however, was open to question after its Permian Basin decision.

On September 17, 1964, Seymour Wenner, previously an employee of the Civil Aeronautics Board and the Interstate Commerce Commission, and whose first major FPC assignment was the Permian Basin rate case, announced the commission's preliminary decision. The objectives of the decision were twofold: to keep gas prices to consumers low and to encourage the discovery of additional supplies of gas. To achieve these aims, Wenner decided to set different ceiling prices on Permian Basin gas from a variety of sources. With a view to spurring exploration for gas, rather than for oil and coincidentally gas, he set the highest ceiling price, 16.75 cents per Mcf, on new gas. From that high, prices graduated downward: 15 cents per Mcf for new residue gas, 11 cents per Mcf for new casinghead gas, and 10 cents per Mcf for old casinghead gas. New gas was any gas first sold after January 1, 1961; old gas was gas first sold before that date. Wenner arrived at his figures by applying a novel formula: averaging what he took to be the costs of both large and small producers to arrive at a national average cost; deducting a small amount to reflect the market position of Permian Basin gas; tacking on a penny; and rounding off the result to the nearest quarter-cent, thereby arriving at his top ceiling price of 16.75 cents per Mcf. This was 3.25 cents less than Permian Basin producers had sought; they had hoped for a 20-cent price without a ladder of prices based on the sources of gas. Wenner exempted producers of less than 10 million cubic feet of gas a year from regulatory price ceilings, though he admitted that purchasers were unlikely to give higher prices to the small independents.[47] All gas producers were affected by the FPC price ceilings, directly or indirectly.

The decision stunned the Permian Basin's gas producers. It was not just that they had not received the price rise they felt was due; it had been hard to be optimistic about that when the FPC staff let it be known they had hoped for prices even lower than those proposed by Wenner.

Indeed, the FPC staff advanced the incredible theory that low gas prices would of themselves indirectly spur exploration by creating increased demand. Wenner, by contrast, thought price differentials based on the gas's source and date of first sale would encourage exploration exclusively for large amounts of gas. But Wenner's arbitrary division between old and new gas and his method of setting prices left producers both amazed and outraged. The IPAA called the whole proceeding a "metaphysical excursion," while one independent termed the decision "inadequate and unrealistic." Whatever one called it, the decision became permanent in 1965, prices were frozen without review for two and a half years, producers were obliged to refund over $30 million from gas sales made after January 1, 1961, that did not conform to FPC ceilings, and precedent was set for FPC regulation throughout the country.[48]

The end result of the FPC's low gas ceilings was in fact an increase in the demand for gas. But the policy also choked off one source of capital for finding additional supplies and discouraged the search for new reserves. By directing the sellers of natural gas toward relatively unregulated intrastate markets, the FPC also encouraged the movement of energy-reliant industry away from those older industrial states of the North and Midwest, the original plaintiffs for gas regulation, to the Sun Belt in search of secure sources of gas. Before the Permian rate case, half the region's natural gas was sold to interstate purchasers. Within a decade of the decision, more than three quarters of Permian Basin gas was sold on the intrastate market, at prices of 8 to 12 cents per Mcf higher than those for regulated interstate gas.[49]

During the years of controversy over FPC policy, petroleum imports continued to be a major issue in domestic politics for most independents. Though the Eisenhower administration had sponsored a voluntary imports limitation program, it, like most easy political answers to difficult economic questions, accomplished little. Rising costs and stable prices in the domestic industry continued to encourage the majors to import as much foreign oil as possible. In 1959, Eisenhower abandoned voluntary limitation in favor of mandatory import controls, an action predictably opposed by Mobil, Standard Oil of Indiana, Jersey Standard, and the editors of the *New York Times*. But because Eisenhower's limit on imports fixed them at a historically high ratio to domestic production, independents continued their political battle on the issue, pushing to change the ratio. Their political lobbying failed: Presidents John F. Kennedy and Lyndon B. Johnson held to the fixed formula.[50]

Washington's disappointing response to domestic industry problems during the sixties encouraged an increasing number of independents to take an active role in politics. The IPAA rallied independents to participate in the election campaigns of conservative candidates sympathetic to their industry position. Similarly, Jake Hamon encouraged his fellow independents to write to their congressmen to support higher crude prices and to fight tighter federal regulation of offshore exploration in the Gulf of Mexico: "Just because you are a little fellow," argued Hamon, "does not excuse your sitting on your behind and doing nothing. It is your fight, if you are to stay in business, and it is your neighbor's fight, too. So get busy, and don't get discouraged."[51]

The result of stepped-up political involvement, however, was not particularly encouraging. While independents could work to elect persons sympathetic to their interests, they found that the immediate source of much aggravation, the federal bureaucracy, was beyond their reach. Independent frustration with "mindless federal bureaucrats," as more than one oilman called them, mounted steadily during the sixties. It was intensified by a series of federal fact-finding efforts whose intention seemed hostile to the petroleum industry and whose implementation added to oilmen's overhead at a time when most of them were trying to cut costs. The first federal fact-finding campaign of the sixties began with the Justice Department's effort to examine the structure of the petroleum industry with a view to antimerger prosecutions. FBI agents circulated a standard questionnaire, beginning in Fort Worth, that included specific questions about ABC transactions and sales of crude oil and producing properties. Some producers dismissed this endeavor as a pointless fishing expedition, while others picked over the questions for useful evidence of obvious bureaucratic incompetence and ignorance of the industry. Such evidence was not hard to find. Commonly, the questionnaire solicited opinions on matters that were amply supported by harder data. Question 24, for example, read like a poorly constructed examination in an undergraduate economics course:

> Would you say that the entire United States constitutes a single market for the crude oil production of producers located anywhere in the United States, or would you say that there are two or more distinct markets due to geographic or other factors? For example, would you say that the area east of the Rocky Mountains and the West Coast area constitute separate crude oil markets for domestic producers? Please discuss.

Few independents filled out the forms, but a great number of them objected to their distribution by the FBI as a strong-arm tactic; many believed the questionnaire to be the work of Robert Kennedy, the attorney general and a firm ally of critics of petroleum industry.[52]

Regardless of oilmen's opposition, federal data gatherers did not retreat, and in 1963 a petroleum statistics study group was organized to coordinate data-gathering projects within the federal bureaucracy. Officials of the Department of the Interior, that department with the most extensive experience in monitoring petroleum, resisted this move;

Interior officials maintained that the federal government lacked both the personnel and the expertise to accumulate and analyze information independent of industry sources. Liberal activists who wanted new sources of information reached a compromise with Interior officials when they agreed that the Bureau of Mines, in the Department of the Interior, and the Census Bureau, of the Department of Commerce, would gather statistics on upstream petroleum operation. These two agencies continued to depend on producers and state regulatory agencies for data.[53]

Oilmen's fears of harassment from federal data gatherers abated temporarily in early 1964, when Lyndon Johnson signed an executive order reducing the amount of information federal agencies could demand from the petroleum industry. Like the import controls of the Eisenhower administration, however, Johnson's directive proved little more than a sign of his good intentions. Several months later the FPC circulated its famous ten-pound questionnaire. Despite objections from Johnson's Committee on Petroleum and Natural Gas, as well as from industry associations ranging from the American Petroleum Institute to the newly formed Permian Basin Petroleum Association, FPC chairman Joseph Swidler insisted that operators complete it.[54]

In dealing with elected officials and bureaucrats in Washington, oilmen were handicapped by their unfavorable public image, which dated from the days of the turn-of-the-century muckrakers. Much to the misfortune of domestic producers, just as the petroleum industry sought to fight off growing regulation by rallying political supporters, a natural and unpredictable calamity tarnished its image yet further. In 1969, a major oil spill took place in the Santa Barbara Channel, off the coast of California, sending a tide of heavy, stinking crude to foul some of the most scenic shoreline on the Pacific Coast. As major television networks dramatized the event with close-ups of oil-soaked seagulls and dying wildlife, the Santa Barbara oil spill became a public relations catastrophe for the petroleum industry. Never in recent times had it been subject to such widespread criticism. The *New York Times* alone published nearly 300 articles on oil pollution following the spill. Between March 1969 and March 1970, more than 30 articles on the Santa Barbara disaster appeared in mass-circulation magazines and influential smaller-circulation publications; multiple reports appeared in *Time*, the *Audubon Magazine*, *Life*, and *Business Week*, while single-article coverage appeared in *Environment*, *National Wildlife*, *Senior Scholastic*, the *Saturday Review*, *Newsweek*, *Science News*, *Commonweal*, *Science*, *Yachting*, the *Nation*, the *New Republic*, *U.S. News and World Report*, *Ramparts*, *Motor*, and *Sea Front*. The federal government responded to the disaster and the surge of publicity that followed by passing the National Environmental Policy Act. Among this act's provisions was the requirement of extensive environmental impact studies prior to drilling on federal lands; environmental protection groups could trigger reviews of these studies in advance of any drilling. In short, oilmen, seen by the public as destroyers of the environment, acquired a new bundle of federal regulation.[55]

As unwelcome as new environmental regulation was to independents, it was a minor problem compared to that created by growing federal concern about inflation. In August 1971, President Richard M. Nixon ordered a ninety-day freeze on wages and prices. Even the modest price increases achieved in 1970 came under attack as U.S. Senator William Proxmire, a liberal Democrat from Wisconsin, urged Nixon to roll back crude oil prices. To the relief of small and intermediate independents, those with less than $100 million income from sales of crude oil per year were not required to obtain contract clearances for sales from the price commission. Natural gas producers were not as lucky; the Cost of Living Council denied all gas price increases, including those granted by the FPC, pending its own investigations.

For independents, price commission policy meant even longer payout periods. Producer requests for rate increases were already backed up at the FPC, which had a backlog of some 1820 rate requests pending at the end of 1971. Following its decision on gas prices, the price commission altered Nixon's earlier policy and placed a freeze on all crude oil prices, covering sales by both large and small producers. This move put independents back where they had been at the beginning of the price regulation process. In response, the IPAA's executive committee prepared a request for a 4 percent hike in crude oil prices, arguing that costs had increased 6.4 percent since the last price rise. The request was turned down; indeed, it prompted senators Proxmire and Philip A. Hart to demand a Justice Department investigation of the IPAA for "possible antitrust violations." A skillful manipulator of anti-oil-industry sentiment, Proxmire accused the IPAA of a "conspiracy to fix prices," a curious allegation at a time when all prices were being set by a federal commission.[56]

Despite their tangles with the Nixon administration, independent preference for Republican candidates for office continued to grow in the late sixties and early seventies. In no small measure, the presence of the petroleum industry's harshest critics on the Democratic side of the aisle in Congress and the presidential candidacy of George McGovern in 1972 reinforced this tendency. McGovern's energy policy, intended to take advantage of strong anti-oil-industry sentiment in the Northeast and upper Midwest, seemed to single out independents for especially adverse treatment. Reverting to federal policy of the late twenties, McGovern criticized what he saw as the Nixon administration's "drain America first" policy and proposed an end to all import quotas. Two other parts of McGovern's eight-point energy program aimed squarely at the financing of exploration and development; McGovern called for an end of both percentage depletion and the practice of expensing intangible drilling costs. These three points together were perceived by most independents as sufficient to put them out of business. It came as no surprise when they supported Nixon for reelection, almost to a man. However unpalatable Nixon's price and energy policies, they were preferable to McGovern's proposals.[57]

By 1972 some federal policymakers had begun to rethink their positions on oil and gas prices. FPC chairman John N. Nassikas, reacting to looming natural gas shortages in the Midwest, came around to admitting that prices probably should be raised; with better political than economic logic, however, he thought it would be "inopportune" to raise prices while shortages persisted. Former FPC chairman Lee C. White, long an opponent of deregulating gas prices, now sided with industry spokesmen on lifting price ceilings, as did two prominent energy economists, M. A. Adelman and Paul T. MacAvoy. The FPC abandoned its long-frozen price scale in some instances. In the Permian Basin, for example, the newly founded Adobe Oil Corporation negotiated a twenty-year contract to sell gas produced in New Mexico for 51 cents per Mcf, 35.5 cents above the area-rate ceiling, under the small-producer exemption in FPC rules. The gain was short-lived. One month after the commission approved the Adobe contract, the U.S. Court of Appeals for the District of Columbia threw out the entire small-producer rule by a two-to-one vote. As a result, prices were rolled back, further discouraging the search for gas for the interstate market. Without the small-producer exemption, independents curtailed activity in many areas, including the Anadarko and Permian basins. To no avail, the administrative judge of the FPC urged an increase in the Permian area rate to 35 cents, up from the 1965 level of 16.75 cents: at the end of 1972, producers were still mired in federal price controls, and gas shortages continued on the interstate market.[58]

Neither a Republican administration nor a change of outlook among federal regulators brought any relief to hard-pressed independents in the early seventies. Independents had responded to slack times with increased political involvement, particularly on behalf of the Republican party, but their friends in office succeeded in protecting them only from the most hostile designs of the liberal wing of the Democratic party; federal measures to counteract inflation left independents saddled with the low prices that kept the domestic petroleum industry in the doldrums.

Slack times came to a dramatic end, not because of Republicans in Washington but because of an ambitious Near Eastern leader. In September 1973, Libya's Colonel Muammar el-Qaddafi halted sales of oil to the United States in retaliation for American support of Israel in the most recent Arab-Israeli conflict. Six weeks later, the Saudi, Kuwaiti, and other Middle Eastern governments halted oil shipments to the United States; the Arab oil embargo was under way, and the liability of an energy policy tied to imported oil quickly became obvious. Arab actions finally brought both federal policymakers and the American petroleum industry to a major reassessment of the role of domestic production and reserves in the nation's energy future. For independents, it was clear that the climate of business was finally changing — in all likelihood, for the better.

7: TULIPOMANIA IN
THE OIL PATCH

Compared to the bleak years of the sixties, the seven years following 1973 marked a period of striking revival and optimism, culminating in a highly speculative drilling boom in 1980 and 1981. The greatest stimuli of this remarkable revival in the independent sector were the rising prices of oil and gas; they surpassed levels that could only have been imagined in 1970. These price rises turned independents strongly toward exploration, and they enabled independents to take advantage of many opportunities that under former circumstances would not have been economically feasible. Higher prices made it possible to test new geological theories and to find new oil and gas; they also gave a strong impetus to stripper well operation. Even during the boom, however, there were significant drags on activity. During the years of peak activity, skyrocketing costs — of operation, of complying with regulation, and of money — offset some of the economic benefits of rising prices. Oilmen, moreover, continued to face hostile congressmen and regulators in Washington; passage of the windfall profit tax clearly demonstrated the extent of their political vulnerability. During the upswing, successful independent strategy depended not only upon taking advantage of rising prices but also upon careful economic planning and coping with costs and regulation. Spectacular price rises overshadowed the growing liabilities of costs and regulation to such a degree that it was easy to overlook the possibility that demand for petroleum could decline and that prices could fall. It seemed safe to assume that prices had nowhere to go but up.

The progressive rise of domestic petroleum prices in the seventies took place within the context of federal price regulation, directed for the most part toward keeping prices artificially low. As federal policymakers gave priority to controlling inflation, they placed the burden of keeping the cost of energy low upon the petroleum industry. At the same time, however, they were obliged to reckon with the dominance of foreign producers. America could no longer assume the availability of unlimited cheap foreign oil. When the political and economic necessity of domestic reserves was obvious, independent producers acquired a new importance.

The shapers of federal energy policy reluctantly conceded that something would have to be done to motivate domestic producers to find more oil.

Washington's initial effort was a complex and cumbersome system of petroleum pricing tied to an arbitrary classification of production. Phase four of the Economic Stabilization Act, effected in August 1973, defined oil production in the categories of old oil (oil produced from properties in production in 1972), released oil (oil from old reservoirs in excess of the amount produced in 1972), stripper oil, and new oil. Only old oil was subject to a price ceiling. Later in the year, however, as the Arab oil embargo and the rising price of Persian Gulf crude pushed world petroleum prices higher, the Emergency Petroleum Allocation Act (EPAA) adjusted the ceiling price of old oil upward, to a national average of $5.05. The prices of new, released, and stripper oil remained uncontrolled; in response to world market conditions, they rose rapidly, reaching an average price of $10.82 per barrel in December 1973. In the same month, the price ceiling on old oil was raised $1. With good reason, one independent geologist reflected, "The best thing that ever happened to me was the Arabs' embargo."[1]

The rise in crude oil prices in 1973 caused a burst of upstream activity in the domestic petroleum industry. By the beginning of 1974, more drilling rigs were at work than at any time since 1969. The surge of activity continued until 1976, when federal tinkering with prices had a dampening effect. As inflation once again assumed paramount importance for policymakers, they brought both new and stripper oil under price regulation. The Energy Policy and Conservation Act (EPCA) of 1976 reorganized crude oil price categories, changing the classification of old oil to "lower-tier" oil and of new and stripper oil to "upper-tier" oil, abandoning the classification of released oil. The EPCA "rolled back" the price of upper-tier oil by more than $1.30 a barrel and placed ceilings on the prices of both lower- and upper-tier oil. Six months later, the Energy Conservation and Production Act (ECPA) deregulated stripper production prices; in another six months, stripper production fetched an average of over $14 a barrel, while upper-tier oil had a ceiling price of approximately $13 a barrel. Lower-tier oil prices were held at an average of $5.25 a barrel.[2]

The extension of federal price regulation to new oil had an immediate effect upon activity. In the Permian Basin, for example, wildcatting, which had risen by 21.6 percent in 1974 and 12 percent in 1975, rose only 6.3 percent in 1976 and 1.1 percent in 1977, and it dropped 0.3 percent in 1978. Similarly, while total well completions rose 30.8 percent in 1975, they fell 4.3 percent in 1976. National operations reflected some slowdown of activity at the same time: between 1976 and 1977 the percentage of wildcats drilled by independents dropped from 91 percent to 86 percent. Price ceilings temporarily discouraged oilmen and investors, but the price of oil was still higher than it had ever been, and the classifications and regulations of the EPCA were limited to forty months' duration. Independent activity bounced back before long.[3]

From 1979 to 1980 crude oil prices rose from a national average of $12.64 to $21.59 per barrel. But the prices set by the Organization of Petroleum Exporting Countries (OPEC) were much higher, averaging $30.87 per barrel in August 1980 and $34.70 in April 1981. Early in 1981 the new Republican president, Ronald Reagan, who had received strong support from independent oilmen, deregulated crude oil prices, and in a free market, the national average price of crude oil per barrel soared upward to $31.77. Without a doubt, producers now had strong encouragement for exploration and development of reserves. In one decade the price of oil had risen tenfold; in one year, 1979–80, industry revenues from production increased 56 percent. Not since the grim days of the Depression and the climb back from 10-cent-a-barrel oil had price rises of such magnitude taken place so rapidly in the domestic crude oil market.[4]

In Texas, rising prices combined with regulatory changes helped boost the income of oil producers. In March 1972, the Texas Railroad Commission reacted to world market conditions by setting allowable production at 100 percent, thus ending decades of trimming back production levels to support prices. This move did not result in a sudden flood of oil on the market, for production from many older wells was already at capacity even under restricted allowables. But it did mean that the payout on new finds might be quicker, and it encouraged investor optimism. Prospects once economically marginal could be seen in a new light.

Though gas producers still had to contend with relatively low interstate prices and FPC regulation, they saw a dramatic improvement in business conditions during the seventies. Despite opposition in the courts and from consumer advocates, the FPC gradually eased price ceilings and approved a growing number of contracts with higher prices. Such price increases prompted purchasers to sign advance-payment contracts to keep ahead of anticipated price rises. As a result, more than a half-billion additional dollars were committed to producers within a few months in 1973, funding a tremendous increase in exploration for gas. During the first six months of 1973, gas wells accounted for 22.3 percent of all U.S. drilling, up by two thirds from the 1970 level. In late summer of that year, the FPC approved gas prices as high as 52 cents per Mcf; price increases sustained the lively revival in exploration for gas.[5]

Though the FPC abandoned area-rate pricing of gas and permitted a gradual raising of price ceilings to an average of $1.43 per Mcf in 1977, the agency's attempt to redirect the flow of gas into interstate markets was only partially effective because producers continued to receive higher prices in unregulated intrastate markets. In 1977, the average intrastate price of gas reached $2 per Mcf. A year later, however, the tremendous expansion of exploration and production of gas began to accomplish what the FPC could not directly effect: the intrastate market now had more gas than it could absorb. Oversupply, along with new regulation of the intrastate market through provisions of the Natural Gas Policy Act (NGPA), brought more gas to the interstate market.[6]

Higher petroleum prices during the seventies were matched by spectacular increases in the costs of operation. In the decade before 1972, for example, an IPAA industry survey indicated that drilling costs rose an average of 6.3 percent a year, a dire development at a time when petroleum prices rose so little. These cost increases seemed paltry, however, compared to those following 1973. Between 1974 and 1976 alone, the rate of increase in costs of services and equipment doubled. Thereafter, between 1976 and 1979, competition for contractors' services helped bring about a truly stunning increase of more than 33 percent every year! The costs independents faced, of course, varied widely with the type of projects they pursued, the regional conditions they coped with, and the depths they drilled to reach pays. As usual, Anadarko and Permian basin costs were relatively high, reflecting the expense of deep drilling; during 1978 the cost of a deep gas well in these regions rose by more than a third.[7] Nor were there easy ways to cut corners, especially in deep drilling. Unlike the poor-boy operators of the thirties, no modern operator drilling below 10,000 feet could afford to use junk equipment and amateur theories.

Drilling was by no means the only cost that increased after 1973, for as rising petroleum prices made the industry's future look bright, the expense of leasing land increased markedly. While the cost of bonuses and rents varied greatly from region to region and from prospect to prospect, some indication of the magnitude of the increase in the price of Permian Basin leases, as well as of the acceleration of regional activity, may be gathered from the lease bonus payments obtained by the University of Texas System in its public auctions of leases. In April 1973, before the Arab embargo, the system leased 53,940 acres for a total bonus of $3,559,300 and an average bonus per acre of $65.99; at the next sale in December 1973, with the embargo under way, the total sale bonus leaped more than threefold, and the average bonus per acre doubled. In September 1980, the average bonus was five times the pre-embargo level, and it nearly doubled at the auction held six months later. Over the whole period, the bonus paid per acre increased nearly 900 percent.[8]

The records of these auctions, in which bidding is public, also shed considerable light upon who drove the prices up. In the September 1980 sale, which broke all prior lease bonus records, Texaco paid $3.6 million, or $11,250 per acre, for a 320-acre lease in Ward County, while Mobil paid $1.6 million for two other Ward County tracts. Exxon spent nearly $3 million on seventeen tracts, Getty $1.7 million on twenty-seven tracts, and Monsanto $7.1 million for sixty-seven tracts. The majors and other large companies, then, invested heavily in regional exploration. Independents did not go unrepresented in this particular spending spree — Midland's MGF and Mid-America Petroleum spent $835,000 and $350,000, respectively, for various tracts — but the scale on which the major companies spent money dwarfed that of the independents as a group. Nor was this new in 1980; since 1973, domestic investment by large American oil companies had grown by leaps and bounds. After the Arab embargo, for example, a group of companies studied by the Chase Manhattan Bank spent roughly two thirds of their worldwide exploration and development capital for 1974 inside the United States. Capital expenditure by the U.S. petroleum industry increased from $4,250 million in 1966 to $14,510 million in 1976. When major companies spent big money at home, American independents faced competition for land, goods, services, and prospects — competition of an intensity they had not seen before.[9]

As major companies made the competition for land keener, landowners drove harder bargains with oil operators. Terms of leases shortened, from five years to three or less. As one mineral owner reflected, "They will ask for five, but they'll settle for three." Royalties rose from an eighth or a sixth to three sixteenths or even one fourth in many areas. As activity in the Austin Chalk area in Central Texas reached a fevered pitch in the mid-seventies, some landowners demanded and received 50 percent royalties.[10]

While leasing and drilling grew ever more costly, the cost of borrowing money rose to heights without precedent in five decades. The cost of borrowing, as reflected in the prime rate, edged upward from 10.81 percent in 1974 to 18.87 percent 1981. The rate at which the independents could obtain oil loans from their bankers varied to some extent, depending on their past records of loan repayments, the type of loans they sought, and the kind of collateral they offered, but they usually obtained money for 1 to 4 percent above the prime rate. Even then, special conditions sometimes limited their use of this capital. Bankers commonly required the borrowers to maintain substantial deposits, often equal to 15 or 20 percent of the loans.[11] During the seventies, then, oilmen found it relatively easy to borrow money, but like services and land, it was ever more expensive. While some independents limited borrowing at high interest rates, most of them accepted the increased cost of capital with equanimity. They assumed that higher prices for oil and gas would increase their income sufficiently to cover repayments and that a high rate of inflation would continue to reduce the real cost of borrowing money.

Both assumptions were parts of the conventional wisdom of borrowers and lenders alike by 1979.

The rising costs of complying with the expanding maze of federal regulations, by contrast, were universally condemned within the oil industry. These costs, unlike the others, had to be borne without hope of return to the independent. Since the Santa Barbara oil spill, the most rapidly proliferating variety of federal regulation was that relating to the environment. In December 1973, for example, the Environmental Protection Agency (EPA) issued oil spill regulations requiring all operators who might discharge oil into navigable water, or water ultimately reaching navigable water, to devise a field plan for prevention and cleanup of spill damage. The plan, certified by a "registered engineer," had to be accessible in the field. Not everyone was impressed by the EPA's scheme; Charles Nesbitt, chairman of the Oklahoma Corporation Commission, called it "a stupid federal program, . . . total bureaucratic nonsense" that his commission would do nothing to enforce. By 1980 there were over fifty federal land-use acts to be observed in all onshore operations; to these were added a host of other regulations relating to drilling on federal land.[12]

Such regulations, while annoying, were by no means as important to independents as the Natural Gas Policy Act of 1978 and the windfall profit tax on crude oil in 1980. These two pieces of legislation directly affected the income they could apply to operations and investments, as well as the amount of time they had to devote to complying with federal law.

From the gas producer's perspective, the most important provisions in the NGPA were those bearing on prices and intrastate markets. One of the Carter administration's objectives in devising this legislation was to provide economic incentives for exploration and development of new gas reserves of types so costly to find and produce that they could not be economically attractive under existing federal price ceilings. Section 107 of the NGPA allowed the Federal Energy Regulatory Commission (FERC), as the FPC had been renamed, to set greatly increased price ceilings on new gas produced from tight-sand formations, and it deregulated wellhead prices of gas produced from formations below 15,000 feet. Producers of tight-sand gas were allowed to sell their gas for as much as 200 percent over average interstate price ceilings; producers of deep gas could sell gas for whatever it would fetch. Both types of gas production, however, involved greater-than-average expenses in operations. Tight-sand gas production required sophisticated fracturing treatments and meticulous well monitoring; drilling for deep gas involved higher drilling costs and, in some cases, unusually challenging technological problems. In both instances, gas producers would have faced discouragingly long payout periods without federal approval of higher prices.[13]

The reaction of individual independents to the NGPA, then, depended in part on whether they were well enough financed to enter relatively expensive exploration for tight-sand or deep gas and hence able to profit from higher prices for new gas placed in these categories. The NGPA offered no advantages to independents too small to enter such exploration, to those already producing from substantial gas reserves, or to specialists in shallow gas. Worse yet, from the small producers' perspective, the NGPA extended federal regulation to intrastate markets. As one result, operators were required to file a sheaf of forms with the FERC for sales from every gas well, thus greatly increasing their paperwork. As a sign of what could be expected, the FERC issued 365 pages of interim regulations relating to the NGPA on December 1, 1978, the date the act became operative. Until the FERC processed the forms operators submitted for new wells, moreover, those wells would be shut in. The length of time between discovery and payout was thus directly tied to the progress of federal bureaucracy, a depressing development indeed. It is not surprising that the IPAA strenuously opposed the NGPA; for small independents, its liabilities greatly outweighed its benefits.[14]

Though independents as a group were not of one opinion regarding the NGPA, they had no trouble uniting in opposition to the crude oil windfall profit tax of 1980. In April 1979, the Carter administration announced a phased decontrol of U.S. crude oil prices, accompanied by a new tax on the windfall, the profit yielded by decontrol. The tax, paid by purchasers, producers, and royalty owners, was in theory a temporary tax, to be phased out beginning in January 1988 or when $227.3 billion had been raised. But as Texas congressman Bill Archer pointed out, "Once you put a tax in place and the government begins to depend on those revenues, it becomes very difficult to change." The tax, moreover, was levied on income and not on profits, despite its title and announced purpose. Texas senator Lloyd Bentsen spoke for many of his oil-producing constituents when he called the windfall profit tax "one more sorry example of the government offering the carrot of decontrol and then taking it away with the stick of punitive taxation."[15]

In its final form, the tax was more damaging to majors than to independents. Indeed, it gave special consideration to small producers who neither refined nor retailed oil or gasoline in a given tax period. Its specific provisions made sense only to oil and gas accountants. The windfall profit on a barrel of crude oil was defined as the difference between the removal price of that barrel of crude oil on the one hand and the sum of the adjusted base price of that oil under prior regulation plus the severance tax adjustment on the other. It taxed what had been classed as upper- and lower-tier oil, newly termed tier 1 oil, at the rate of 70 percent; stripper oil, newly termed tier 2 oil, at the rate of 50 percent; and newly discovered oil, some heavy oils of sixteen-degree gravity or below, and oil from tertiary recovery, all termed tier 3 oil, at 30 percent. But independents could qualify for a lower tax rate on combined production from tiers 1 and 2 of 1000 barrels a day, a reduction to 50 percent for tier 1 and 30 percent for tier 2.[16] Production beyond 1000 barrels per day was taxed at the higher rates. Presumably the tax reduction for small producers implied recognition of the role of independents in finding new oil.

This relatively favorable treatment did not make the windfall profit tax more palatable to independents. It placed those producers, independents and majors alike, who had succeeded in developing substantial production in the past at a disadvantage. One Midland independent found that the new tax amounted to roughly 31 percent of his gross income; Noble Affiliates of Ardmore, Oklahoma, while posting record sales during the first half of 1980, saw profits fall because the tax carved a $3 million bite from its revenue.[17]

The objectionable features of the tax, however, were not limited to loss of capital. Almost as great a burden was the demand it placed on recordkeeping and personnel. Veteran independents who had picked up numerous fractional interests in ventures over the years now faced the enormous headache of complex accounting for every barrel of oil they produced in order to calculate their taxes. As the managing supervisor of one older firm explained, "We had to change our accounting setup to include windfall profit tax in all our royalties, production papers, our lease records, and everything else." The complexity of the tax made professional expertise indispensable and, hence, expensive. One large Midland firm, MGF, claimed that it needed an entire floor of a large office building to accommodate its post–windfall profit tax accounting staff; other independents offered premium wages when they raided public accounting firms for personnel to handle the new tax. The cost of complying with what Oklahoma congressman James R. Jones called the lawyers and accountants' relief act of 1980 was high. B. J. Pevehouse, head of Adobe Oil, estimated that over a ten-year period ending in 1982, regulation increased the firm's operating and staff costs by as much as 25 percent; on the proliferating mass of regulation, recordkeeping, and red tape, he reflected, "It's spooky, it's so crazy."[18]

The rising petroleum prices of the seventies and early eighties were thus partly offset by a tremendous increase in the cost of doing business. Though many independents responded to this development by basing business strategies on the expectation of constantly rising prices, doing so obscured the reality of declining profit margins. Among independents, the veterans who had weathered the slack times of the sixties were more prone to notice diminished profit margins than the novices. As one independent noted in 1981, "If you can sell oil for $30 a barrel but it costs you three or four times more to drill a well, you're not really better off than when you were selling oil at $3 a barrel and producing eight days a month. . . .The payout hasn't changed that much." Another independent noted, "A lot of deals in the last half of 1981, in practice, are not any better margins than they were in 1965." A developer of high-priced tight-sand gas made a similar observation on the rising cost of drilling and services in the early eighties: "The economic impact was to almost bring us back in line to where we were with $2 gas." Despite record-high prices, business was not as good as it seemed. Reflecting on business in 1980, after passage of the windfall profit tax, one small operator summed matters up: "You know, I get roughly $8000 a month, and if I don't work it right close, I'd write $9000 worth of checks paying bills. Where the hell is that big windfall profit?"[19]

Despite rising costs and bureaucratic constraints, the expectation of increasingly high prices made it possible for independents to reassess the potential of projects that had been economically unattractive during slack times. Deep exploration in the Rocky Mountain Overthrust Belt, the Anadarko Basin, the Hugoton Embayment in Kansas, and the Tuscaloosa Trend of southern Louisiana and southwestern Mississippi became economically attractive, as did exploration for oil in the Texas Austin Chalk, in which the presence of oil had long been recognized but economic development had hitherto been barely possible. Higher prices also enhanced the attraction of secondary and tertiary recovery projects, as well as of stripper well production. As independents recalculated the economics of a wide variety of projects, they found many attractive areas for activity.

Beyond a doubt, the most promising area for exploration was the Rocky Mountain Overthrust Belt. During the forties and fifties, it had been known as an oilman's graveyard, for most attempts to find oil ended in expensive dry holes. The existing seismic techniques could not locate traps at great depths and in "high-dip-angle" surroundings. Nonetheless, during the mid-fifties, Pan American Petroleum, a subsidiary of Amoco, approached the region's largest landowner, the Union Pacific Railroad, with a proposal to explore on farmed-out acreage. Union Pacific had done little to test its vast holdings for petroleum; when prospectors sought farmouts, it had seldom offered them more than a niggardly single section of land. But in 1969 Amoco succeeded in striking a bargain through which it received the exclusive right — for only three years — to evaluate 7.4 million acres in a forty-mile-wide belt stretching through Utah, Colorado, Wyoming, and Nebraska. With a vast amount of acreage to explore, Amoco looked for customers for farmouts. It offered dry-hole money and relatively generous terms, but overthrust tests nonetheless remained beyond the small independent's reach. The economics were discouraging: it cost $8 million to $12 million, exclusive of completion costs, to drill a hole to 15,000 to 19,000 feet, and high-pressure hydrogen sulphide gas made drilling especially expensive and hazardous in many areas. The Rocky Mountain Overthrust Belt, however, was one of the few remaining areas in the United States that held tempting possibilities of big production. Striking successes increased the allure of the region. One discovery, the giant Anschutz Ranch East field, discovered at the end of 1979, had reserves estimated at more than 800 million barrels of petroleum liquids.[20] The possibility of replacing reserves through rank wildcatting appealed to many intermediate independents, making Denver the hottest exploration center in the country. Independents from coast to coast joined the latest rush to the Rockies.

Independents looking for less expensive prospects in other areas were attracted to the Anadarko Basin and the Tuscaloosa Trend. Whereas the majors dominated Rocky Mountain Overthrust exploration, independents predominated in the Anadarko; in 1982, according to one observer, close to 95 percent of all Anadarko exploration was conducted by independents. There were practical reasons behind Anadarko's special appeal to independents. Land in the region was generally in the hands of relatively small property owners, making assembly of a block of acreage the kind of time-consuming job major companies tried to avoid, so independents were not shut out of participation by preeminent leasing campaigns of majors. Deep Anadarko projects, moreover, became known for their high production rates, their long reserve life, and, above all, their high drilling success rate, 97 percent in parts of the lower trend. Moreover, it was not uncommon for an unsuccessful deep test to uncover profitable amounts of oil in shallower pays. All these attractions made Anadarko projects relatively easy to sell to investors and bankers. A bit of quick work with a pencil made them look even better. Once the NGPA sanctioned high prices for deep gas, the optimists in the Anadarko expected gas prices to average more than $10 per Mcf over the life of a well. Such a figure could go a long way toward overcoming economic reservations about drilling a deep well costing between $7 million and $10 million. Similarly, in the deep Tuscaloosa Trend, the combination of high prices and big production made gas projects attractive.[21]

Within Texas, new applications of sophisticated technology made the Austin Chalk the liveliest area of independent activity. Though oilmen had known since the twenties that the Austin Chalk could yield oil, the typical test yielded either meager production or impressive initial production that rapidly fizzled out. High oil prices, however, made even small and short-lived production profitable and justified employing expensive science and technology to locate oil.

Like that in the Spraberry Trend, production in the Austin Chalk had to be understood by studying complex fracture patterns in the formation, and to do this, sophisticated seismic techniques were necessary. Once wells were drilled, operators boosted production with fracturing techniques. Even with this treatment, however, a well's production commonly declined by 50 percent within six months. By the end of its economic life, the average well had produced 50,000 to 80,000 barrels, with very good wells yielding as much as 120,000 barrels. With these relatively low yields, independents who held costs down profited in the Austin Chalk. Most of the Permian Basin independents in the Austin Chalk play, such as Clayton Williams, Jr., BTA, Tipperary, and MGF, were intermediate-sized operators with engineering staffs to control costs and nurture production. Other independents in the play, many of them small and new to the business, took roles closer to that of the promoters of an earlier age. They acquired relatively cheap leases away from the profitable "sweet spots" developed by Williams and others and sold their deals to outside investors with a "can't-miss" promise. Of course, given the extent of the productive formation, their promises were not totally empty; most tests found some oil. As the more responsible operators knew, however, the depth and permeability of the productive formation varied widely, making the promotion of an oil well often more profitable than the production of oil. With both types of independents at work in the Austin Chalk, the trend was both highly active and largely the preserve of the independents, who drilled nearly 95 percent of all of the wells in it.[22]

In mature areas like the Permian Basin, high prices stimulated increased activity and new types of projects. Drilling for gas, for example, continued in the Delaware and Val Verde basins, and in Lea and Eddy counties, New Mexico, but a few prospectors took on a new objective, the location of carbon dioxide. The impetus for tertiary recovery projects that both high prices and changes in tax law gave major-company producers created a new demand for huge quantities of carbon dioxide. Though a find of carbon dioxide without accompanying hydrocarbons was not profitable, Delaware Basin formations likely to contain both became increasingly attractive prospects. In the search for oil, new objectives developed from prospecting on the Abo Reef Trend, along the northern and eastern edges of the Midland Basin, often beneath shallower pay zones. As in the Rocky Mountain Overthrust, greatly improved prospecting technology played a major part in the new discoveries; in Abo prospecting, the borehole gravimeter was especially useful. Exploration for Abo oil was much cheaper than looking for deep gas; the average well cost roughly $350,000 to drill, well within the reach of many small independents.[23]

The rising cost of finding oil, taken with federal price and tax regulation, enhanced the appeal of stripper well properties. Indeed, so attractive did once-marginal properties become that established stripper and secondary recovery specialists found it increasingly costly to acquire new properties. The small tracts that the majors once farmed out became profitable enough for them to continue to manage; small producers saw their two- and three-barrel-per-day wells begin to yield profits, and as one independent noted, they were not inclined "to give it up for peanuts." The diminishing availability of properties led some small stripper and waterflood specialists to revise their business strategies. The intermediate-sized firm of Wood, McShane, and Thams, for example, redirected its efforts from secondary recovery to exploration. Between 1977 and 1979, this firm undertook a successful exploration program for shallow gas in Andrews County, looking for production in an area where, in past decades, wells producing gas had been plugged and abandoned as uneconomical. Both familiarity with a mature producing region and the geological expertise of one of the partners aided the firm in the redirection of its strategy. By 1981, the firm had broadened its search for shallow gas to the Raton Basin of Colorado, where it brought in several successful wildcat wells. The firm made this move out of the more familiar Mid-Continent region in order to find reserves at a lower cost than that at which they could be obtained nearer home. Thus, radically changed business conditions after 1973 brought Wood, McShane, and Thams not only to pursue new activities but also to enter a different region.[24]

During the worldwide petroleum boom that began in 1973, a commonplace observation in Tulsa, Oklahoma City, Denver, Houston, and Midland was that a horde of newcomers had descended upon the oil and gas community. This observation was not merely the populace's startled reaction to livelier times in the industry. In Midland, for example, during the twelve-year period from 1969 through 1981, the number of listings for independents in business directories increased by nearly 90 percent, with more than two thirds of the growth occurring between 1969 and 1975. As in earlier expansions of activity in the region, some of the newcomers were established intermediate and large independents from other regions who were undertaking new or broadened activity in the Permian Basin, such as Mitchell Energy of Houston and Saxon Oil of Dallas. A significant number of the newcomers, however, were small independents who went into business for themselves. The expansion of activity, reflected in the dramatic increase in drilling, created expectations of greater opportunity; scores of landmen, geologists, and engineers responded to promising possibilities by going independent, much as their counterparts had during the good times of the late thirties and during the postwar boom.[25]

The greatest number of new independents were already in Midland when they took that step. Nearly one third of the new entries were employees of other independents or major companies before going independent. The greatest number in this group were landmen; half of them worked for other independents just before going into business for themselves. The largest single group had been employed by Adobe Oil Corporation, an aggressive Midland company likely to foster the urge to "get in on the action," as several new independents described the situation. About one quarter of the newly independent landmen had worked for major oil companies, while an equal proportion worked for companies that either were being reorganized or had been acquired: the Atlantic Oil Company, Amerada, Sinclair, Getty, and Midwest. Most often these landmen left their companies because they expected to lose standing in new organizations or to lose their jobs during staff consolidations. Their decision to go independent was generally a response to higher pay for day work and to their perception of expanding opportunities in Midland, where prosperous and well-known operators had gone independent during earlier times and other company employees were following a like course during the current boom.[26]

Like landmen, many geologists and engineers gave up the security of a regular paycheck to become independents. In Midland, nearly three quarters of this group had been employees of independents, while the next-largest number worked for companies that were either acquired or reorganized. These new independents paid their personal and business expenses with fees earned by undertaking consultation work for intermediate and large independents. When the demand for geological prospects increased after 1973, they commonly received an overriding royalty interest on their prospects, and when exploration was successful, this income supplemented the fees they received from consulting, stabilized their personal finances, and gave the more successful scientists the options of investing in ventures or of promoting prospects with investors.[27]

During the boom, few of the new independents grew beyond small size. The most important limitations on their growth were their lack of substantial financial resources and their inability to enter established oil and gas circles. Rather than speculate on small newcomers, banks preferred to lend funds to small independents with known track records and to the emerging intermediate independents. It simply took time for a new independent to develop the performance history that made him competitive in borrowing. His modest consultation and royalty income, moreover, was rarely adequate to launch a venture with a relatively high probability of success; newcomers seldom came to participate in the deals of larger established independents because they lacked sufficient capital to participate in projects on a regular basis and because they did not have what the independents call staying power, the capital necessary to meet unanticipated exploration costs and the heavy expenses of developing some types of proven properties. For these reasons, though small independents performed highly useful consultation functions in the oil and gas community, they seldom advanced quickly to the intermediate level. The new independents, in particular, continued to rely on fees for their living.

Some of the feeling that the oil and gas community was being inundated with new members came from the proliferation of new companies that were, nonetheless, the ventures of established community members. Thus, in Midland, many directory listings for apparently new firms were in fact either new listings for independents identified differently in 1969 or new multiple entries for operators already established in town before the boom. In many instances, these new companies were partnerships, created to structure cooperation between general partners and to manage the investments of limited partners. Arden Grover, for example, had merged his company, Pomokai, into Flag-Redfern in 1972, and he entered the company as vice president for acquisitions. With the upturn in activity, however, he went independent again in 1977, working through the Arden, Kenyon, and other oil companies of his creation. Similarly, Kelly Bell did business both under his own name and as the Troporo Oil Company. Earle M. Craig, Jr., one of Midland's Ivy Leaguers, continued to do business under his own name and through additional oil companies, including the Chartiers Oil Company and the Chartiers Production Company. In these examples, even when business directories seemed to indicate that there were new faces, veteran oilmen were simply wearing new hats.[28]

The independents who were already in business when the boom began enjoyed the special advantage of having both access to capital and position in the oil and gas community. They shared that advantage, but as the subsequent development of two intermediate independents indicates, they pursued differing strategies.

During the entire boom-to-bust period, the Flag-Redfern Oil Company operated under the leadership of its founder, John J. Redfern, Jr., and his perspectives, personality, and strategies determined company policies. They were, for the most part, conservative, directed at building the assets of the closely held corporation. Redfern's relatively cautious approach to business was a direct reflection of the time and terms of his entry to the industry. He completed his undergraduate degree in civil engineering at Rensselaer Polytechnic Institute during the Depression and struggled along during hard times by working for a plumbing wholesaler. In 1937, an alternative appeared: Redfern read of heightened oil activity in the Southwest. With his small savings and some backing from his family, Redfern moved to Oklahoma City to enter the oil business. For a year, he attended classes in petroleum geology and petroleum engineering at the University of Oklahoma in Norman; at the same time, he looked for a likely place to begin business. In 1939 activity in the Permian Basin was somewhat slow, and opportunities for purchases of royalties were appealing. Redfern set out to try his hand at being a West Texas independent.[29]

John Redfern was not cut after the pattern of the romantic wildcatter; during his early years he used the income from relatively low-risk ventures to provide a living and to acquire royalty interests. When Flag-Redfern was created in 1970, therefore, it bore the marks of Redfern's experience. The new company comprised Redfern's various companies and properties in New Mexico, Texas, and Canada; it included the Flag Oil Company of Delaware, a royalty company that had acquired mineral interests during the twenties and thirties as part of an imaginative royalty pooling scheme. Redfern obtained control of Flag by cash tender, acquiring 97,276.78 net royalty acres in six states, principally in Oklahoma and Texas. This investment in royalties incurred low costs and relatively low risks. It also gave Redfern a large spread of undeveloped acreage, mainly in South Texas and in the Anadarko Basin of Oklahoma, with lesser amounts of acreage in Colorado, Kansas, Nebraska, and New Mexico. These interests required little day-to-day management, and consequently, they generated few operating expenses. Apart from maintaining legal records relating to titles, the only ongoing work was that of tracking development in the various areas to keep up with the prevailing prices of properties.[30]

Throughout the seventies, Redfern expanded Flag-Redfern's assets through acquisition, functional integration, and heightened activity in exploration and production. During the first half of the decade, Flag-Redfern acquired the producing properties and undeveloped leases of six other operators and companies, through merger or purchase. While prices of oil and gas were still held back by federal regulation, Redfern found it more economical to replace and build his reserves through acquisition than through exploration. By the end of 1974, he had built Flag-Redfern to its historically high level of 6.5 million barrels of oil in reserves. Thereafter, reserves declined slowly, by less than 3 percent per year. In only one year, 1976, was the downward trend of reserves interrupted, and then by the purchase of properties from the Great Expectations Oil Company of Fort Worth. After that, no more economical purchases came Redfern's way; rising prices of oil and gas in the intrastate market raised the value of reserves and inclined their owners to ask high prices, some of them based on expectations that the price of oil would rise to $80 per barrel by the mid-eighties. The relatively inflated cost of petroleum in the ground effectively blocked acquisition as a means of replacing and building reserves.[31]

In response, Redfern expanded the company's involvement in exploration and development. During the latter half of the seventies, he both enlarged his own staff and increased the company's participation in the ventures of other independents. By the end of his expansion program, Flag-Redfern employed five geologists working in three locations, three petroleum engineers, two landmen, and an in-house lawyer, in addition to a greater number of support personnel. This staff generated more geological prospects and managed more properties; it evaluated the prospects and properties of other independents with whom Flag-Redfern participated. In 1979, the company either drilled or participated in 102 wells, compared to 29 at the beginning of the company's life. In the same year, it operated 409 wells, about eight times the number reported in 1970. Even so, by the end of the decade, the return from the increased activity declined for reasons that went beyond the management of the company to the prevailing economic conditions in the petroleum industry.[32]

Like other independents of the seventies, Flag-Redfern faced rising costs of money, land, and services; shrinking profit margins; and shortages of experienced personnel. Taken with stepped-up competition for attractive geological prospects, these conditions encouraged Redfern to modify his business strategy. In exploration, this meant increasing exposure and trying for bigger finds, at the cost of both greater investment and higher risk. Like the Midland-based firms of Adobe, Coquina, Tipperary, Mallard, C&K, and MGF, Flag-Redfern continued to invest outside the Permian Basin, to acquire interests in foreign countries as well as other domestic producing regions. The company added to its modest holdings in Canada, keeping them until the late seventies, when it responded to adverse tax laws and a hostile political climate by selling them. During the early seventies, Flag-Redfern also made small investments in leases in both the British sector of the North Sea and offshore Sicily. When these foreign ventures failed to live up to expectations, however, the company disposed of them.

Domestic prospects outside the Permian Basin proved to have a more enduring attraction. Flag-Redfern followed prospects in areas of lively activity, particularly on emerging geological frontiers. The firm not only increased its operations and investments in areas like South and Central Texas, where the original Flag Oil Company had substantial royalty interests, but also drilled three shallow wells in Tennessee when outside interest in that area was keen. In 1981, when Rocky Mountain Overthrust Belt activity reached its highest pitch, Flag-Redfern joined a number of other independents in an ambitious and costly venture there. In exchange for leases covering nearly a township, Flag-Redfern agreed to undertake seismic work that could be expected to cost at least $300,000. Responding to encouraging geophysical data, Flag-Redfern and its associates drilled two tests to hold their leases. Both wells were dry. The expense and the risk of this venture were greater than Flag-Redfern usually accepted, but the only reasonable answer to the problem of declining reserves was to try for large reserves that might be found in underexplored areas. The lure of finding something big — or, as Redfern described it, the romance and excitement of prospecting on a frontier — persuaded the firm to try its luck in this area.[33]

Apart from this sizable risk, Redfern, like many other veteran independents, took a conservative approach to operations, especially to risk and debt. As costs of reserve purchases climbed, Redfern bought shares in royalty trusts, which he perceived as the most economical reserves available. In some measure, rising costs were offset by minor economies of scale as the company increased the number of properties it operated. As contractors' rates rose sharply, Flag-Redfern performed more work for itself, and it entered the service sector of the industry in a modest way.[34] Redfern, like other veteran intermediate independents, responded to the soaring cost of borrowing by reverting to the Depression tactic of drilling out of income and by reducing both debt and costs. During 1977, for example, the company retained 95 percent of its earnings to provide additional operating capital, and it lowered its debt to less than $2 million, about 2 percent of the assets of the corporation. During the same year, more than 90 percent of the company's working capital came from operation. At the same time, the company tried to keep overhead low. To minimize these costs, the company continued to lease office space and computer equipment. With single-minded emphasis on finding petroleum, Flag-Redfern resisted the temptation common among successful Midland oilmen to change the city's skyline with a personalized office building.[35]

With a view to minimizing risks, during the late seventies and early eighties Flag-Redfern divided funds equally between exploration and development. Most exploratory activity was in the form of stepouts, extensions of known pools. These wells could still be risky: they could be dry, or, more likely, they might not produce enough oil to return investments and operating costs within a reasonable period of time. Thus even in these ventures, Flag-Redfern drilled with partners and limited its own investment to $500,000, an amount not often approached in its exploration program. The company also sought to offset higher costs by drilling on properties in which it already had an interest, and it took on some drilling and service work to avoid ever-steeper contractors' bills. As leasing costs rose, the company curtailed purchases of leases. A few ventures involved relatively greater costs and risks, which Redfern undertook in search of sizable reserves: "Everybody has to find something reasonably big once in a while — once every five years in my case — just to stay in business." But Flag-Redfern assumed its risks with retained earnings, and by the end of the boom, the firm carried no significant debt. For that reason, in 1982, when other intermediates were pressed for cash to meet interest payments, Flag-Redfern reported record income and expanded its activities to take advantage of falling lease and drilling costs. With the boom's end, Redfern's conservative approach was amply vindicated.[36]

The strategy of financing operations from retained income ultimately served Flag-Redfern well, but it was ill suited to the firm whose objective was rapid growth. One such Midland company was the MGF Oil Corporation, which responded to higher petroleum prices with a spectacular increase in size and scope of operations. MGF grew out of a partnership; the original partners, R. O. "Jack" Major and Aaron F. Giebel, were a geologist and a petroleum engineer, respectively. Both had worked for other independents before they became consultants in 1957. Like other small independents, they supported themselves with fee work until they acquired sufficient capital to undertake operations with joint venture investors, in 1962. Three years later, Major and Giebel sold their interests and those of investors to clear debts and to obtain additional working capital. After two more years of small-scale activity, they began to expand their operations by taking Fred Forster, Jr., a drilling contractor, into the partnership. With the capacity both to generate and to drill prospects, the new partners were in a position to increase their level of activity and profits; all they lacked was adequate funding.[37]

Like other growing independents, the partners had largely abandoned consultation in favor of operation, which provided 90 percent of their revenues. This shift had posed several serious problems for the partnership. During 1969, for example, they decided to try for the one big discovery that small independents typically seek to achieve rapid growth. The vehicle for their aspirations was a joint venture to drill and operate a series of twelve wildcat wells. In addition to providing the prospects and managing the venture, the partners assumed some of the drilling costs of this ambitious project. When it ended in eleven dry holes, they faced the alternative of either curtailing their business and reverting largely to drilling and consultation or reorganizing and refinancing for another try. They settled on the latter course.[38]

In revamping their operations, a major feature of the partners' strategy was the limitation of their own financial commitments by selling interests in drilling funds to limited partners. Their first fund, MGF 70-A, Ltd., brought in nearly $1.25 million, paying about half of the overhead costs of the entire MGF operation and enabling the partners to work more prospects and keep their drilling rigs busy. Continued reliance on fund money after 1971, when MGF was reorganized as a public company, remained a key element of corporate strategy. Indeed, sale of limited partnerships in drilling funds often yielded more capital than income from the firm's operations. The company also borrowed heavily, but it received more money from limited partners than from bankers. Within a decade, MGF's long-term debt grew from $111,693 to $125 million. During the same period, the company raised nearly $140 million through its fund offerings.[39]

The growth of MGF accelerated after 1974; as Aaron Giebel expressed it, the company was "absolutely growing out of sight." The nature of the business changed dramatically: "The bigger we got, the more trips there were to New York, to placate the securities people, the Internal Revenue Service, investors, promotional people, and others." By the end of 1981, the partners had built MGF into one of the larger intermediate independent companies, with 1450 employees and an annual operating budget of nearly $300 million. During the same period the company's oil and gas reserves increased to the equivalent of more than 8.7 million barrels of oil. At 1981 prices, these reserves were worth about $150 million. Other assets included 44 drilling rigs, valued at $89 million, and nearly 700,000 net acres of undeveloped acreage, valued at about $49 million, plus other properties that raised the company's total assets to about $320 million.[40]

By the standards of the independent sector, this was truly dramatic growth. It was also highly risky. The rapid expansion of the MGF rig fleet, for example, rested on the assumption that demand and prices would hold. Construction and management of the large organization, moreover, required continuing subscriptions to drilling funds and rising oil prices. MGF assumed that improved net revenues and inflation would make it increasingly easy to pay large debts, which MGF incurred not only to purchase rigs but also to acquire three small independents, Beaver Mesa Exploration and Griffin Petroleum, both of Denver, and NFC Corporation, an intermediate-sized Oklahoma company. These acquisitions in 1979, 1980, and 1981 cost more than $100 million, and they expanded MGF's operations and risks into the Anadarko Basin and Rocky Mountain areas, where the company's management had little experience.[41]

Expanded operations required more staff, more public funds, and more borrowed money. MGF acquired them at high cost, because technical staff was in critically short supply after 1975. Throughout the industry, experienced geologists and engineers received great inducements to change jobs, and untrained scientists and technicians found jobs even before they received baccalaureate degrees. As Jack Major put it, "I found that we'd been completely without people to interview for some of our key jobs. They just weren't available." It was hard to sustain efficiency in a rapidly growing company when experienced personnel were in short supply.[42]

Operating with this serious handicap, compounded by the inexperience of top management in operating a large company, MGF still bagged some big game in its hunt for geological elephants. Its Permian Basin drilling campaigns produced profitable results for its limited partners early in the company's history, and activity in South Texas from 1974 to 1976 produced more profits. During the next four years, MGF completed successful projects in the Permian Basin and the Gulf Coast area of Texas and expanded drilling operations in Colorado and Oklahoma. In 1981, MGF made significant discoveries in the Williston Basin of North Dakota, the Anadarko Basin, and the Gulf Coast area, and it completed a development project in Reagan County. But even in these successes, the company's weakness was exposed: funds for these ambitious projects were largely raised from stockholders and borrowed from banks rather than generated from operations. In 1982, for example, only 12.26 percent of the company's working capital was provided by its operations; nearly three fourths of its budget was funded by long-term borrowing, while about 10 percent was raised by issuing additional common shares. The costs of borrowing were also apparent. In 1981, MGF used about 35 percent of all revenue to make interest and principal payments on long-term debts; the sum nearly equaled the amount spent to acquire reserves, and it surpassed funds spent in exploration and development. It was clear that both the management and its creditors had taken a massive gamble on continued demand for drilling services and on rising prices of oil and natural gas.[43]

MGF's risk did not seem daunting when it was taken. The rising oil and gas prices of the seventies culminated in gigantic upward leaps in the price of crude oil at the beginning of the eighties. Following deregulation, crude oil prices shot past $30 a barrel. When industry analysts predicted that oil prices would rise more than 13 percent annually to exceed $75 a barrel by the mid-eighties, the most optimistic perspectives on oil economics became plausible, especially to those unfamiliar with the ups and downs of past years. It was easy for oilmen and investors alike to assume that the spectacular increases they had already seen merely foreshadowed prices of $80 or even $100 a barrel by the end of the eighties.[44] With these figures in mind, almost any project yielding production could seem profitable in spite of staggering increases in operating costs. As a result of these expectations, in 1980 most oil-producing regions in the United States went into an all-out drilling boom.

Faced with keener competition than ever for land, prospects, employees, and services, intermediate and large independents scrambled to assemble leases, find materials, and line up contractors. Farmouts of acreage virtually disappeared in most regions; as one independent put it, between 1980 and 1982 "everybody was drilling everything they had." Prospects brought ever-higher prices, and they involved ever-higher risks. Drilling contractors not only raised day rates but often made operators pay separate charges for setup and rig fuel. High prices, along with long waits for drilling and services, led many operators to enter these businesses themselves; large independent companies with drilling operations, like MGF, profitably expanded their rig fleets. In the first half of 1981, for example, Tom Brown, Inc., and Midland Southwest, both companies with extensive drilling contracting operations, recorded profit increases of 122.8 percent and 184.9 percent, respectively. One did not need drilling rigs, however, to make handsome profits, and as oilmen made money, the skylines of oil towns like Midland showed unmistakable signs of unprecedented profit: proud towers sheathed in silver reflective glass sprang up like mushrooms after a rain.[45]

While the oil industry boomed, other basic domestic industries — home building, auto manufacturing, and steel making, for example — were awash in red ink. With good reason, large and small investors alike plunged into oil. Their enthusiasm was spurred by stories like the *New York Times*'s feature on a twenty-six-year-old millionaire from Odessa, Texas, who started out as a tennis pro and emerged as head of a public oil company, as operator or investor in forty-eight consecutive successful wells in the Austin Chalk, and as partner in the construction of two Houston office buildings. Oil, the source of quick and near-inevitable fortune, was the fast lane toward the American dream. To the amazement of veteran Midland oilmen, by mid-1981 a host of persons who had never before invested in oil were now steady customers of promoters. Independent John Hendrix, owner of a large company, compared this phenomenon to Holland's tulipomania of the seventeenth century:

> There's a real desire to shoot the dice. Just about all segments of our community are cutting however much they can comfortably stand, some they can't comfortably stand. They probably can't get into my deals or some other people's deals. But we have another level or two of people [small operators in Midland] who will gladly take $1000 or $5000 . . . and sell them what I think are marginal prospects. Even if they hit, they won't get their money back.

There was more money for investment than there were prospects likely to yield profit: to use the oilman's derisive phrase, money was chasing deals. As Kenneth Hooper, an employee of the Texas State Securities

Board, observed, "With oil priced at $35 a barrel, everybody and his damn dog is getting into the oil business."[46]

As investors rushed to get in on the 1980–81 oil boom, fraudulent promoters and con men seized the opportunity for ready profit. Some of these operators stayed just inside the boundaries of the law by using investors' money to find oil — but in old fields and in quantities so small that the investors would have gotten a better return if they had put their money in savings banks. As Mike Armstrong, another State Securities Board employee explained, "These promoters will tell investors they have hit 20 out of 22 wells, which they may have, but what they don't tell is that it will take investors twenty years to recoup their investment." Other promoters were not as scrupulous: they sold interests in nonexistent oil wells; sold interests in drilling ventures with no reasonable possibility of finding any oil; oversold interests in wells; and took money from the sale of interests for their private enrichment without making a bona fide search for oil. One Dallas promoter was indicted for bilking retired military officers by claiming to have high-ranking military participants; one of his victims confessed, "I was really relying a lot on the fact that there were a lot of generals and other military-types investing in it."[47] Such persons, eager to invest in oil but having no knowledge of it, were easy marks for fraudulent promoters.

One of the most bizarre promotional approaches was that used by an Oklahoma promoter who named "God Almighty" as his firm's director:

> If and when thou art ready, willing, and able to invest large sums of cash money in the United States Domestic Oil & Gas Play (It's currently the greatest, biggest, hottest, wildest, most exciting and most profitable oil & gas boom anywhere on this earth in all of history up to the present time): The wisest and best move that thou couldst possibly make, in pursuit of good investments, is a mailing of thy good checks for substantial amounts of cash money unto GOD & SON at the above address; without any further stalls, delays, excuses, questions, provisions, requirements, directions or instructions, hanky-panky, or any other sort of idiocy; so We shall be pleased to transfer over unto thee good title in and to those oil & gas prospects, properties, leases, mineral & royalty interests, etc., that We shall, when thou has so done, transfer unto thee from time to time as We see fit in Our infinite wisdom to so do.[48]

The Oklahoma Securities Commission did not share his religious enthusiasm.

Even as investment and drilling activity reached the most fevered pitch the petroleum industry had seen in decades, some oil industry veterans grew wary. To the old-timers, the prices of land and services had grown beyond reasonable bounds to levels one experienced operator thought were "wild, terrible"; they saw rapidly vanishing profit margins behind the high prices. Such oilmen grew increasingly skeptical that highly risky prospects, whose attraction rested primarily on assumptions of oil priced above $50 a barrel, would ever pay out. Charles Henderson, an independent geologist who had weathered the sixties, explained:

> We see deals where people are buying something based on what will happen in the next ten years. They build into their formula price escalation for oil every year for ten years, so they're in the $50- and $60- and $70-a-barrel [range]. Well, I think that is pretty thin ice on which to base a deal, because if you're wrong, you've created a disaster.

He preferred to work with a conservative estimate of $30 a barrel: "If it works out that way as a good deal, fine; if the price goes to $50, then we're twice as smart." He added, "I do think you need to use prudence and common sense."[49]

To the cautious oilman, dwindling profit margins were not the only sign that the future of the boom might be uncertain. In January 1981, U.S. demand for petroleum began its second year of steady decline, a decline tied to worsening economic conditions in the nation. Would petroleum prices continue to rise in the face of declining demand and deepening world recession? Certainly there was no historical precedent to indicate that they would. Perhaps the long years during which petroleum had experienced doldrums while other American industries made record profits led some oilmen to overlook the state of the national economy in making their plans. It had long seemed that the economic health of oil and gas was determined more by government regulation than by the state of the domestic economy, whose ups and downs had relatively little apparent effect on the independents' fortunes. Still, to conservative operators and investors, declining demand for oil and gas was not reassuring. By the fourth quarter of 1981, world spot market prices of oil had fallen and domestic gas consumption declined.[50]

Despite these ominous signs, during the last quarter of 1981 the domestic oil boom continued, and U.S. independents continued to drill at what industry observers described as "a blistering pace." Spending on drilling and completion rose to a record $36.6 billion in 1981, a 60 percent increase over the previous year.[51] Such a breakneck pace of activity made the reversal of industry fortunes in 1982 all the more dramatic when it took place.

It was obvious that the boom was over when the University of Texas held its land auction on February 3, 1982. For the first time since 1978, bidders passed over a tenth of the tracts offered. More striking yet was the drop in the average lease bonus bid per acre. In March 1981, the average bonus had reached a record-breaking $634.30; less than a year later, it dropped to $244.79. The following month world spot market prices for crude oil dipped to $28 a barrel. Posted domestic crude oil prices averaged between $32 and $34 a barrel, only slightly lower than the average of a year before, but a far cry from the $40 or more that many independents, investors, and bankers had been counting on. By June 1982, domestic demand for petroleum and products had slipped below 15 million barrels a day, the lowest level since the early seventies. Still, many optimists predicted that demand for petroleum would improve over the course of the summer and that the industry would emerge from its slump in the final quarter of 1982.[52]

By the end of the year, however, the optimists were proved wrong. Prices of crude oil slid further, and the price of fuel oil followed, bringing about decreased demand for natural gas. Domestic petroleum producers thus found income doubly reduced. As crude oil prices fell, their income from sale of oil declined. Gas prices stayed high, but producers were selling far less of it. The decline of both oil and gas meant that recovery from the slump would not be as rapid as some had hoped.[53]

While lower crude oil prices and a glut of high-priced gas on the market would have, in all likelihood, slowed the feverish activity characteristic of 1980–81, the abruptness with which action turned down cannot be entirely explained by prices and markets. As one operator noted in June 1982, "It's just like turning off a water tap, the way business has turned around."[54]

It took a combination of market conditions and new federal tax legislation to produce the sharp downturn. In 1981, while the market was changing, Congress passed the Economic Recovery Tax Act (ERTA), at best a mixed blessing for oilmen. The features of the act most directly affecting them were its provisions for reducing the maximum income tax rate from 70 to 50 percent, for creating minimum tax requirements, and for gradually scaling down the windfall profit tax. On the one hand, oil producers were given a tax cut. But on the other, the lowering of the maximum tax rate and the inclusion of IDC exemptions in the calculation of the minimum tax reduced the incentive of wealthy investors to place money in exploration; they looked for investments safer than wildcat drilling. Before 1982, such tax-motivated investors, both inside and outside the petroleum industry, had provided a substantial proportion of capital for high-risk ventures; indeed, one oilman noted in 1977 that the risk of exploratory dry holes was primarily borne by $1.5 billion from tax-motivated investors.[55] In 1982, oilmen saw the ranks of these investors dwindle. Capital for the exploration necessary to maintain reserves correspondingly declined. It was this development, above all others that made the end of the boom an abrupt one.

Within the independent sector of the domestic petroleum industry, three groups were hit hardest by the sudden end of the boom: small independents who were just starting their own businesses, the operators who had made large investments in rigs, and the intermediate independents who were heavily in debt.

For the new small independents, the downturn came before they had done enough business to develop a stable circle of investors who were willing and able to place money behind prospects during both good times and bad. Nor had many of the newest independents had time to build up sufficient production to generate enough income to meet expenses when prices fell. Those who entered business after 1979, moreover, entered at a time of fierce competition for the safest and most lucrative prospects; those prospects likely to come to the attention of the new small independent, the prospects whose terms he could meet, were often high in risk and profitable only under optimal conditions. Conditions in 1982 emerged far short of being optimal. Indeed, by the spring of 1982, industry observers began to speak of a "shakeout" of weaker operators. Some comforted themselves with the notion that those shaken out were fly-by-nighters, or persons who probably never should have gone into business in the first place — as their failure seemed to make obvious.[56] But before many more months had passed, it was clear that many legitimate and capable small and intermediate independents faced grave difficulties.

Those who had banked on an ever-swifter pace of drilling in 1982 were left high and dry as the tide of industry fortune receded. In July 1982, roughly half as many drilling rigs were at work as had been in use a year earlier. As operators sought to trim expenditures to fit lower incomes, and as they directed exploration strategy away from high-priced deep gas, for which purchasers were scarce, they planned an increasing proportion of shallower tests. In short, they looked to drill less expensive wells. Drilling contractors thus faced not only a lower level of business activity but less lucrative jobs as well. With competition stronger, they were obliged to trim prices and to return to less profitable footage rates; by midyear drilling costs had dropped by as much as one third to one half in many areas.[57] Even at that, however, most drilling contractors had idle rigs stacked in their yards. Delta Drilling, for example, saw its land rig utilization rate drop from 75 percent to 64 percent in 1981–82; MGF, which had invested heavily in contract drilling, from which it made handsome profits in 1981, saw its rig utilization rate drop from 94 percent to 55 percent; it responded by cutting jobs, hours, and wages in its drilling operations. So grim was the outlook for drilling contractors by the beginning of 1983 that T. Boone Pickens, the head of Mesa Petroleum, forecast, "I don't think in my lifetime I'm going to see a rig built again. . . . There'll be some specialty rigs . . . built, but I don't think you'll see full, complete drilling rigs manufactured again." He added, "We're down to [the level of drilling activity in] 1957, and it's in the trenches."[58]

Those who most keenly felt a sense of being under fire were the independent public companies that had borrowed large sums at high rates, on the expectation of rising income from production. During the boom such companies had found eager lenders among financial institutions. One independent reflected, "Everybody was carried away by reserve estimates, and sometimes there was inadequate investigation of those reserves."[59] Optimism about future prices and readily available loans led a great number of public companies to take on capital expenditures far exceeding after-tax income. In 1981, the height of the boom, for example, Chaparral Resources spent more than thirty-two times its income after taxes; Saxon Oil of Dallas, deep in exploration for gas reserves in the Fletcher area of the Anadarko Basin, spent more than fourteen times its income after taxes. On a lesser scale, MGF and Tom Brown, Inc., respectively, spent 5.63 and 2.17 times their income after taxes. When production income dipped in 1982 as crude prices fell and gas takes were cut, companies with heavy loan obligations faced the problem of meeting staggering payments from diminished revenue. Worse yet, the ERTA cut the amount of capital coming from tax-motivated investors for future projects; sales of drilling funds plummeted as oil lost its luster.[60] Many a public independent company, then, was left with a crushing debt from past projects and scant likelihood of raising funds for current and future use.

Among the many public companies facing rough water for these reasons were MGF and Tom Brown, Inc. During the first quarter of 1982, Jack Major anticipated a decline both in drilling and in rig utilization rates, which did not augur well for that sector of the firm's activity. Despite slumping sales in drilling funds in the industry at large, however, aggressive salesmanship enabled MGF to sell $26.5 million in limited partnerships to drilling fund investors in the first half of 1982, placing the company in the leading group nationally for such sales. This achievement could not be repeated. When the next MGF fund fell $13.5 million short of its $40 million goal, the company withdrew the subsequent offering it planned. At the end of the third quarter of 1982, MGF reported a loss of $21.7 million; by the end of the year, there were further losses of more than $80 million.[61]

MGF responded with further cutbacks. By November 1982, it had cut its staff, acquired with difficulty and expense during highly competitive times, by nearly half. It closed out-of-town offices, centralizing operations in Midland. Its executives took a series of pay cuts amounting to a minimum of 25 percent. It scrapped its ambitious plans for building a luxury hotel-office building designed by I. M. Pei in Midland. Yet, even with these strenuous measures, it became obvious early in 1983 that more would be necessary. The company made additional staff and salary cuts and, in March 1983, started to sell its undeveloped leases. A local news story on MGF ended with the chilling observation "The company does not plan to spend any significant amount of money in 1983 for exploration or development." Its total losses for 1982 amounted to $80,273,000 on revenues of $104,838,000.[62] The risks in MGF's strategy for rapid growth became clearly visible when the boom ended.

Many other bold strategists faced equally tough times. Tom Brown, Inc., founded by an enterprising salesman, had developed into a substantial intermediate drilling and production company, with 1700 employees, 32 rigs, and a division that manufactured drilling tools. With the downturn of the industry, the company saw the utilization rate of its rigs fall below 50 percent. Profits of $20 million in 1981 were followed by losses of $16 million during 1982. As business continued to decline, the company terminated nearly two thirds of its employees. The company sold its Giddings, Texas, drilling yard and a manufacturing subsidiary and closed its drilling division in the Rockies. Tom Brown held on for better times.[63]

The reversal of fortunes of such independent companies rapidly extended to their bankers. During the boom years, traditional energy leaders like Continental Illinois and Chase Manhattan, as well as other major banks in financial and energy centers, rushed to place funds at high interest in oil and gas industries. In Midland, for example, the First National Bank expanded its lending capacity during the speculative phase of the boom, from 1979 to 1981, by acquiring more than a half-billion dollars of additional short-term deposits through money brokers. In their haste to get on the energy bandwagon, many bankers gave borrowers' financial statements and collateral only superficial scrutiny; it hardly seemed necessary to be careful when industry predictions of $80-a-barrel oil kept drilling rigs working around the clock. The bankers thus fueled highly speculative activity and contributed to inflated costs. But in July 1982, with the collapse of the Penn Square Bank of Oklahoma City, bankers' expectations came face to face with grim reality. Many oilmen were not going to be able to make their scheduled loan payments. A succession of large lenders, including Continental Illinois, Chase Manhattan, and Seafirst Corporation of Seattle, disclosed that they held large portfolios of problem energy loans.[64]

Within Texas, nonperforming energy loans piled up at many larger banks as drilling declined and prices did not rise. The InterFirst group of banks reported losses of more than $100 million on energy loans.

Regional banks with smaller assets were hit harder. The First National Bank of Midland, for example, had more than $300 million in nonperforming loans on June 30, 1983, and losses of more than $120 million during the first eight months of the year. As larger depositors steadily withdrew their money from First National, its loan funds for small and intermediate local independents dried up. Finally, in October, the bank failed and was taken over by the Federal Deposit Insurance Corporation, a painful blow to the Midland oil and gas community.[65]

The independents who had followed more conservative strategies did not usually face dire problems with the end of the boom. Indeed, the independents who entered the downturn with substantial production developed in good times, with established business circles, and with relatively little debt could find attractive opportunities in the changed business climate. Like other independents, they faced diminished income from production. Unlike those who had to scramble to pay off large loans, however, the conservative small and intermediate independents could apply their income in an arena where costs dropped far more dramatically than prices. As hard-pressed companies turned to farming out leases, attractive opportunities emerged in many areas. Once the fever of oil speculation broke, prospects of better quality became available at lower costs. Thus one independent noted that he had seen more good prospects in the spring of 1982 than he had in all of 1981. Another independent reflected in June 1982, "Anyone sitting here with cash at a time like this is really in the driver's seat. You can make your dollars go a long way."[66]

For independents whose finances were stable and relatively unencumbered, then, the downturn of 1982 brought opportunities for profit. Flag-Redfern took advantage of lower crude prices by purchasing the reserves of two small independents, thereby replacing their own for less than the cost of drilling to do so. Another intermediate that thrived during the downturn was Adobe Oil. Having correctly anticipated changes in business conditions, Adobe sold North Sea properties in 1981 and whittled down its debt. It emerged from the first half of 1982 with a healthy profit of $11.7 million. Other independents took advantage of lower costs to increase drilling. The owner of one established firm explained in 1982, "We're going to drill 50 percent more wells this year than we did last year. Better prospects and better drilling costs. Even though the price of crude is down, probably overall the economics are as good or better." With interest rates still high and prices slipping, other small and intermediate independents were inclined to shift toward less risky development drilling, financing projects from cash flow rather than borrowing. Business strategists took a less daring course in tighter times.[67]

To the intermediate and established small independents whose financial position permitted them to maximize opportunities offered by the downturn, the end of the boom of 1980–81 was not entirely unwelcome. One large veteran independent observed, "It's probably as well that things are a bit slower. It got too fast . . . it got a little out of hand. It was wasting money." How much activity in exploration would slow down or how far prices would fall was not clear by mid-1983, nor was it certain that new government regulation would not force more changes in business. These uncertainties complicated the planning of independents. Still, for those who weathered the most recent storm, the future held promise. As one independent reflected, "We're in a downturn now, but there's always opportunity. Whether the market moves up or the market moves down, there's opportunity."[68]

CONCLUSION

Far and away the most important function independent oilmen perform in the American petroleum industry is that of finding and producing oil. As the history of domestic exploration amply illustrates, independents rush in where the major oil companies, wary of high risks and small returns, fear to tread. Independents have made most of America's oil and gas discoveries; they have drilled the overwhelming majority of wildcat tests.

For independents, taking exploratory long shots is not merely quixotic adventuring. Particularly since scientific and technological progress advanced prospecting from the realm of guesswork, hunch, and creekology, major companies have used their ample capital to identify the most promising prospects, those likely to have the lowest risk and highest return; they have been quick to take up the most attractive possibilities, outbidding and outbuying independents to do so. Independents, therefore, have been most active where the majors have not cornered promising acreage, where the majors have not pursued many geological possibilities, or where the majors have decided that prospects are not worth their while. In such areas, often exploratory frontiers, independents have tried their luck at proving the majors wrong. Often they have done so.

Various incentives tempt independents to take on prospects that do not appeal to major companies. There is, of course, the hope of making a big find in an untried area. This means more than romance and quick profits: a big find can add up to a secure and stable business future for a small or intermediate independent. Indeed, established independents find that a substantial discovery every few years is necessary for a firm's continued prosperity. In recent years relatively few independents have succeeded in making the kind of giant discovery that grabs the headlines: most have had to settle for a lot less. Still, independents have been able to realize comfortable profits from finds too small to interest major companies. Able to work with lower returns, independents have been able to do stepouts in mature areas, "mopping up the edges of the plate," taking on projects not big enough to be worth major-company investment.

Economic motives are not always the independents' entire reason for trying their luck in an area shunned by major companies. Particularly for the geologist independents, prospects turned down by a major company as too daring may be appealing as opportunities to test novel or unconventional scientific speculation. Scientific curiosity thus goes hand in hand with the desire to make money. Proving new theories has occasionally returned a profit. But there have also been those tests that, though scientific successes, were economic failures.

Much of the oil that independents find, then, is oil that the major companies did not look for. Similarly, over the years, independents have produced much oil that major companies could not have produced profitably. Since 1973, rising crude oil prices have led many major companies to retain stripper properties and take on elaborate enhanced oil recovery projects, but when prices were much lower, the majors commonly disposed of wells producing less than 10 barrels a day to independents, who then kept them in production. Since the early Pennsylvania fields, there have been independent producers who, unlike any major company, specialize in stripper production. Often working on a very small scale, such stripper operators make profits by keeping all costs low. In recent years an increasing number of stripper specialists have been petroleum engineers, who have applied science to enhance production from marginal properties. These independents have produced much oil that otherwise would not have been recovered.

Industry observers have long noted these important functions of independents. But there is another important part independents have played that is ordinarily misunderstood, and that is the independents' role in raising large quantities of capital outside the petroleum industry for high-risk ventures. From Dr. Frederick Cook and other oilmen who solicited capital through mail order schemes to the oilmen who courted Hollywood celebrities to John King and the other giant fund operators of recent times, independents raised large sums of money outside the oil community. Over the years, shadier fund-raisers often made it seem that "promoter" was synonymous with "crook." Not infrequently, uninformed investors found it difficult to believe that a dry hole was an honest possibility; it has often been assumed that a promoted venture was necessarily a dubious proposition. A closer look, however, makes it clear that the promoter's role was and is legitimate and significant. Though independents obtain outside capital to cover the direct costs of ventures in order to spread their own risks in a risky business, their contributions of prospects and venture management are both valuable and essential to exploration and development projects. The capital they raise outside the industry has funded some of the most spectacular American petroleum discoveries.

Federal tax policy has generally facilitated the raising of capital both inside and outside the industry, by encouraging investors to place money in oil-related ventures to lower their tax liability. Such tax-motivated investment has often financed high-risk exploration that could not have been funded in other ways. Whenever national economic conditions or changes in tax policy slow the flow of capital into petroleum investments, the effect on independent activity is dramatically visible in declining levels of exploration.

In these respects, then, independents perform functions in the industry distinct from those carried out by the major companies. Yet it would be a mistake to assume, from the difference between independent and major-company roles, that these two sectors of the industry work at variance with one another or that their interests are usually at odds. Overall, in the upstream sector of the industry, relations between independents and majors have been cooperative. As in the opening of the Permian Basin, independents took risks major companies did not wish to take, but they frequently had financial encouragement from the majors. In turn, the majors bought the oil independents found. Sometimes they did not buy as much oil as independents hoped. More often than not, however, the business interests of the two sectors have been compatible though not identical. The greatest exception to this general observation was not, as has most often been claimed, the dispute over production regulation in the late twenties and early thirties; in that instance, the business interests of each company, rather than its major or independent status, determined its position on regulation. The greatest real difference between majors and independents has been over imports, for most of the oil produced by independents has been domestic. For that reason, the independents' chief representative industry association, the IPAA, has consistently opposed increasing oil imports since its founding in 1929.

On the occasions when the independents' business interests have run counter to the majors' business strategies, as they have on imports, differences between the two sectors have reflected contrasting approaches to business opportunities. For the major companies, and for the largest independents, scope and scale of operations require keying business strategy to long-term developments in the national and world economy. Such large companies plan strategies for decades rather than weeks, months, or years; decision making in these large corporations is still a lengthy process in which many persons play a part, and the result is the commitment of large sums of capital over a long period. The development of petroleum production on Alaska's North Slope offers a good example of large-company long-term planning. But independents, particularly the smaller ones, have been far less prone to perceive business opportunity in the context of long-term economic development or of national and world conditions than to see it in the light of short-term and local industry conditions. In large measure, this independent approach to business opportunity reflects the independents' access to capital. When slender resources limit the scope of ventures and rule out tying up capital for long periods, business is geared to the local and short-term. Independents are affected directly by the long-term national and world conditions because major-company purchasing policies respond to such conditions. But the smaller independents are likely to ignore what happens in Rotterdam or New York as they concentrate on the current week's developments in, say, Pecos County: operating on a limited and local scale, they are more alert to short-term local conditions.

The more limited the independents' access to capital, then, the more closely their business strategies are keyed to highly specific and local conditions. For this reason, the nature of business opportunity for some independents is not infrequently counter to business trends in the national and world economies. Thus, in the sixties, as the national market for natural gas grew by leaps and bounds, Permian Basin gas producers responded to low regional prices by cutting down exploration and shifting gas away from the interstate market. In the late seventies, as national economic conditions turned down, Permian Basin independents enjoyed high petroleum prices and booming prosperity; then, in 1982, as the national economy began to revive, falling international crude oil prices and glutted gas markets brought the boom to an end many independents did not foresee because of their essentially local and short-term orientation. Still, as the end of the boom revealed, many of those independents — like John J. Redfern, Jr., whose perception of business opportunity was broadened beyond the narrow short-term focus by reflection on past experiences — were able to avoid calamity when prices turned down. Those independents who responded to declining profit margins at the end of the seventies by paying off debts and cutting back on activity were, in effect, working against the prevailing independent trend. They remembered the mid-fifties and opted for caution.

Over the course of six decades, independents have used a wide variety of business strategies to make money; there has never been one strategy uniformly applied by all independents to produce profit. Given the local, short-term, and highly specific orientation to business opportunity of most independents, this is scarcely surprising. Over the years, the spectrum of money-making opportunities has changed, particularly as a result of developments in science and technology on the one hand and regulation on the other. Generally speaking, scientific and technological progress has tended to broaden the range of opportunities for independents, while regulation has tended to limit them. The independents of the twenties responded to low crude oil prices by running their wells wide open, looking for the maximal short-term return. When regulation in many oil-producing regions came to restrict such a practice, other strategies were necessary to offset low prices. Here, science and technology eventually came into play; John L. Cox and other independents of the sixties were able to use increasingly sophisticated engineering technology to counteract the effects of low prices and allowables with more efficient production and recovery techniques. Strategy thus took on a longer-term dimension. It also became more complex, tied to scientific and technological specializations. At the same time, independents themselves have increasingly been highly trained specialists. Whether in geology, engineering, finance, or other fields, the specialists have found ways to apply their particular skills.

The kinds of opportunities independents pursued have been influenced not only by training and skills but also by membership in oil and gas communities. When new regions like the Permian Basin first opened, there were no indigenous oil and gas communities; the people and the capital necessary for exploration and development came from outside the region. As the region matured, however, oil and gas communities of varying size developed in a number of towns, that of Midland being the most important and enduring. The growth of the Midland community made it easier for independents, doing business with major companies and other independents, to raise money for local projects and to broaden the scope of their activity in the region. By the fifties, the Midland oil and gas community had gotten big enough to permit small independents to raise funds for projects without leaving town to look for investors or obliging bankers. By that time, independents had formed stable business circles within the community; being part of such circles and being known locally helped many Midland independents to weather the slack times of the sixties.

While small independents usually pursued localized opportunities, as they grew to intermediate size their perspective upon opportunity changed. Growth, in essence, meant access to increasingly large amounts of capital. With capital, independents looked to increase their production and reserves in a greater number of places; they moved outside mature regions like the Permian Basin to new domestic frontiers and to foreign areas. Other independents diversified by picking up additional types of operations, like drilling or oil field equipment supply. They resorted to increasingly complex financial tactics in order to accelerate their rate of growth. For most independents, growth from small to intermediate size brought problems as well as rewards. As the scope of these independents' operations moved to include ever-wider horizons, managerial skills were increasingly important, and these skills were largely unrelated to those that brought earlier successes in exploration and production. Oilmen who headed intermediate-sized firms generally continued to participate in most operating decisions, and they still made them rapidly. At some point in the company's growth, however, they crossed a managerial threshold, giving more of their time to directing the work of employees and less time to finding and producing oil. Many of these intermediates were not highly successful at their new tasks. They often failed to repeat the earlier successes that set them on the road to expansion.

One demand upon the time of all independents in recent years has been regulation. The gradual increase in state and federal regulation from 1920 onward has had a profound effect upon independent business strategies. Regulation has affected independents of all sizes, but it has unquestionably been most burdensome to the small independents. Early regulation of production pressed hardest on the small independents with operations in only one or two local fields; reduced allowables in one field could not be offset by production from other fields. Complying with wartime red tape placed a greater burden on the independents with one-man offices than on the larger companies with office staffs. Even regulation that ostensibly gave the small independents a break at the expense of larger operators and producers, the windfall profit tax, caused independents of all sizes to rush to tax accountants and attorneys for expensive help that took a bigger bite from small incomes than from large. For all independents, however, complying with regulation has required the use of financial and human resources that would otherwise be directed toward finding and producing oil.

Over the years it has been common for independents to react to new types of regulation with the cry that it will drive them to extinction. Indeed, with every industry downturn since the twenties, pessimists have come forward to argue that independents cannot possibly survive the latest plunge in fortune. But as Mark Twain said about his premature obituary, the reports of the death of the independent have proved to be greatly exaggerated. Even in the darkest days of the Depression, independents like Ed Landreth made enough money to stay in business; even in the bleak sixties, independents like Midland's Ivy Leaguers adapted their strategies to yield modest prosperity. At any time, there have been independents entering and leaving the industry; in the most recent downturn, while some independents, facing impatient creditors and production incomes that did not pay bills, went out of business, others, including many victims of company layoffs, decided to go independent. Thus far in the American petroleum industry, there has never been a development that eliminated the independent sector.

Sudden or prolonged slumps in petroleum prices, however, have time and again thinned independent ranks. The historical evidence makes it clear that independent numbers and industry activity have grown whenever capital — from production income, from investors, from lenders — was readily available. It is equally clear that the independent sector shrank when prices fell or were kept low, when markets for production contracted, and when fewer investors put money in the industry.

Whenever the independent sector contracted, so did exploration and, particularly, wildcatting. History bears out the commonsense observation that petroleum prices have a direct effect upon the level of exploratory activity. No example demonstrates this more clearly than the FPC's flight from common sense in the early sixties, when it kept gas prices low with the stated aim of encouraging exploration and production: it was abundantly clear by the early seventies that FPC price policy had exactly the opposite effect. The pronounced sensitivity of exploration activity to changes in prices reflected the independents' importance in looking for oil and gas. When independents' incomes dropped, they were able to take on fewer exploratory ventures. The exploration that took place, moreover, was less likely to be geared to new or unconventional prospecting methods than to more conservative strategies, looking for safer if slower returns on investments.

In recent years prices have presented independents with fewer problems than national politics, and in the political arena, independents have long been vulnerable. It is not easy to think of a single economic development likely to take place in the near future that could put independents as a group out of business, but there are potentially disastrous public policies that could do so. For example, a policy affecting those tax provisions that favor independents in raising capital — eliminating IDC write-offs, lowering tax brackets to thin yet further the ranks of tax-motivated investors, ending the depletion allowance — would certainly deal relatively new independents a blow from which few could recover. A return to artificially low, frozen petroleum prices would have a harmful effect on all independents. Independents have not always fared well in national politics, and it is in the political arena that their future is most precarious.

If independents can cope with the policies that emerge from Washington, however, it is likely that they will continue to play an important role in the American petroleum industry. Conditions and opportunities have changed, but independents have always found strategies that worked in new business climates. For these reasons, despite the most recent downturn, public and private comments on business by independents are generally inclined toward optimism: the most common observation among independents is still "If I weren't an optimist, I wouldn't be in the oil business."

NOTES

All the sources for a paragraph are combined in one note, in most instances, and listed in order of occurrence. Shortened forms are used after the first reference; a cross-reference to the first citation is provided when it occurs in another chapter. Interviews conducted by the authors are cited in full in the bibliography.

The following abbreviations for periodical titles have been used in citations:

IPM   *IPAA Monthly* (to 1961), *Independent Petroleum Monthly* (1961–71), and the *Petroleum Independent* (1971–).
JPT   *Journal of Petroleum Technology*
MRT   *Midland Reporter-Telegram*
NYT   *New York Times*
OGJ   *Oil and Gas Journal*
OW   *Oil Weekly*
PE   *Petroleum Engineer*
SADS   *San Angelo Daily Standard*
SAES   *San Angelo Evening Standard*
SAST   *San Angelo Standard-Times*
WO   *World Oil*
WSJ   *Wall Street Journal*

Chapter 1

1. Sanford E. McCormick, "U.S. Oil and Gas: An Independent's View," WO 191:7 (Dec. 1980), pp. 35–42. See also William H. Strang, "Independents Drill 72% of Current U.S. Wells," OW 95:9 (Nov. 6, 1939), pp. 19–20; "Independents Drill Three-Fourths of Wells," OW 122:9 (July 29, 1946), p. 59; L. J. Logan, "Independents' Role in Finding Oil Reserves," OW 129:4 (June 23, 1947), pp. 54–55; "Independents Do Big Part of Drilling in All Areas," WO 144:7 (June 1957), p. 180.

2. U.S. Senate, Seventy-Ninth Congress, Second Session, *Hearings Before a Special Committee Investigating Petroleum Resources* (Washington, D.C.: U.S. Government Printing Office, 1946), p. 4; Wallace E. Pratt, "Independents and Independence in Oil Finding," IPM 20:1 (May 1949), p. 24.

3. Ralph W. Hidy and Muriel E. Hidy, *History of Standard Oil Company (New Jersey): Pioneering in Big Business, 1882–1911* (New York: Harper & Brothers, 1955), pp. 708–14; Leonard M. Logan, Jr., *Stabilization of the Petroleum Industry* (Norman, Okla.: University of Oklahoma Press, 1930), pp. 17–20.

4. "IPAA's Tenth Anniversary," IPM 10:2 (June 1939), p. 9; Wirt Franklin, "Economic Situation Demands Immediate Action," OW 60:6 (Jan. 23, 1931), p. 31; "Fort Worth Delegation to Austin Seeks Pipe Line Law Changes," OW 56:11 (Feb. 28, 1930), p. 52.

5. John Blair, *The Control of Oil* (New York: Pantheon Books, 1976), pp. 128–29; McCormick, "U.S. Oil and Gas," pp. 35–42; Peter R. Odell, *Oil and World Power,* 5th ed. (New York: Penguin Books, 1979), p. 16.

6. Jim Landers, "Economy Drains Small Texas Oil Firms," *Dallas Morning News,* Mar. 31, 1982; U.S. Senate, *Hearings,* pp. 27, 53.

7. For a general account of the development of the structures and practices of "big business," including the major oil companies, see Alfred D. Chandler, Jr., *The Visible Hand: The Managerial Revolution in American Business* (Cambridge, Mass.: Harvard University Press, 1977).

8. Penn, West, and Craig interviews.

9. Ibid; Paul R. Schultz, "Economic Factors Involved in Operations by Large vs. Small Companies," IPM 26:12 (Apr. 1956), pp. 38–40, 72–75; C. Jackson Grayson, Jr., *Decisions Under Uncertainty: Drilling Decisions by Oil and Gas Operators* (Boston: Division of Research, Graduate School of Business Administration, Harvard University, 1960).

Chapter 2

1. Harold F. Williamson, Ralph L. Andreano, Arnold R. Daum, and Gilbert C. Klose, *The American Petroleum Industry: The Age of Energy, 1899–1959* (Evanston, Ill.: Northwestern University Press, 1963), pp. 261, 294–95, 444–48; Kendall Beaton, *Enterprise in Oil: A History of Shell in the United States* (New York: Appleton-Century-Crofts, 1957), p.155.

2. Gerald D. Nash, *United States Oil Policy, 1890–1964* (Westport, Conn.: Greenwood Press Publishers, 1968), pp. 8–9; Williamson et al., *Age of Energy,* p. 295; Sam H. Schurr, *Historical Sketches of Minerals in the United States* (Washington, D.C.: Reserves for the Future, 1960, 1966), M133–37, p. 12, M152–67, p. 14; Robert E. Hardwicke, *Antitrust Laws, et al. v. Unit Operation of Oil or Gas Pools,* rev. ed. (Dallas: Society of

Petroleum Engineers of AIME, 1961), pp. 1–6; Grady Triplett, "How Long Will Our Oil Last?" OW 40:4 (Jan. 5, 1926), pp. 50, 147; "Wilbur Outlines Government Policy," OW 55:12 (Dec. 6, 1929), p. 41.

3. Henrietta M. Larson and Kenneth Wiggins Porter, *History of Humble Oil & Refining Company: A Study in Industrial Growth* (New York: Harper & Brothers, 1959), pp. 171–91; John G. McLean and Robert Wm. Haigh, *The Growth of Integrated Oil Companies* (Boston: Division of Research, Graduate School of Business Administration, Harvard University, 1954), pp. 377, 381, 384–85; Logan, *Stabilization* (see ch. 1, n. 3), pp. 130–32; OW 51:5 (Oct. 19, 1928), p. 126.

4. Joseph A. Kornfeld, "A Half Century of Exploration in the Southwest," OGJ 50:4 (May 1951, Golden Anniversary Number), pp. 186, 190–97; Larson and Porter, *History of Humble,* pp. 64–65, 114–66; Beaton, *Shell,* pp. 105, 152.

5. Penson interview.

6. Berte R. Haigh, interviewed by Samuel D. Myres, n.d., n.p., and Harwell H. King, interviewed by S. D. Myres, Feb. 9, 1971, Fort Worth, Tex. (these and the interviews by Myres cited hereafter may be found in the Abell-Hanger Collection, Permian Basin Petroleum Museum, Library, and Hall of Fame, Midland, Tex.); H. H. King, "Three Wells Extend Winkler Field Quarter Mile," OW 53:3 (Apr. 5. 1929), p. 61; "Wildcatting Campaign Plans for 1929," OGJ 27:37 (Jan. 31, 1929), p. 199; William V. Gross, "February Crude Production Tops January Despite Handicap," OW 53:1 (Mar. 22, 1929), p. 36; Jones interview; Beaton, *Shell,* p. 333.

7. James C. Young, "Wildcat Oil Stock Lure Still Has Powerful Effect," NYT, Mar. 9, 1924.

8. "Texas Panhandle Development Responsible for 110 Companies with Big Capital," OW 44:11 (Mar. 4, 1927), p. 38.

9. NYT, Mar. 25, 1923.

10. Harwell H. King, interviewed by S. D. Myres.

11. Young, "Wildcat Oil Stock."

12. N. H. Darton, "Geologic Structures of Parts of New Mexico," in David White and M. R. Campbell, eds., *Contributions to Economic Geology,* U.S. Geological Survey, Bulletin 726 (Washington, D.C.: U.S. Government Printing Office, 1922), pp. 210–11; Samuel D. Myres, *The Permian Basin, Petroleum Empire of the Southwest: Era of Discovery* (El Paso: Permian Press, 1973), pp. 95–105; David T. Day, "The Petroleum Resources of the United States," in *Papers on the Conservation of Mineral Resources,* U.S. Geological Survey, Bulletin 394 (Washington, D.C.: U.S. Government Printing Office, 1909), pp. 30, 45.

13. OW 54:13 (Sept. 13, 1929), p. 112. The author of the OW's joke did not know that Wink did not exist before oil was discovered. See Roger M. Olien and Diana Davids Olien, *Oil Booms: Social Change in Five Texas*

Towns (Lincoln, Neb.: University of Nebraska Press, 1982), pp. 11, 13, 15.

14. Darton, "Geologic Structure," pp. 174–75; American Petroleum Institute, *American Petroleum, Supply and Demand* (New York: McGraw-Hill Book Company, 1925), p. 73; Walter A. Ver Wiebe, *Oil Fields in the United States* (New York: McGraw-Hill Book Company, 1930), p. 427; William B. Phillips, *The Mineral Resources of Texas,* University of Texas Bulletin No. 365 (Austin: University of Texas, Bureau of Economic Geology and Technology, 1914), pp. 105, 126, 129, 214, 222, 224, 234, and passim.

15. J. A. Udden, *Notes on the Geology of the Glass Mountains,* University of Texas Bulletin No. 1753 (Austin: University of Texas, Bureau of Economic Geology and Technology, 1917), pp. 56–58; R. A. Liddle, *The Marathon Fold and Its Influence on Petroleum Accumulation,* University of Texas Bulletin No. 1847 (1918), pp. 9–10, 16; R. A. Liddle and T. M. Prettyman, *Geology and Mineral Resources of Crockett County with Notes on the Stratigraphy, Structure, and Oil Prospects of the Central Pecos Valley,* University of Texas Bulletin No. 1857 (1918), p. 89.

16. American Petroleum Institute, *American Petroleum, Supply and Demand,* p. 73; Ver Wiebe, *Oil Fields,* p. 437; H. H. King, "Big Lake Performance Attracts Wildcatting," OW 36:5 (Jan. 23, 1925), p. 19; Charles D. Vertrees and George Abell, interviewed by S. D. Myres, Feb. 21, 1971, Midland, Tex.; H. H. King, "Third Pecos County Well Marks Half Mile Extension," OW 44:11 (Mar. 4, 1927), p. 36.

17. Myres, *Era of Discovery,* pp. 140–50, 152–56, 159–66.

18. Winkler County, *Oil and Gas Lease Record,* vol. 1, pp. 143–44, 176; *Ozona Stockman,* July 31, 1941.

19. Winkler County, *Oil and Gas Lease Record,* vol. 1, pp. 143–44, 305; Barton interview.

20. Myres, *Era of Discovery,* pp. 194–273; Frank Pickrell, interviewed by S. D. Myres, Sept. 2, 1971, El Paso, Tex.

21. Myres, *Era of Discovery,* pp. 199–200.

22. Ibid., pp. 200–206; Pickrell interview.

23. Myres, *Era of Discovery,* pp. 206–207, 211, 216–17.

24. Ibid., pp. 222–23; King, "Big Lake Performance," p. 19; H. H. King, "Over Eight Million Barrels Produced by Big Lake Wells," OW 39:8 (Nov. 13, 1926), p. 51; Richard A. Jones, "Review of Drilling Below 5000 Feet in West Texas," OW 57:12 (June 6, 1930), p. 28.

25. Myres, *Era of Discovery,* pp. 223–29; King, "Big Lake Performance," p. 19; "Marland Oil Company Buys Interest in Texon Oil and Land," OW 53:10 (May 24, 1929), p. 36; "Greatest Wildcatters Made Greatest Oil Strikes in West Texas," SAST, May 28, 1933; Sam T. Mallison, *The Great Wildcatter* (Charleston, W.V.: Education Foundation of West Virginia, 1953), pp. 331–34, 340–41; Reigle interview.

26. Larson and Porter, *History of Humble,* pp. 172–76, 185–86, 188–89; McLean and Haigh, *Growth of Integrated Oil Companies,* pp. 377, 381, 384–85; OW 39:2 (Oct. 2, 1925), p. 36; OW 39:10 (Nov. 27, 1925), p. 51; Grady Triplett, "More Wells, More Oil, and More Consumption," OW 40:4 (Jan. 15, 1926), pp. 43–44; H. H. King, "Mexia-Corsicana Decline Rapid During Last Half of 1925," OW 40:5 (Jan. 22, 1926), p.36.

27. "Inside Completions Send Big Lake Production Up," OW 38:13 (Sept. 18, 1925), p. 94; Richard Jones, "Development of the Big Lake Oil Field," OW 37:9 (June 12, 1925), p. 37; R. L. Dudley and H. H. King, "What Is on the Horizon," OW 41:9 (May 21, 1926), pp. 25–26; H. H. King, "Big Lake Field Responsible for Much Wildcat Drilling in Western Texas," OW 42:6 (July 30, 1926), p. 68; "Humble Seeks Three-Year Contracts in West Texas," OW 48:2 (Dec. 30, 1927), p. 26; King, "Over Eight Million Barrels," p. 52; Larson and Porter, *History of Humble,* p. 189.

28. King, "Big Lake Performance," p. 19; Jones, "Development," p. 40; H. H. King, "Wells in Big Lake Field Maintain Average of 400 Barrels," OW 40:10 (Feb. 26, 1926), pp. 51–52; OW 44:3 (Jan. 7, 1927), p. 34; H. H. King, "Water Intrusion Hurries Work in Yates Field," OW 48:9 (Feb. 3, 1928), p. 31.

29. H. H. King, "Crockett County Test May Mean New Field," OW 37:9 (June 11, 1925), p. 28; *Fort Worth Star-Telegram,* Mar. 4, 1934; Myres, *Era of Discovery,* pp. 312–14.

30. H. H. King, "Intensive Drilling in Prospect for Crockett County Area," OW 38:1 (June 26, 1925), p. 80; H. H. King, "Wildcat Activity Spreading over West Texas," OW 38:3 (July 10, 1925), p. 28; H. H. King, "Three Completions Add 10,000 Barrels to Big Lake Production," OW 38:5 (July 24, 1925), p. 56; Paul Wagner, "Powell District, South of Big Lake, Still Producing Enigma," *National Petroleum News,* May 26, 1926, p. 46; *Ozona Stockman,* July 31, 1941.

31. James McIntyre, "Big Leasing Campaign in New Mexico," OGJ 24:3 (May 3, 1928), p. 80; Kornfeld, "A Half Century," pp. 186, 190–98, 209, 213; Mrs. Charles Vertrees and Spencer interviews.

32. "Index to West Texas Oil and Gas Fields," OW 86:6 (July 19, 1937), pp. 122, 128, 138, 144.

33. C. D. Lockwood, "Hendricks Pool Already a Big Field," OGJ 26:12 (Aug. 11, 1927), p. 138; H. H. King, "West Texas Test Opens Producing Area," OW 38:10 (Aug. 28, 1925), p. 28; "Drilling Program Launched Northwest of Crane County Production," OW 41:4 (Apr. 16, 1926), p. 57; H. H. King, "Enough Oil Land in West Texas to Keep Drills Busy Many Years," OW 42:6 (July 30, 1926), p. 162; *Odessa News and Ector County News,* Aug. 12, 1927; James H. Dameron, "Sky Is Limit in Lea County Campaign," OGJ 27:41 (Feb. 28, 1929), p. 38; H. J.

Struth, "Pioneer Spirit Exists in Remote West Texas Camp," OW 53:10 (May 24, 1929), p. 26; H. H. King, "Unit Control and Proration Pacts Limit West Texas Drilling," OW 54:6 (July 26, 1929), p. 74; "Index to West Texas," pp. 99, 134, 136; H. H. King, "Duplicate of Big Lake Object of Extensive Exploration," OW 41:10 (May 28, 1926), p. 26.

34. King, "Wildcat Activity," p. 28; SADS, Sept. 12, 1926; "Large Virgin Area Attracts Operators to West Texas," OW 39:8 (Nov. 13, 1925), p. 55; Beaton, *Shell*, p. 333.

35. Myres, *Era of Discovery*, pp. 344–49; H. H. King, "Texas Wildcats Show Favorably for Two New Fields," OW 38:13 (Sept. 18, 1925), p. 28; "Major Companies Betting on Deep Oil in Upton-Howard Counties," OW 39:1 (Sept. 25, 1925), p. 52.

36. "Large Virgin Area," p. 55; King, "Duplicate," p. 27; "Crane-Upton Crude Cut to $1.00 per Barrel and Nobody Wants It," OW 43:1 (Sept. 24, 1926), p. 66; SADS, Mar. 27, 1927; "Wildcatting Campaign Plans for 1929," OGJ 27:37 (Jan. 31, 1929), p. 199; H. H. King, "West Texas Wildcat Effort Nets 13 New Producing Spots," OW 32:10 (Feb. 22, 1929), p. 56; William Gross, "February Crude Production Tops January Despite Handicap," OW 53:1 (Mar. 22, 1929), p. 36; H. H. King, "West Texas Operators Complete 1007 Wells During Year," OW 54:6 (July 26, 1929), p. 88; H. H. King, "West Texas Has 303 Dry Holes During Past Year," OW 58:7 (Aug. 1, 1930), pp. 144–48.

37. Files TMD 20, 81, 119, 130, 132, WD 132, Rector Oil Company Papers, Flag-Redfern Oil Company, Midland, Tex.

38. H. H. King, "McCamey-Hurdle District Crowding Handling Facilities," OW 44:8 (Feb. 11, 1927), p. 27; C. D. Lockwood, "West Texas Fields Not a Menace," OGJ 25:50 (May 5, 1927), p. 29; A. R. McTee, "West Texas Field Development Calls for Best of Engineering Skill," OW 46:9 (Aug. 12, 1927), p. 41.

39. W. A. Moncrief, Sr., "Plaudits for Ed: Remarks at the Presentation of a Life Membership Award to E. A. Landreth, During the General Session, 42nd Annual Meeting, Texas Mid-Continent Oil and Gas Association, Hotel Texas, Fort Worth, September 26, 1961," E. A. Landreth Papers, Fort Worth, Tex.; Hines Baker, "Remarks on Presentation of Distinguished Service Award to E. A. Landreth," *Proceedings of the 35th Annual Meeting of the Texas Mid-Continent Oil and Gas Association*, San Antonio, Tex., Oct. 5–6, 1954, E. A. Landreth Papers; Landreth interview.

40. A. W. Thomas, "Oil and Its Relation to Banking," OGJ 25:40 (Feb. 24, 1927), p. 32; Wallace Davis, "Change in Finance Methods Benefits Industry," OW 51:8 (Nov. 9, 1928), p. 37; Harold Vance, "Bank Loans on Oil and Gas Production," PE 26:11 (Oct. 1954), p. E4.

41. Baker, "Remarks"; *Abilene Reporter-News*, Oct. 17, 1965; "Landreth Properties Sold to Phillips Petroleum," OW 41:3 (Apr. 9, 1926), p. 62.

42. H. H. King, "Noble-Dyson Potentially Important Light Oil Field,"

OW 39:12 (Dec. 11, 1925), pp. 27–28; "Landreth Well in Stephens County Again Increases Flow," OW 40:2 (Jan. 1, 1926), p. 46; H. H. King, "The Texas Company Buys Landreth West Texas Properties," OW 50:2 (June 29, 1928), p. 26.

43. Crane County, *Deed Records,* vol. 19, p. 257; A. N. Hendrickson to Landreth stockholders, Sept. 8, 1975, Landreth Papers; King, "Texas Company Buys," p. 25.

44. Hendrickson to stockholders; *Odessa News and Ector County News,* Sept. 13, 1927; King, "Texas Company Buys," p. 25.

45. Hendrickson to stockholders; SAES, June 17, 20, 1927; *Odessa News and Ector County News,* Aug. 30, 1927.

46. Hendrickson to stockholders; *Odessa Times,* Oct. 21, 1927; H. H. King, "West Texas Has Big Tank Building Program Under Way," OW 47:4 (Oct. 14, 1927), p. 27.

47. Winkler County, *Deed Records,* vol. 45, pp. 443, 618; A. R. McTee, "Yates Field Shows No Bad Effect from Shut-In," OW 47:5 (Oct. 21, 1927), p. 37; SADS, Oct. 7, 9, 27, 1927, Feb. 27, May 11, June 8, July 23, 1928; King, "Big Tank Building Program," p. 27; "Five New Producers in Northwest of Yates Field," OW 47:3 (Oct. 7, 1927), p. 36; "Ask Royalty Owners to Pay Transportation," OGJ 26:45 (Mar. 29, 1928), p. 25; "Royalty Owners Organize Texas Division," OW 52:5 (Jan. 18, 1929), p. 52.

48. Hendrickson to stockholders; "Bargains Offered West Texas Crude Buyers," OW 48:4 (Jan. 13, 1928), p. 27; Kent Ridley, "West Texas Is Weak Spot in Crude Market," OW 48:13 (Mar. 16, 1928), pp. 23–24; Winkler County, *Deed Records,* vol. 26, p. 604; Winkler County, *Liens,* vol. 1, pp. 119, 122.

49. Hendrickson to stockholders; King, "Texas Company Buys," p. 25; Kent Ridley, "Proration Strengthens Market But Prevents Advance," OW 50:1 (June 22, 1928), p. 25; SAES, Sept. 26, 1928.

50. H. H. King, "Taylor-Link Pool Promises Big Flush Production," OW 59:10 (Aug. 23, 1929), p. 51; *Odessa News-Times,* Sept. 6, 1929; SADS, Apr. 7, 1927, Oct. 21, Nov. 1, 1928, July 25, 29, 31, Aug. 16, 18, 23, 1929; "Pecos County Will Have Big Wildcat Campaign," OW 54:3 (July 5, 1929), p. 66.

51. Hendrickson to stockholders; SADS, Aug. 14, 15, 18, Sept. 5, 13, 16, 26, 29, Oct. 8, 15, Dec. 9, 11, 16, 1929; H. H. King, "New Pecos County Area to Get Thorough Testing," OW 54:5 (July 19, 1929), p. 43; H. H. King, "New Pecos County Areas Appear Probable Market Threats," OW 54:12 (Sept. 6, 1929), p. 87; H. H. King, "Drilling Rush Gets Underway in New Pecos County Areas," OW 55:14 (Oct. 11, 1929), p. 196; *Odessa News-Times,* Sept. 6, 13, 1929.

52. SAES, Aug. 7, 28, 29, 30, Sept. 4, 9, 17, 20, 27, Oct. 3, 11, 21, 1929; Well Log, Independent and Rowan and Tong, McDonald Lease, by John Emery Adams, Pecos County files, Permian Basin

Petroleum Museum, Library, and Hall of Fame; Landreth interview; Hendrickson to stockholders; King, "Drilling Rush," p. 197.

53. SAES, Aug. 15, 16, 17, Sept. 4, 26, Oct. 10, 15, 16, 24, 25, Dec. 9, 1929; Hendrickson to stockholders; King, "West Texas Operators Complete 1007 Wells," p. 226.

54. SAES, Sept. 4, 26, Oct. 8, 15, 1929; H. H. King, "Pecos Pools Get Pipelines and Prorated Runs," OW 55:1 (Sept. 20, 1929), p. 69; Landreth interview; Hendrickson to stockholders; H. H. King, "Shell Purchase of Taylor-Link Pipeline," OW 56:3 (Jan. 4, 1930), p. 55; "Tidal Buys Landreth Tank Farm and Other Properties at McCamey," OW 58:13 (Sept. 12, 1930), p. 69; "Shell Company Takes Over Landreth Line," OW 56:5 (Jan. 17, 1930), p. 39; "Landreth Sells Out Again," OW 58:5 (July 18, 1930), p. 64.

55. "Reeser Again Elected President — Penn Vice President for Production," OW 59:10 (Nov. 21, 1930), p. 27; MRT, Dec. 20, 1931; "Robert R. Penn," OGJ 30:32 (Dec. 24, 1931), p. 14; Penson interview.

56. The partnerships are indicated by purchase and sale documents, files TxR 48, 50, 66, 88, 102, 177, Mrs. Robert R. Penn Papers, Dallas, Tex.; H. H. King, "Modern Rigs Replace Make-Shift Outfits in West Texas," OW 56:4 (Apr. 9, 1926), p. 52.

57. Purchase and sale documents, files TxR 133, 137, Penn Papers; King, "Modern Rigs," p. 52.

58. I. G. Yates to Robert R. Penn, July 2, 1927, Penn Papers; Penson interview.

59. "West Texas Producing Area Crosses Pecos," OW 43:8 (Nov. 5, 1926), p. 40; SADS, Feb. 13, 1927; purchase and sale documents, file TxR 81, Penn Papers.

60. Purchase and sale documents, files TxR 136, 149, 181, Penn Papers.

61. Winkler County, *Deed Records,* vol. 18, p. 93; vol. 19, p. 93; vol. 22, pp. 181, 356; vol. 20, p. 512; vol. 24, p. 94; vol. 28, p. 43; vol. 3, p. 44; vol. 17, p. 100; vol. 23, p. 117; vol. 25, pp. 25, 381.

62. OW 40:2 (Jan. 1, 1926), p. 19.

63. Purchase and sale documents, file TxR 171, Penn Papers.

64. Undated note by W. Y. Penn, file TxR 147, Penn Papers.

65. SADS, Jan. 21, Apr. 8, 9, 11, 22, 30, May 6, June 11, 1929; H. H. King, "Two New West Texas Pools," OW 53:4 (Apr. 12, 1929), p. 76; Jones, "Review of Drilling," p. 112; King, "West Texas Operators Complete 1007 Wells," p. 90.

66. SADS, May 9, Oct. 10, 1929, Jan. 13, 1930; King, "Pecos Pools," p. 69; purchase and sale documents, file TxR 293, Penn Papers.

67. Penson interview.

68. Penson interview; Hardwicke, *Antitrust Laws,* p. 88.

69. Penson interview; Robert R. Penn obituary, OGJ 30:32 (Dec. 24, 1931), p. 14.

Chapter 3

1. Henrietta M. Larson, Evelyn H. Knowlton, and Charles S. Popple, *History of Standard Oil Company (New Jersey): New Horizons, 1927–1950* (New York: Harper & Row Publishers, 1971), p. 75.

2. "Oklahoma Operators Initiate Proration Order," OW 58:3 (July 4, 1930), pp. 34, 72.

3. Erich W. Zimmermann, *Conservation in the Production of Petroleum: A Study in Industrial Control* (New Haven, Conn.: Yale University Press, 1957), pp. 89–100; Hardwicke, *Antitrust Laws* (see ch. 2, n. 2), p. 57.

4. Larson and Porter, *History of Humble* (see ch. 2, n. 3), p. 308. See also Hardwicke, *Antitrust Laws,* pp. 1–9, 22; Zimmermann, *Conservation,* pp. 122–27.

5. Mallison, *Great Wildcatter* (see ch. 2, n. 25), pp. 293–94, 308; SADS, July 28, 31, Aug. 9, 19, Oct. 31, 1926; "West Texas Producing Area" (see ch. 2, n. 59), p. 40; C. D. Lockwood, "Big Promise in Pecos Shallow Pool," OGJ 25:41 (Mar. 3, 1927), p. 31; Well Log, California Company Yates No. 1, by John Emery Adams, Pecos County files, Permian Basin Petroleum Museum, Library, and Hall of Fame, Midland, Tex.; James H. Dameron, "Peculiarities of the Pecos Oil Field," OGJ 26:15 (Sept. 1, 1927), p. 29. Eventually other companies' lines reached the field, after agreement to limit production had been reached.

6. SADS, Feb. 4, 13, 14, Mar. 3, 10, 1929; "Upton County Well Registering Formation High," OW 44:7 (Feb. 4, 1927), p. 68; "Three West Texas Counties Have Big Flush Wells," OW 44:9 (Feb. 18, 1927), p. 64; Myres, *Era of Discovery* (see ch. 2, n. 12), p. 449.

7. Larson and Porter, *History of Humble,* p. 288; SADS, Aug. 15, 18, 1927; H. H. King, "Gauge Shows Yates Field Possibilities Larger than Believed," OW 47:3 (Oct. 7, 1927), p. 41.

8. SADS, Sept. 8, 1927; H. H. King, "Committee Prepares for Proration of Yates Production," OW 47:2 (Sept. 30, 1927), pp. 36–37; J. Elmer Thomas, "Production Curtailment in Texas," OW 51:12 (Dec. 7, 1928), p. 55.

9. "Five New Producers in Northwest of Yates Field; Much New Drilling in Hendricks," OW 47:13 (Oct. 7, 1927), p. 36; H. H. King, "Gauge Reveals Yates Field Capable of 313,381 Barrels," OW 47:8 (Nov. 11, 1927), p. 29. For the prevailing thought on water incursion at the time, see American Petroleum Institute, *American Petroleum, Supply and Demand* (see ch. 2, n. 14), pp. 88–90.

10. Thomas, "Production Curtailment," pp. 54–55; H. H. King, "Revise Basis of Proration in Yates Field," OW 49:10 (May 25, 1928), p. 45; "Yates Proration Order Held Up by Commission," OW 49:13 (June 15, 1928), p. 33.

11. H. H. King, "Yates Field Proration Plan Change Due First of Year," OW 47:11 (Dec. 2, 1927), p. 71; Thomas, "Production Curtail-

ment," p. 55; King, "Revise Basis," p. 45; H. H. King, "Hendrick Operators Protest Output Cut But Comply," OW 51:4 (Oct. 12, 1928), p. 33; H. H. King, "Yates Proration Increased 15,000 Barrels by Commission," OW 52:5 (Jan. 15, 1929), p. 38; SADS, Jan. 13, 1929; "Ohio Gains in Texas by Transcontinental Merger," OW 58:1 (June 20, 1930), pp. 54, 60.

12. Thomas, "Production Curtailment," p. 55. As Norman E. Nordhauser points out, some industry leaders found the combination of voluntary agreement reinforced by state regulatory supervision particularly appealing; see Nordhauser, *The Quest for Stability: Domestic Oil Regulation, 1917–1935* (New York: Garland Publishing, 1979), p. 14.

13. Winkler County, *Oil and Gas Lease Records,* vol. 1, pp. 143–44, 156, 305; vol. 3, pp. 11–117, 487–88; H. H. King, "Southern Withdrawing as West Texas Crude Buyer," OW 47:11 (Dec. 2, 1927), p. 66; "Humble Seeks Three-Year Contracts in West Texas," OW 48:2 (Dec. 30, 1927), pp. 26, 40; H. H. King, "Hendrick Extension Starts Big Offset Campaign," OW 48:12 (Mar. 9, 1928), p. 40; H. H. King, "West Texas Has 200,000 Barrel Pipe Line Outlet," OW 49:10 (May 25, 1928), p. 51; "Bargains Offered" (see ch.2, n. 48), p. 27; Ridley, "West Texas Is Weak Spot" (see ch. 2, n. 48), pp. 23–24.

14. H. H. King, "Peculiar Water Trouble Develops in Hendrick Field," OW 48:4 (Jan. 13, 1928), p. 37; King, "Water Intrusion" (see ch. 2, n. 28), p. 31; SADS, Dec. 25, 1927, Jan. 15, 18, 1928.

15. H. H. King, "Hendrick Field Operators Appoint Conservation Committee," OW 48:8 (Feb. 10, 1928), p. 23; E. N. Van Duzee, "Effects of Choking Wells in Winkler County, Texas," OW 53:4 (Apr. 12, 1929), p. 43.

16. A. R. McTee, "Winkler Conservation Move Follows Commission Conference," OW 48:13 (Mar. 16, 1928), pp. 25–27. On the Railroad Commission's powers, see Robert E. Hardwicke, "Legal History of Conservation of Oil in Texas," in *Legal History of Conservation of Oil and Gas: A Symposium* (Baltimore: Section of Mineral Law, American Bar Association, 1938), pp. 217–19.

17. A. R. McTee, "Commission Promises to Select Plan for Hendrick Situation," OW 49:5 (Apr. 20, 1928), pp. 27–28, 48; "Texas Commission Calls Another Proration Meeting at Austin," OW 49:4 (Apr. 13, 1928), p. 42.

18. "Commission Orders Proration for Hendrick Field," OW 49:6 (Apr. 27, 1928), p. 27.

19. H. H. King, "Hendrick 'Umpire' Arranging Details of Proration Order," OW 49:7 (May 4, 1928), p. 28; "Court Ruling Removes Cloud from West Texas Titles," OW 50:2 (June 29, 1928), p. 35.

20. H. J. Struth, "Feasibility of Nationwide Control Exemplified by Winkler Plan," OW 53:3 (Apr. 5, 1929), p. 21.

21. H. J. Struth, "Extended Proration or Future Reduction Is Ultimatum," OW 52:9 (Feb. 15, 1929), pp. 39–40; H. J. Struth, "Lower Crude Market Only Alternative to Expedite Control," OW 52:11 (Mar. 1, 1929), p. 38; "Regional Committees Acting on Conservation Plan," OW 53:2 (Mar. 29, 1929), p. 51; H. H. King, "Winkler County Proration Has Increased Recovery," OW 54:7 (July 2, 1929), p. 35; H. H. King, "Commission Extends Winkler County Proration Rules," OW 55:10 (Nov. 8, 1929), p. 49.

22. "Power of Texas Commission to Prorate Gets Court Test," OW 52:2 (Dec. 28, 1928), p. 27; H. H. King, "Water Encroachment Brings Vote on Winkler Curtailment," OW 52:11 (Mar. 1, 1929), p. 46; "Winkler Operator Protests Water Encroachment Report," OW 52:13 (Mar. 15, 1929), p. 58; H. H. King, "Plan to Curtail Winkler Output Dropped," OW 52:12 (Mar. 8, 1929), p. 34. The violations of proration in Winkler County foreshadowed events in East Texas three years later.

23. Gulf resisted the initial move to Hendrick proration as well; see McTee, "Commission Promises to Select Plan," pp. 27–28.

24. H. H. King, "Committee Seeks Permit to Increase Hendrick Runs," OW 49:12 (June 8, 1929), p. 34.

25. Logan, *Stabilization* (see ch. 1, n. 3), pp. 159–63; "Curtailment Reduces Output 525,000 Barrels a Day in 1930," OW 60:10 (Feb. 20, 1931), p. 35; "Oklahoma Allowable Production Raised to 725,000 Barrels," OW 53:9 (May 17, 1929), p. 66; Ray M. Collins, "Production Control," OW 51:12 (Dec. 7, 1928), p. 51; Wallace Davis, "Commission Order Fails to Lower Oklahoma Output," OW 51:2 (Sept. 28, 1928), p. 27; H. J. Struth, "Oklahoma Proration Opponents May Take Question Before Legislature," OW 59:13 (Dec. 12, 1930), p. 53.

26. "Curtailment Reduces Output," pp. 40, 44; Logan, *Stabilization,* p. 168; Brad Mills, "Curtailment Proves No Cure-All for California Ills," OW 58:3 (July 4, 1930), p. 31.

27. Clarence L. Linz, Washington Withholds Approval of Institute's Conservation Plan," OW 53:4 (Apr. 12, 1929), p. 37; Wallace Davis, "Limitation of Crude Output up to Regional Committees," OW 53:1 (Mar. 22, 1929), p. 19; Hardwicke, *Antitrust Laws,* p. 36.

28. Larson and Porter, *History of Humble,* p. 316; "Texas Independents Oppose Unit Operation," OW 64:1 (Dec. 18, 1931), p. 39; J. R. Parten, "Unit Operation Wouldn't Work to Good of the Majority," OW 64:1 (Dec. 18, 1931), pp. 20, 69–71; H. H. King, "Big Companies Pool Interests in New Van Field," OW 55:8 (Nov. 8, 1929), p. 30. For a detailed definition of unitization, see Logan, *Stabilization,* pp. 171–72.

29. "Wilbur Outlines Government Policy," OW 55:12 (Dec. 6, 1929), p. 41. For a useful, recent perspective on federal policy, see August W. Giebelhaus, *Business and Government in the Oil Industry: A Case Study of Sun*

Oil, 1876–1945 (Greenwich, Conn.: JAI Press, 1980), pp. 130–40. See also Triplett, "How Long Will Our Oil Last?" (see ch. 2, n. 2), pp. 50, 147; "Curtailment Board Suggests Unrestricted Imports," OW 52:12 (Mar. 8, 1929), p. 50.

30. Nash, *Oil Policy* (see ch. 2, n. 2), pp. 104–105; Giebelhaus, *Business and Government,* pp. 137–40; Davis, "Limitation," p. 19; George L. Sweet, *Gentleman in Oil* (Los Angeles: Science Press, 1966), p. 50; "IPAA's Tenth Anniversary" (see ch. 1, n. 4), p. 9.

31. Wirt Franklin, "Economic Situation Demands Immediate Action," OW 60:6 (Jan. 23, 1931), p. 31.

32. H. H. King, "Mid-Continent Association Favors Oil Tariff," OW 59:13 (Dec. 12, 1930), p. 26; "Oil Tariff Beaten in Senate Vote," OW 56:12 (Mar. 7, 1930), p. 45; "Seek Conference of Oil Men from Nine States," OW 60:4 (Jan. 9, 1931), p. 57; R. L. Dudley, "Washington Conference Seeks Limiting of Imports," OW 60:6 (Jan. 21, 1931), pp. 23–25.

33. "Oklahoma Independents Make Plea for More Oil," OW 52:11 (Mar. 1, 1929), p. 62; OW 56:10 (Feb. 21, 1930), p. 75; "Texas Independent Oil Operators Organizing," OW 56:10 (Feb. 21, 1930), p. 75; "Fort Worth Delegation to Austin Seeks Pipe Line Law Changes," OW 56:11 (Feb. 28, 1930), p. 52; H. J. Struth, "Independents Seek Better Understanding," OW 59:7 (Oct. 31, 1930), pp. 21–22.

34. "Fort Worth Delegation," p. 52; "Drastic Change in Pipe Line Laws Before Texas Legislature," OW 56:12 (Mar. 7, 1930), p. 21; Larson and Porter, *History of Humble,* pp. 322–24; Zimmermann, *Conservation,* p. 146; Hardwicke, "Legal History," pp. 221–22.

35. Jack Logan, "Texas Pipe Line Law Gets Initial Application at Darst Creek," OW 58:3 (July 4, 1930), pp. 43, 46; "Darst Creek Proration Collapses, Production Jumps," OW 58:10 (Feb. 20, 1931), p. 24; Hardwicke, "Legal History," pp. 228–29.

36. James A. Clark and Michel T. Halbouty, *The Last Boom* (New York: Random House, 1972), pp. 9, 25–27; J. Evetts Haley, " 'Dad' Joiner, Wildcatter," *The Shamrock* (autumn, 1962); James A. Clark, *An Oilman's Oilman: A Biographical Treatment of Walter W. Lechner,* ed. by Judith King (Houston: Gulf Publishing Company, 1979), pp. 65–66; "A Decade of East Texas: Colossus of Oil," OW 99:5 (Oct. 7, 1940), pp. 19–40; "Joiner Future Depends on Pending Completions," OW 59:9 (Nov. 14, 1930), p. 77; "Joiner Area Records Two Failures During Week," OW 59:10 (Nov. 21, 1930), p. 79.

37. Davis interview.

38. Brad Mills, "East Texas Ranks High," OW 81:4 (Feb. 17, 1936), pp. 17–25; "A Decade of East Texas," pp. 20–24.

39. "Many Operators Are Attracted to Rusk County Oil Area," OW 60:4 (Jan. 9, 1931), p. 60; Jack Logan, "Fast Drilling in Soft Forma-

tions Makes for Low Drilling Costs in East Texas," OW 60:12 (Mar. 6, 1931), pp. 28–29; H. H. King, "East Texas Drilling Cost," OW 61:10 (May 22, 1931), p. 66; Jack Logan, "Economies Imperative in East Texas Field Work," OW 62:7 (July 31, 1931), pp. 40–41; H. H. King, "East Texas Contractors Held to Top Price of $2 per Foot," OW 63:7 (Oct. 30, 1931), p. 49.

40. "Large Operators Acquire Leases in Joiner Section," OW 60:5 (Jan. 16, 1931), p. 72; "Joiner Future," p. 77; Jack Logan, "Future of East Texas Important Question Before Industry," OW 60:12 (Mar. 6, 1931), p. 38; Davis interview; Larson and Porter, *History of Humble,* pp. 397–99; "Humble Buys Bateman Block Paying Two Million Dollars," OW 60:5, (Jan. 16, 1931), p. 70.

41. Jack Logan, "East Texas—Whether One Pool or a Series of Pools—It's a Big Oil Field," OW 60:11 (Feb. 27, 1931), pp. 27–29; H. H. King, "East Texas Oil Attractive to Small Refiners," OW 60:12 (Mar. 6, 1931), p. 55; H. H. King, "Rapid Refinery Development Takes Place in East Texas," OW 62:12 (Sept. 4, 1931), p. 24.

By March 1933, there were 48 loading racks, 48 pipelines, and 35 sizable refineries active in the East Texas field; see OW 68:12 (Mar. 6, 1933), p. 9.

42. H. J. Struth, "Price Cut Follows Rising East Texas Production," OW 61:11 (May 29, 1931), p. 43; "Lowered Price Promises to Curtail Drilling Orgy," OW 61:12 (June 5, 1931), p. 64; H. J. Struth, "East Texas Breaking General Crude Market," OW 61:12 (June 5, 1931), p. 43; James McIntyre, "Crude Prices Below Lifting Costs," OGJ 30:3 (June 4, 1931), p. 19; OGJ 30:8 (July 9, 1931), p. 24; Larson and Porter, *History of Humble,* pp. 452–53.

43. David F. Prindle, *Petroleum Politics and the Texas Railroad Commission* (Austin: University of Texas Press, 1981), pp. 33–34; H. H. King, "Rapid Development of East Texas Bars Proration Idea," OW 60:12 (Mar. 6, 1931), p. 85.

44. Warner E. Mills, Jr., *Martial Law in East Texas,* Inter-University Case Program No. 53 (Indianapolis: Bobbs-Merrill Company, 1960), pp. 14–16; Larson and Porter, *History of Humble,* pp. 453–54; Zimmermann, *Conservation,* pp. 151–53; "East Texas Injunction Not Applicable to Whole Area," OW 61:5 (Apr. 17, 1931), p. 75; L. E. Bredberg, "East Texas Operators Adopt Unit Plan," OGJ 30:5 (June 18, 1931), p. 13; Raymond Brooks, "Lucey Has New Plan for East Texas," OGJ 30:7 (July 2, 1931), p. 13; "Abandonment of Cranfill Plan Seems Inevitable," OW 62:3 (July 3, 1931), p. 15.

45. Mills, *Martial Law,* p. 19.

46. Prindle, *Petroleum Politics,* pp. 27–29, 32–33; Zimmermann, *Conservation,* pp. 145, 152–53; Larson and Porter, *History of Humble,* pp. 458–59; "Court Decides Proration Orders of Commission Are 'Usurpa-

tions,' " OGJ 30:11 (July 30, 1931), p. 155; Hardwicke, *Antitrust Laws,* p. 206.

47. Mills, *Martial Law,* pp. 23–28; Zimmermann, *Conservation,* p. 153; "Troops Shut Down East Texas Fields," OGJ 30:14 (Aug. 20, 1931), pp. 15, 20; Hardwicke, *Antitrust Laws,* p. 206.

48. Larson and Porter, *History of Humble,* p. 460.

49. Hardwicke, *Antitrust Laws,* p. 206; "Governor to Enforce East Texas Legislation Despite Federal Order," OW 63:5 (Oct. 16, 1931), p. 41; Larson and Porter, *History of Humble,* pp. 460, 464–65; H. H. King, "Acreage Basis Plan Proposed for East Texas Proration," OW 63:7 (Oct. 30, 1931), p. 13; "Organization of Conservation Association Finally Completed," OW 64:1 (Dec. 18, 1931), p. 39; L. E. Bredberg, "Texans Organize to Conserve Their Oil and Gas," OGJ 30:26 (Nov. 12, 1931), p. 156; "Texas Independents Oppose Unit Operation: Approve Anti-Trust Suit and Tariff," OW 64:1 (Dec. 18, 1931), p. 39; "IPA of Texas Opposes Present Proration Rules," OGJ 31:30 (Dec. 15, 1932), p. 31; "The Texas Free-for-All," OW 69:7 (May 1, 1933), p. 11.

50. "Texas House for New Oil Commission," OGJ 31:49 (Apr. 27, 1933), p. 11; "Texas Free-for-All," p. 11; Larson and Porter, *History of Humble,* pp. 476–77.

51. "Warner-Quinlan Deprived of Pipe Line Connections," OW 61:1 (Mar. 20, 1931), p. 57; "Make Plea for More Oil from West Texas," OW 72:6 (Jan. 22, 1934), pp. 42–43; "West Texas Operators Want Increased Output Allowable," OW 72:10 (Feb. 19, 1934), p. 53.

52. L. E. Bredberg, "Consider Shutting In West Texas Wells," OGJ 30:9 (July 16, 1931), p. 32; OGJ 30:11 (July 30, 1931), p. 34; OGJ 31:50 (May 4, 1933), p. 9; L. J. Logan, "Profits Following 1929 Pattern," OW 86:4 (July 5, 1937), pp. 15–18; "Wirt Franklin Petroleum Corporation Creditors Paid," OW 86:4 (July 5, 1937), p. 69; IPM 3:7 (Nov. 1932), p. 8. Gulf, which went into the Depression with heavy financial obligations, did not resume paying dividends until 1935, a gap of four and a half years; see "Dividends Higher," OW 81:1 (Mar. 16, 1936), p. 22.

53. Larson and Porter, *History of Humble,* pp. 479–80; "Interior Secretary Not to Be Dictator Under Revised Bill," OW 69:11 (May 29, 1933), p. 10; Wirt Franklin, "Independents Win at Conference," IPM 4:1 (Apr. 1933), p. 5; Russell B. Brown, "Record of Hearings on Oil Control," IPM 4:3 (June 1933), pp. 7–8; Nash, *Oil Policy,* pp. 130–32.

54. Nash, *Oil Policy,* p. 139; "This Is Independents' Day, Says Franklin," IPM 4:8 (Dec. 1933), pp. 8–9.

55. "Government Control of Oil Industry Proposed in New Bill," OW 73:8 (May 7, 1934), pp. 7–8, 36; Jack Logan, "Ickes Bill Dominates Oil Scene," OW 73:9 (May 14, 1934), pp. 9–10; "President's Approval of Ickes Oil Control Bill Does Not Stop Fight," OW 73:11 (May 28,

1934), pp. 12–14, 52; "Committee Holds Petroleum Bill Fate," IPM 5:3 (June 1934), pp. 7–8, 15.

56. Nash, *Oil Policy,* p. 145; Zimmermann, *Conservation,* p. 158; Hardwicke, *Antitrust Laws,* pp. 206–207; "Texans Urge Passage of Connally Control Bill," OW 76:9 (Feb. 11, 1935), p. 11; Jack Logan, "Stabilization Is in Prospect," OW 76:11 (Feb. 25, 1935), p. 9.

57. "East Texas Production Trading Remains Active," OW 72:1 (Dec. 18, 1933), p. 43.

58. Zimmermann, *Conservation,* p. 154.

59. Prindle, *Petroleum Politics,* p. 35; Hardwicke, "Legal History," p. 239; Zimmermann, *Conservation,* pp. 156–58; Larson and Porter, *History of Humble,* p. 476; "Court Upholds Texas Well Spacing Order," OW 72:2 (Dec. 25, 1933), p. 38; "Proration Valid," OW 78:4 (July 8, 1935), p. 8; "Rehearing Denied," OW 79:12 (Dec. 2, 1935), p. 9; "Important Decision," OW 85:8 (May 3, 1937), p. 41. Among producing states, California and Illinois continued without such a body.

60. "Control Bill Rewritten," OW 76:10 (Feb. 18, 1935), p. 9; Giebelhaus, *Business and Government,* p. 215; Brown, "Record of Hearings," p. 8.

61. "Prorated Production and Minimum Profit Level," OW 98:8 (July 29, 1940), p. 51.

62. Prindle, *Petroleum Politics,* p. 43; H. H. King, "Older Areas Lose Outlets as Buyers Adjust to Higher Prices," OW 65:9 (May 16, 1932), p. 16; "Cores Indicate Crockett Ordovician Well Producer," OW 67:13 (Dec. 12, 1932), p. 56; "West Texas Fields," OW 90:4 (July 4, 1938), p. 57; Z. H. Mischka, "U.S. Continues to Find Many New Fields," OW 98:6 (July 15, 1940), pp. 15–18; H. H. King, "Permian Basin Oil to Get Full Outlet," WO 128:1 (May 1948), p. 79; Robert E. Sullivan, ed., *Conservation of Oil & Gas: A Legal History* (Chicago: Section of Minerals and Natural Resources Law, American Bar Association, 1960), p. 241.

63. "Proration and Financing," OW 84:7 (Jan. 25, 1937), p. 8.

Chapter 4

1. "Two Small Pumpers Are Completed in West Texas," OW 70:6 (July 24, 1933), p. 48; OW 82:7 (July 27, 1936), p. 12.

2. *The Texas Oil Directory* (San Angelo: Oil Directory Publishing Company, 1929); *Midland City Directory,* 1928 (El Paso: Hudspeth Directory Company, 1928).

3. *Midland City Directory,* 1930, 1937, 1940; Penn and W. A. Yeager, Sr., interviews.

4. *Petroleum: Industry Hearings Before the Temporary National Economic Committee* (New York: American Petroleum Institute, 1942), p. 456; Tucker and Reigle interviews.

5. H. H. King, "Second Andrews County Test Better than Discovery," OW 65:9 (May 16, 1932), p. 57; L. E. Bredberg, "Ordovician Test in Southeastern Reagan County," OGJ 33:8 (July 12, 1934), p. 44; Fred H. Fuhrman, interviewed by S. D. Myres, Mar. 18, 1975, Midland, Tex.; Samuel D. Myres, *The Permian Basin, Petroleum Empire of the Southwest: Era of Advancement* (El Paso: Permian Press, 1977), p. 178.

6. "Cores Indicate" (see ch. 3, n. 62), p. 56; "Gulf, Humble Each Starting Tests for West Texas Ordovician," OW 68:11 (Feb. 27, 1933), p. 43; "Ordovician Test Earns Its Objective Cautiously," OW 71:6 (Nov. 27, 1933), p. 39; "Ordovician High," OW 79:5 (Oct. 14, 1935), p. 61; Addison Young, "Current Knowledge of West Texas Ordovician Leaves Much to Learn," OW 67:12 (Dec. 5, 1932), pp. 12–13.

7. Penn and Hills interviews.

8. Ford Chapman, recorded recollections, Nov. 8, 1978, tape in the Abell Hanger Collection, Permian Basin Museum, Library, and Hall of Fame, Midland, Tex.

9. Chapman interview.

10. George Bentley, interviewed by S. D. Myres, May 20, 1970, Monahans, Tex.

11. Myres, *Era of Discovery* (see ch. 2, n. 12), p. 472; Myres, *Era of Advancement,* pp. 153–54; scout tickets, Pecos County, vols. 1–6, Midland County Library; "Producing Oil Wells and Crude Oil Production in U.S. Fields," OW 116:9 (Jan. 29, 1945), pp. 198–200.

12. H. H. King, " 'Mid-Continent' Texas Drilling More than Any Other Area," OW 72:7 (Jan. 29, 1934), p. 26; "West Texas Active," OW 79:2 (Sept. 23, 1935), p. 55; "Work Increase," OW 80:3 (Dec. 30, 1935), p. 49; "Drilling Gains," OW 83:6 (Oct. 19, 1936), p. 72.

13. Reigle interview.

14. "Yoakum County Strike," OW 79:4 (Oct. 7, 1935), p. 71; "Outpost Produces," OW 81:1 (Mar. 16, 1936), p. 184; "Wildcat Produces," OW 80:12 (Mar. 2, 1936), p. 54; "Back in the Limelight," OW 81:2 (Mar. 23, 1936), p. 56; "Cores Saturated," OW 82:4 (July 6, 1936), p. 58.

15. Reigle interview.

16. Noel interview.

17. "Encounter Delay," OW 80:13 (Mar. 9, 1936), p. 54; Reigle interview.

18. "Leases Assigned," OW 78:13 (Sept. 9, 1935), p. 71.

19. "Jones Ranch Is Gaines County Hot Spot," OW 86:2 (June 21, 1937), p. 90; "Wasson Area Extended Three Miles Northeast," OW 86:8 (Aug. 2, 1937), p. 63; "Harper Field Extended," OW 86:13 (Sept. 30, 1937), p. 70; OW 99:4 (Sept. 30, 1940), p. 45; OW 99:6 (Oct. 14, 1940), p. 58; OW 118:3 (June 25, 1945), p. 82.

20. Myres, *Era of Advancement,* pp. 127–28; R. T. German, George

Abell, and Berte Haigh, interviewed by S. D. Myres, n.d., n.p.; Chapman and Linebery interviews.

21. Chapman and Linebery interviews.

22. Linebery interview; Winkler County, *Deeds of Trust,* vol. 4, pp. 262, 576; vol. 5, p. 274; vol. 6, p. 444; vol. 8, pp. 24, 34.

23. Winkler County, *Deed Records,* vol. 41, p. 383; vol. 48, pp. 553, 575, 578; vol. 49, pp. 221, 565; vol. 50, p. 239; Winkler County, *Mechanic's Liens,* vol. 1, pp. 46, 419, 421, 425, 427, 429, 446, 448, 450; OW 67:8 (Nov. 7, 1932), p. 43; OW 71:1 (Sept. 18, 1933), p. 44; OW 78:6 (July 22, 1935), pp. 53–54; OW 78:11 (Aug. 26, 1935), p. 14; OW 87:4 (Oct. 4, 1937), p. 39; Myres, *Era of Advancement,* pp. 121, 127–28, 139; Texas Railroad Commission, *Individual Lease Records,* District 8, vols. 2, 4, 5, 6, 8 (1940); "Occurrence of Oil and Gas in West Texas," Publication 5716, Bureau of Economic Geology (Austin: University of Texas, 1957).

24. OW 101:3 (Mar. 24, 1941), p. 46; OW 101:7 (Apr. 21, 1941), p. 56.

25. "New Delaware Field Opened in Reeves County," OW 86:9 (Aug. 9, 1937), pp. 65–66; Brad Mills, "Geophysical Advancements," OW 84:6 (Jan. 18, 1937), p. 38.

26. "Drilling Ahead," OW 80:7 (Jan. 27, 1936), p. 180; W. A. Yeager, Sr., and Davis interviews.

27. Myres, *Era of Advancement,* pp. 175-79; "Biggest Means Well," OW 78:4 (July 8, 1935), pp. 56–57; "Yoakum County Strike," pp. 70–71; "To Test Wildcat," OW 80:10 (Feb. 17, 1936), p. 66; "Permian Test," OW 81:5 (Apr. 13, 1936), p. 60; C. J. "Red" Davidson, interviewed by S. D. Myres, Mar. 19, 1971, Fort Worth, Tex.; "Leasing Activity," OW 79:10 (Nov. 18, 1935), p. 66; "Permian Failure," OW 79:11 (Nov. 25, 1935), p. 70.

28. Winkler County, *Deeds,* vol. 51, pp. 446, 459; vol. 54, pp. 417, 418, 573; vol. 56, pp. 232, 234, 255; "United States Well Completions," OW 104:2 (Dec. 15, 1941), p. 68; "New Ector Field," OW 78:8 (Aug. 5, 1935), p. 70.

29. *Midland City Directory,* 1929, 1939; Sloan and McRae interviews.

30. Myres, *Era of Advancement,* pp. 155–56; W. A. Yeager, Sr., Davis, Penn, and Williamson interviews.

31. Myres, *Era of Advancement,* p. 71; Penn, Sauer, Hills, Phillips, Sloan, and McRae interviews.

32. "Harper Field, Ector County, Becomes Important Area," OW 87:1 (Sept. 13, 1937), p. 72; OW 88:1 (Dec. 13, 1937), p. 72; Penn and Sauer interviews; Myres, *Era of Advancement,* p. 73.

33. Butler, Penn, and Hills interviews; "Proration and Financing," OW 84:7 (Jan. 25, 1937), p. 8; "Bank Loans and the Oil Business," OW 98:8 (July 29, 1940), p. 119.

34. Joseph E. Pogue, "Economic Effects of Recent Oil Discoveries in Illinois," OW 95:2 (Sept. 18, 1939), pp. 13–15; "Illinois Independents to Fight Conservation Law," OW 92:2 (Dec. 19, 1938), p. 69; Frank B. Taylor, "Western Kansas Oil Fields," OW 85:8 (May 3, 1937), pp. 85–100; "Oil and Gas Fields in Illinois, Indiana, Kentucky Basin," OW 93:13 (June 5, 1939), pp. 94–100.

35. OW Crude Oil Price Schedules: 85:4 (Apr. 5, 1937), p. 97, 88:4 (Jan. 3, 1938), p. 46, 92:4 (Jan. 2, 1939), p. 50, 96:4 (Jan. 1, 1940), p. 50, 104:5 (Jan. 5, 1942), p. 45; King, "Older Areas Lose Outlets" (see ch. 3, n. 62) p. 16; "Price Justified," OW 85:1 (Mar. 15, 1937), p. 11.

36. OW 95:13 (Dec. 4, 1939), p. 70; OW 97:3 (Mar. 25, 1940), p. 60; H. H. King, "Pipe Line Facilities Retard Permian Basin Expansion," OW 87:12 (Nov. 29, 1937), p. 62; "Pipe Line Proration Grows with Increased Allowables," OW 96:13 (Mar. 4, 1940), p. 62; "Nomination Proration in Texas Results in Selective Buying," OW 105:12 (May 25, 1942), p. 45; "West Texas' Day Is Coming," OW 109:3 (Mar. 22, 1943), p. 11.

37. William E. Hubbard, "Diminishing Allowable per Well," OW 83:7 (Oct. 26, 1936), p. 36; "Allowable Picture," OW 93:4 (Apr. 3, 1939), p. 43; "Six States Close In Production," OW 94:11 (Aug. 21, 1939), p. 58; "Texas Fields to Shut In 13 Days During January," OW 96:2 (Dec. 25, 1939), p. 45; "Prorated Production and Minimum Profit Level," OW 98:8 (July 29, 1940), p. 51; Penn interview.

38. "Wildcats Boom," OW 85:1 (Mar. 15, 1937), p. 74; Brad Mills, "Drilling Costs Have Many Factors," OW 91:3 (Sept. 26, 1938), p. 32; H. H. King, "Permian Basin Assumes Greater Importance as a Source of Oil," OW 111:1 (Sept. 6, 1943), p. 43; Penn and Tucker interviews.

39. L. J. Logan, "Surplus Gasoline and Smaller Exports Handicap Industry," OW 98:1 (June 10, 1940), pp. 12–14, 44; "War Brings Crisis to Texas Oil Markets," OW 98:4 (June 24, 1940), p. 41; "Texas Curtails Production in Emergency Move," OW 98:4 (June 24, 1940), p. 41; "Texas Allowable Slashed in New 90-Day Order," OW 98:13 (Sept. 2, 1940), p. 41; OW 98:2 (June 17, 1940), p. 53.

40. L. J. Logan and H. H. King, "Permian Basin Fields Can Fill Urgent Need for Crude When Pipe Lines Are Expanded," OW 107:12 (Nov. 23, 1942), pp. 8–10; Williamson et al., *Age of Energy* (see ch. 2, n. 1), p. 763; H. H. King, "Daily Movement of Permian Basin Oil Sets New All-Time Record," OW 114:3 (June 19, 1944), pp. 50–52.

41. Williamson et al., *Age of Energy*, pp. 753–56; Hardwicke, *Antitrust Laws* (see ch. 2, n. 2), pp. 104–105; OW 105:13 (June 1, 1942), p. 46.

42. "Oil Placed Under Virtual Wartime Federal Control," OW 104:4 (Dec. 29, 1941), pp. 11–12; OW 106:1 (June 8, 1942), p. 8; OW 106:4 (June 29, 1942), p. 7; Warren L. Baker, "Extraordinary Half Year of Shifting to War Footing," OW 106:6 (July 20, 1942), pp. 15–16;

Frederick H. Lahee, "Wildcat Drilling in 1940 More Successful," OW 101:4 (Mar. 31, 1941), p. 37.

43. Williamson et al., *Age of Energy,* pp. 763–64; "Paper Work Wasting Many, Many Hours," OW 105:6 (Apr. 13, 1942), p. 10; "Coordinator's Office Issues Detailed Instructions on Getting Priorities," OW 103:8 (Oct. 27, 1941), pp. 52–54; Arch H. Rowan, "Drilling Efficiency Under War-time Conditions," PE 15:3 (Dec. 1943), pp. 92–96; W. H. Morrison, "Drilling Materials Under Wartime Conditions," PE 15:12 (Aug. 1944), p. 17; Porter and Reigle interviews.

44. *Midland City Directory,* 1941, 1945; Penn and Hills interviews.

45. "The Changing Panorama, 1944–1945," OW 116:9 (Jan. 29, 1945), pp. 85–86; Everette De Golyer, "Petroleum Exploration and Development in Wartime," PE 14:10 (Reference Annual, 1943), pp. 37–43; Noel interview.

46. Scout tickets: Ector County, vol. 8, Gaines County, vol. 3, Yoakum County, vol. 4, Lea County, New Mexico, vol. 8, Midland County Library.

47. Harold L. Ickes to Prentiss M. Brown, June 10, 1943, reprinted in OW 110:5 (June 28, 1943), p. 47; Warren L. Baker, "Independents Declare Only Higher Prices Will Prevent Oil Shortage," OW 107:8 (Oct. 26, 1942), pp. 42–44; "Resolutions Adopted at IPAA Mid-Year Meeting," IPM 14:2 (June 1943), p. 7; "Independent Plight Is Deplorable, Committee Says in Urging Price Increase," OW 115:6 (Oct. 9, 1944), p. 25; OW 109:7 (Apr. 19, 1943), p. 48.

Chapter 5

1. Williamson et al., *Age of Energy* (see ch. 2, n. 1), p. 798; "Early May Announcement Expected on Suspension of All Oil Price Ceilings," OW 121:6 (Apr. 8, 1946), pp. 23–24; OW 121:2 (Mar. 11, 1946), p. 25; "Independents of Texas Perfect New Organization," OW 121:8 (Apr. 22, 1946), p. 27; "Texas Association Organizes," IPM 17:2 (June 1946), p. 12; "Texas Independent Oil Group Approves Aggressive Program," OW 125:7 (Apr. 14, 1947), p. 34; Roger M. Olien, *From Token to Triumph: The Texas Republicans Since 1920* (Dallas: Southern Methodist University Press, 1982), pp. 102–104, 106–108, 112–38.

2. "Effects of Extended Coal Strike," OW 121:11 (May 13, 1946), p. 28, WO 126:6 (July 7, 1947), p. 29; "Texas Independent Oil Group," p. 34; "Oil Field Materials Outlook Continues Uncertain," OW 124:10 (Feb. 24, 1947), pp. 44–45; WO 127:10 (Feb. 1948), p. 24; "Steel to Remain Scarce for Remainder of Year," WO 132:7 (June 1951), p. 45; "Trading Casing for Connections Scored at TIPRO Meeting," IPM 18:12 (Apr. 1948), p. 51.

3. Leigh S. McCaslin, Jr., "Scarcity of Cement for Oil Uses Expected to Last Through 1949," OGJ 47:36 (June 6, 1949), p. 40.

4. H. C. Wiess, "Producers Face Troublesome Times," OW 118:13 (Aug. 27, 1945), pp. 30–31; R. H. Hargrove, "The Gas Industry in 1946," PE 18:4 (Jan. 1947), p. 66; Ernestine Adams, "$4 Billion Marked for 1948 Expansion," PE 19:8 (May 1948), p. 65; John R. Stockton, Richard C. Henshaw, Jr., and Richard W. Graves, *Economics of Natural Gas in Texas* (Austin: Bureau of Business Research, College of Business Administration, University of Texas, 1952), pp. 252–53.

5. L. J. Logan, "Demand Far Exceeds Estimates," OW 125:8 (Apr. 21, 1947), pp. 37–41; WO 127:6 (Oct. 1947), pp. 45–46; Warren L. Baker, "The Changing Panorama, 1947–1948," WO 127:11 (Feb. 1948), p. 64.

6. OW 121:2 (Mar. 11, 1946), p. 25; "Early May Announcement," pp. 23–24; "Additional Advances Likely for Petroleum Prices," WO 128:11 (Feb. 15, 1949), p. 72; "Petroleum Prices Stable After Drop from Postwar Peaks," WO 130:3 (Feb. 1950), pp. 44–47.

7. H. J. Struth, "1947 Oil Discoveries Largest Since 1937," PE 19:4 (Jan. 1948), p. 51; Adams, "$4 Billion," p. 63; John C. Casper, "33,098 Well Completions in 1947 Only 874 Short of All-Time High," OGJ 46:39 (Jan. 29, 1948), pp. 154, 165; Leigh S. McCaslin, Jr., "Exploration Campaign Stepped Up to Highest Level in History," OGJ 46:39 (Jan. 29, 1948), p. 162; Charles J. Dugan, "37,550,137½ Million Feet Predicted for 1949 Drilling," OGJ 47:39 (Jan. 27, 1949), p. 170; "West Texas Has Record Volume of Discoveries and New Pays," WO 128:11 (Feb. 15, 1949), p. 82. See also Franklin M. Fisher, *Supply and Costs in the United States Petroleum Industry: Two Economic Studies* (Baltimore: Johns Hopkins University Press, 1964); M. A. Adelman, *The World Petroleum Market* (Baltimore: Johns Hopkins University Press, 1972).

8. OW 120:12 (Feb. 18, 1946), p. 43; OW 121:6 (Apr. 8, 1946), p. 26; "Texas and Shell to Build New Outlet from Permian Basin to Cushing, Okla.," OW 124:13 (Feb. 24, 1947), p. 29; OW 125:9 (Apr. 28, 1947), p. 28; "Texas–New Mexico Plans Feeders and Trunk Line from West Texas to Gulf," OW 122:1 (June 3, 1946), p. 27; OW 121:6 (Apr. 8, 1946), p. 26; "Higher Texas Allowables for April Appear to Be in Demand for May," OW 121:8 (Apr. 22, 1946), p. 29; H. H. King, "Permian Basin Oil to Get Full Outlet," WO 128:1 (May 1948), pp. 77, 79–80; "Lowered Rail Rates on West Texas Crude May Help Navy Oil Situation," OW 121:6 (Apr. 8, 1946), p. 26; OGJ 46:37 (Jan. 25, 1948), p. 136.

9. L. J. Logan and Cecil W. Smith, "Deeper Pays Provide More Sweet Crude in Permian Basin," WO 131:4 (Sept. 1950), pp. 60, 64; H. H. King, "New Strikes Add Vast Area to Permian Basin," WO 128:4 (Aug. 1948), p. 69.

10. WO 127:10 (Feb. 1948), p. 24; H. H. King, "Midland Basin Oil Possibilities," WO 128:6 (Oct. 1948), pp. 45–46.

11. O'Neill, Sauer, and Kennedy interviews.

12. O'Neill interview; MRT, June 9, July 18, Aug. 23, 1949, Apr. 23, July 7, 1950; SAST, Nov. 12, 1949, Apr. 6, 1950; *Fort Worth Star-Telegram,* Apr. 23, 1950; "Scurry Conservation Plans Envisage Billion Barrel Payoff," WO 133:4 (Sept. 1951), p. 102.

13. *Midland City Directory,* 1946, 1950, 1951; Reigle interview.

14. Penn, Butler, and W. A. Yeager, Jr., interviews.

15. Craig, O'Neill, Kennedy, and Reigle interviews.

16. Polly De Armond, "Wildcat Success Ratio Stays High Though Number Takes Big Jump," OGJ 47:39 (Jan. 27, 1949), p. 176; "Wildcatting Success Shows Gain for 1948," WO 128:11 (Feb. 1949), p. 80; L. J. Logan, "Permian Basin Symbolic of American Enterprise," WO 131:4 (Sept. 1950), pp. 57, 59; Cecil W. Smith, "Permian Basin Maintains Position as Drilling Leader," WO 133:4 (Sept. 1951), p. 106; L. J. Logan, "Permian Basin Yields Fifth of U.S. Oil Production," WO 133:4 (Sept. 1951), pp. 107–11.

17. "Markets Unsteady As Supply Exceeds Needs," WO 128:12 (Mar. 1949), p. 31; "Surplus of Crude Forces New Cuts in Allowables," WO 128:12 (Mar. 1949), p. 32; "Texas Hardest Hit by Cut in U.S. Production," WO 129:5 (Aug. 1949), p. 51; L. J. Logan and Cecil W. Smith, "Oil Demand Rising Less Sharply," WO 131:6 (Nov. 1950), p. 70; L. J. Logan, "Competition Is Becoming Stiffer," WO 136:2 (Feb. 1953), p. 66.

18. Anthony Gibbon, "Utilization and Conservation of Casinghead Gas," OW 124:12 (Feb. 17, 1947), pp. 28–36; L. T. Potter, "Operating Problems of the Independent Gas Producer," WO 128:2 (June 1948). pp. 44–48; Stockton et al., *Economics of Natural Gas,* pp. 230–31.

19. Gibbon, "Utilization and Conservation," p. 32; Warren L. Baker, "Great Strides in Conserving Texas Casinghead Gas," WO 128:9 (Jan. 1949), p. 34; "Baker Says Industry Making Huge Expenditures to Save Texas Gas," OGJ 47:37 (Jan. 13, 1949), p. 37.

20. Prindle, *Petroleum Politics* (see ch. 3, n. 43), pp. 62–66.

21. "Texas Cracks Down on Seeligson Flared Gas," OW 125:4 (Mar. 24, 1947), p. 15; OW 125:8 (Apr. 21, 1947), p. 31; "Texas Would Say Farewell to Flares," OW 125:10 (May 5, 1947), p. 25; "Order to Stop Flaring Is Upheld by Texas Court," WO 128:12 (Mar. 1949), p. 34; Blakely M. Murphey, ed., *Conservation of Oil and Gas, A Legal History, 1948* (Chicago: Section of Mineral and Natural Resources Law, American Bar Association, 1949), p. 472; Sullivan, ed., *Conservation of Oil and Gas* (see ch. 3, n. 62), p. 232; Baker, "Great Strides," pp. 32–34; "Big Gasoline Plant to Be Built at Slaughter," OW 121:9 (Apr. 29, 1946), p. 15.

22. M. Elizabeth Sanders, *The Regulation of Natural Gas: Policy and*

Politics, 1938–1978 (Philadelphia: Temple University Press, 1981), pp. 17–45, 83–86, 94–110.

23. "Petroleum Prices Under Pressure," WO 134:3 (Feb. 15, 1952), p. 55; "Will 12,000 Foot Fields Pay Out?" WO 128:1 (May 1948), pp. 67–72; Warren L. Baker, "Drilling Prices Fail to Keep Pace with Rising Costs," WO 128:6 (Oct. 1948), p. 53; Hines H. Baker, "Rising Costs Industry's Greatest Problem," WO 138:7 (June 1954), p. 65; James V. Brown, "The Trends in Costs of Replacing Petroleum Reserves," IPM 16:1 (Mar. 1946), p. 22; "Study of Industry Problems," IPM 19:7 (Nov. 1948), p. 32; Struth, "1947 Oil Discoveries," p. 51; "Relation of Crude Found to Drilling," WO 144:3 (Feb. 15, 1957), p. 135; H. J. Struth, "Exploratory Costs Soar to New Highs During 1956," WO 145:1 (July 1957), p. 63.

24. Baker, "Drilling Prices Fail to Keep Pace," pp. 52–53; Ray L. Dudley, "Drilling Contracting Situation," WO 127:6 (Oct. 1947), p. 63; J. E. Warren, "Economic Trends in Contract Drilling," PE 19:10 (Reference Annual), pp. 52–54; King, "Midland Basin Oil Possibilities," p. 48; Cecil W. Smith, "Geophysical Costs Go Up As Profits Sag," WO 138.5 (Apr. 1954), p. 90; "Major Drilling Equipment Prices Soaring," WO 146:3 (Feb. 15, 1958), p. 156; "Gas Price Fixing Against Public Good, Says Murray," WO 132:7 (June 1951), p. 48; "Baker Says Industry Making Huge Expenditures," p. 37; Wallace Hawkins, "The Natural Gas Act and the Oil and Gas Producer," OW 125:8 (Apr. 21, 1947), p. 53; WO 127:6 (Oct. 1947), p. 46; Zimmermann, *Conservation* (see ch. 3, n. 3), p. 264; WO 139:1 (July 1954), p. 84.

25. Brown, "The Trends in Costs," p. 22; "Study of Industry Problems," p. 32; Struth, "1947 Oil Discoveries," p. 54; "How the Cost of Finding and Producing Oil Has Increased," WO 142:7 (June 1956), pp. 90, 96; Struth, "Exploratory Costs Soar to New Highs," p. 63.

26. T. W. Kidd, "Workovers in West Texas," PE 23:13 (Dec. 1951), p. 1355.

27. Myres, *Era of Advancement* (see ch. 4, n. 5), p. 501; R. W. Byram, "West Texas Experimental Water Flood Successful," OW 110:3 (June 21, 1943), pp. 15–17; J. C. Hostetler, "Secondary Recovery by Waterflood, West Texas and New Mexico," IPM 25:4 (Aug. 1954), pp. 24, 26, 48–50; WO 133:1 (July 1951), p. 48; "Revival in the Osage," WO 143:2 (Aug. 1956), pp. 44–47; "Waterflooding Trend Shown in Mines Bureau Report," WO 134:1 (Jan. 1952), p. 51.

28. W. B. Berwald, "The Economics of Secondary Oil Recovery," WO 127:4 (Jan. 1948), pp. 142–44; W. W. Wilson, "Water-Flood Prospects Need Analysis," WO 144:7 (June 1957), pp. 238–40; Eugene McElvaney, "Factors in Financing Secondary Recovery Projects," IPM 24:3 (July 1953), p. 41; Eugene McElvaney, "Factors Involved in Financing Oil Properties," WO 127:7 (Nov. 1947), p. 75; Fred F. Florence,

"Financing Oil Properties," WO 130:2 (Feb. 1950), p. 52; D. Clayton Arnold, "How to Get an Oil Loan," PE 24:7 (July 1952), pp. A37–39; Craig interview.

29. "Texas Legislature Enacts Bill to Permit Unitization," WO 129:2 (June 1949), p. 46; Sullivan, ed., *Conservation of Oil and Gas,* p. 220; WO 144:4 (Mar. 1957), p. 59.

30. Bob Senning, "Spraberry May Produce 10 Billion Barrels," SAST, Oct. 14, 1951; R. C. Senning, "The Spraberry Play in West Texas," WO 133:4 (Sept. 1951), p. 125; Myres, *Era of Advancement,* p. 358.

31. Myres, *Era of Advancement,* p. 341; Senning, "The Spraberry Play," pp. 125–26; King, "Midland Basin Oil Possibilities," p. 46; "Is World's Largest Oil Field Looming Up in West Texas?" OGJ 50:23 (Oct. 11, 1951), pp. 98–99; John L. Cox, "That Spectacular Spraberry," OGJ 50:29 (Nov. 27, 1951), pp. 74–82; "Prospecting Outlook Emphasized Deep Drilling," WO 132:3 (Feb. 15, 1951), p. 79; MRT, Jan. 1, Mar. 14, 1950.

32. "Permian Basin's East Side Reflects Steady Buildup," OGJ 49:23 (Oct. 12, 1950), p. 158; Senning, "The Spraberry Play," p. 126; Roy F. Carlson, "West Texas Spraberry," OGJ 49:42 (Feb. 22, 1951), p. 79.

33. Midland, Tex., telephone directories, 1949–52; Philip C. Ingalls, "Midland Basin's Spraberry," OGJ 50:2 (May 17, 1951), p. 163; Thomas interview; Olien and Olien, *Oil Booms* (see ch. 2, n. 13), pp. 13, 78–83.

34. Senning, "The Spraberry Play," p. 130; MRT, Mar. 20, 1951.

35. Reigle interview.

36. Penn, Gibson, Williamson, and Craig interviews.

37. Texas Railroad Commission, *Individual Lease Records,* District 8, vols. S-2, T-1, 1950, vols. S-3, T-1, 1951; Spraberry Area Engineering Committee, *Statistical Report, 1947–1954* (Midland, 1955), pp. 17–21, 59, 63, 64–65, 80, 85.

38. *Statistical Report,* ibid. "Spraberry a Siltstone," WO 133:7 (Dec. 1951), p. 206; "Competition Will Solve Spraberry Problems," WO 133:7 (Dec. 1951), p. 37; Cecil W. Smith, "Permian Basin 'Hot Spot' of U.S. Drilling Activity," WO 135:5 (Oct. 1952), p. 114; "Will the Spraberry Pay Out?" WO 135:1 (July 1952), p. 50; G. Frederick Warn, "Spraberry Structural Conditions," WO 136:4 (Mar. 1953), p. 84; Charles J. Deegan, "Can Industry Recover Hidden Spraberry Hoard?" WO 135:6 (Nov. 1952), pp. 73–75; John L. Cox, "Spraberry Drilling and Completion Methods," PE 24:4 (Apr. 1952), pp. B72, 77.

39. "Tex-Harvey Field Opens Large New Producing Zone," WO 131:4 (Sept. 1950), p. 93; Roy F. Carlson, "Spraberry Spacing Report," OGJ 51:24 (Oct. 20, 1952), p. 102; Roy F. Carlson, "Spraberry Falling Off," OGJ 51:15 (Aug. 18, 1952), p. 76.

40. WO 133:6 (Nov. 1951), p. 37; WO 134:5 (Apr. 1952), p. 35;

Roy F. Carlson, "Wider Spacing Asked," OGJ 51:20 (Sept. 22, 1952), p. 72; Deegan, "Can Industry Recover," pp. 73–75; "Spraberry Spacing Set," OGJ 51:33 (Dec. 22, 1952), p. 47; Sullivan, ed., *Conservation of Oil and Gas* (see ch. 3, n. 62), p. 232.

41. *Statistical Report,* pp. 59, 70, 71, 83, 89, 97; *Individual Lease Records,* vol. S-4, 1954, 1955; "Tricks That Get Oil from Spraberry Field in Texas," *Business Week* (Feb. 16, 1952), pp. 82–85.

42. *Statistical Report,* pp. 59, 70–72, 83, 89, 97; *Individual Lease Records,* vol. S-4, 1954, 1955.

43. *Individual Lease Records,* vols. 2-S, T-1, 1950, vols. S-2, T-1, 1951.

44. Gibbon, "Utilization and Conservation," p. 34; Potter, "Operating Problems," p. 44; Baker, "Great Strides in Conserving," p. 34; Edward J. Neuner, *The Natural Gas Industry: Monopoly and Competition in Field Markets* (Norman, Okla.: Oklahoma University Press, 1960), pp. 128–29.

45. Neuner, *Natural Gas Industry,* pp. 128–29; Nelson Jones, "The Spraberry Decision," in *Supplement to Oil and Gas Law, with Articles Pertaining to Sulphur, Taxation, Tidelands, and Other Related Subjects, Reprinted from Volumes 30, 31, 32 of the Texas Law Review* (Austin: University of Texas Law School, 1954), pp. 2089, 2090–91; "Supreme Court Knocks Out Spraberry Shutdown Order," *TIPRO Reporter* 5:3 (May-June 1953), pp. 21, 32.

46. Jones, "Spraberry Decision," pp. 2091, 2094–96; "Spraberry Suit Opens," OGJ 51:51 (Apr. 27, 1953), p. 129; "Spraberry Appeal Set," OGJ 51:51 (Apr. 27, 1953), p. 129; "Spraberry Order Void," OGJ 52:6 (June 15, 1953), pp. 78–79; "Spraberry Back," *Business Week,* Jan. 2, 1954, p. 54; Sullivan, ed., *Conservation of Oil and Gas,* p. 234; "Supreme Court Knocks Out," pp. 21, 32; *Statistical Report,* pp. 34–35.

47. *Individual Lease Records,* vols. S-2, T-1, 1953, vol. S-4, 1955.

48. W. E. Hasselbrock and A. B. Waters, "Advancements Through 15 Years of Fracturing," JPT 16:7 (July 1964), pp. 760–64; Cox, "Spraberry Drilling and Completion Methods," pp. 72, 77; Gibson interview.

49. *Individual Lease Records,* vol. S-4, 1956, Spraberry vol. 1957; Spraberry Area Engineering Committee, *Statistical Report, Spraberry Fields, 1954–56* (Midland, 1957), p. 212; *Statistical Report, Spraberry Fields, 1957,* p. 124; L. F. Elkins, "64,000 Acre Waterflood Promises Spraberry Payout," PE 30:10 (Sept. 1958), pp. B33–38.

50. Henry Ozanne, "Super-Tankers Threaten U.S. with $2 Middle East Oil," WO 128:13 (Apr. 1949), p. 51; "How the Cost of Finding," pp. 90, 96; Baker, "Rising Costs," p. 65.

51. "Independents Abroad," IPM 18:5 (Sept. 1947), p. 67; "Independents Look Toward Middle East After Organizing $100 Million Concern," WO 126:13 (Aug. 25, 1947), p. 27.

52. "Imports and the Trade Agreements Act," IPM 18:5 (Sept. 1947),

p. 67; *TIPRO Reporter* 10:1 (Jan.-Feb. 1958), p. 9; "Fight Against Imports Greatly Intensified," WO 128:13 (Apr. 1949), p. 42; "Imports Chief Concern at TIPRO Meeting in Austin," IPM 20:2 (June 1949), p. 49; WO 129:1 (May 1949), p. 266; WO 129:2 (June 1949), p. 41; MRT, Jan. 1, Mar. 9, 1950.

53. H. J. Porter, "Business Statesmanship Is Not a Complete Solution to Imports," *TIPRO Reporter* 6:1 (Jan.-Feb. 1954), pp. 12–13; Al Reese, "Texas Independents Propose United Front on Imports," WO 140:1 (Jan. 1955), p. 70.

54. Eugene Miller, "Oil Industry Public Relations Good Locally, Poor Nationally," *TIPRO Reporter* 5:6 (Nov.-Dec. 1953), pp. 26–28; Alwyn P. King, Jr., "Industry Is Target of Abuse by Misinformed and Malicious," *TIPRO Reporter* 5:4 (July-Aug. 1953), p. 27.

55. Ernest O. Thompson, "General Thompson Looks at Imports," IPM 24:8 (Dec. 1953), p. 27; WO 139:1 (July 1954), p. 76.

56. "Texas Allowables Up Again," WO 140:1 (Jan. 1955), p. 68; WO 142:7 (June 1956), p. 75.

57. "Salient Oil and Gas Statistics," WO 142:3 (Feb. 15, 1956), pp. 62–73; Ray L. Dudley and Warren L. Baker, "U.S. Imports Are Too High," WO 145:2 (Aug. 1, 1957), pp. 56–57; Warren L. Baker, "Oil's Economic Outlook Becomes Critical," WO 146:4 (Mar. 1958), pp. 76–77; Richard J. Gonzalez, "Will Texas Oil Remain Competitive?" WO 146:7 (June 1958), pp. 88–90.

Chapter 6

1. Michel T. Halbouty, "An Independent's Blueprint for Survival," WO 147:6 (Nov. 1958), pp. 103–106.

2. "Well-Drilling Costs Still Creeping Up," OGJ 59:45 (Nov. 6, 1961), p. 69; "Where Does Oil Stand in the Cost-Allowable Price Squeeze?" WO 152:4 (Mar. 1961), p. 87; Don E. Lambert, "What's Troubling the Independent Producer," WO 153:1 (July 1961), pp. 37, 39; PE 68:20 (May 18, 1974), p. 69; OGJ 68:20 (May 18, 1970), p. 53; "Drilling Costs Hold the Line," PE 38:1 (Jan. 1966), p. 101; John Scott, "Rig Auctions More than Squeeze Symptom," PE 35:1 (Feb. 1963), pp. 63–64.

3. OGJ 57:15 (Apr. 6, 1959), pp. 77–78; NYT, Mar. 11, 12, 14, 21, 1959; "Crude Prices Get Modest Hike," IPM 38:3 (July 1967), p. 5; "Soaring Tanker Rates Felt in U.S.," OGJ 68:28 (July 13, 1970), p. 36; "Why Oil Price Hike Isn't Activating U.S. Operators," OGJ 69:5 (Feb. 1, 1971), pp. 33–37; Wolf interview.

4. Frank J. Gardner, "Derby Winner's Luck Holds," OGJ 57:20 (May 11, 1959), p. 161; "Texas Goes to 9 Days," OGJ 57:26 (June 22, 1959), p. 82; "Texas Holds Production to 8 Days for June," OGJ 58:21 (May

23, 1960), p. 76; "It's 8 Days for Texas in June," OGJ 59:21 (May 22, 1961), p. 68; Anderson interview.

5. Gene T. Kinney, "What's Behind the Rash of Sellouts by Producers?" OGJ 60:4 (Jan. 22, 1962), p. 30; "Mergers Cut List of Producers," OGJ 60:11 (Mar. 12, 1962), p. 76; "Papers for Sale of Honolulu Signed in $380 Million Oil Deal," IPM 32:2 (June 1961), p. 25; "Indecision Develops in the Midst of a Wave of Selling," OGJ 59:30 (July 24, 1961), pp. 38–39; Young O. Mitchell, "Cost-Price Squeeze," IPM 32:11 (Mar. 1962), p. 23; "Ohio Looks for Big Benefits in Plymouth Deal," OGJ 60:2 (Jan. 8, 1962), pp. 46–47; Deance Beazley, "El Dorado, Boom Town — 1921 and 1971," PE 42:11 (May-June 1971), p. 35; "Monsanto Buys Houston Firm's Oil Properties," OGJ 61:36 (Sept. 9, 1963), p. 93; "Sinclair Oil Strengthens Crude Production," OGJ 61:36 (Sept. 9, 1963), pp. 82–83; Don E. Lambert, "Economic Climate Is Ripe for Another Record-Setting Year," WO 162:5 (Apr. 1966), p. 38; "R. J. Reynolds's Buy," OGJ 68:33 (Aug. 17, 1970), p. 29; Wallace W. Wilson, "Where'll the Money Come From?" IPM 62:2 (July-Aug. 1971), pp. 18–19.

6. Halbouty, "An Independent's Blueprint," p. 104; Don E. Lambert, "Needed: More Wildcatting," WO 168:5 (Apr. 1969), pp. 65–68; "Where Does Oil Stand," p. 86; Frank J. Gardner, "Who Finds Those Fields?" OGJ 63:6 (Feb. 8, 1965), p. 133.

7. Compiled from the *Midland City Directory* (see ch. 4, n. 2) and *Hank Seale's Texas Oil Directory,* 1951–69.

8. Kennedy, Redfern, and Leibrock interviews; C&K Petroleum Corporation annual reports, 1970–74.

9. Leibrock and Gilmore interviews; Paul I. Lyons, "Trends in Exploration," IPM 27:5 (Sept. 1956), pp. 28, 30, 54; IPM 37:8 (Dec. 1966), p. 11; WO 164:5 (Apr. 1967), p. 77; S. J. Pirson, "Needed — The Exploratory Spirit," OGJ 70:39 (Sept. 25, 1972), p. 174; James L. Porter, "Independents Now Hold the Fate of Kansas as an Oil and Gas Producing Province," IPM 41:3 (July 1970), pp. 20–22; Joseph A. Kornfeld and Maury M. Travis, "Muddy Sandstone: Hottest Play in Rockies," WO 165:7 (Dec. 1967), pp. 94–101; John Scott, "Powder River Basin: And the Boom Goes On," PE 40:12 (Nov. 1968), pp. 57–61.

10. Dittman and West interviews.

11. "Independents Thrive in California's Gas Play," OGJ 60:37 (Sept. 10, 1962), pp. 100–101; John Scott, "Oil Country Still Has Prizes," PE 36:1 (Jan. 1964), pp. 64–70; "Mecom," OGJ 63:42 (Oct. 18, 1965), p. 49; "Smaller Firms Score 75% of U.S. Exploratory Hits," OGJ 71:27 (July 2, 1973), pp. 10–13; H. J. Struth, "Interstate Economic Ratios Reveal Serious Inequities," WO 156:4 (Mar. 1963), p. 118; C. F. Barnes and E. W. Caldwell, Jr., "Delaware Basin: The Next Big Boom?" WO 145:2 (Aug. 1957), pp. 68–75.

12. Myres, *Era of Advancement* (see ch.4, n. 5), pp. 392, 395–399; Carl Hoot, "West Texas Drillers to Go Deep," OGJ 57:15 (Apr. 6, 1959), pp. 185–86; "Big New Gas-Condensate Field Takes Shape," OGJ 61:41 (Oct. 14, 1963), pp. 120–21; "Nation's Hottest Drilling Play Has 30 Rigs Working Below 10,000 Feet," WO 161:7 (Dec. 1965), pp. 113–14; Joseph G. Kornfeld, "Deep Ellenburger Gas Play Continues to Pay Off Big," WO 163:2 (Aug. 1966), p. 58.

13. Robert J. Enright, "It's Not All Glamor in Delaware Basin," OGJ 60:24 (June 11, 1962), pp. 102–103; Frank J. Gardner, "Texans Attack Deep Delaware," OGJ 63:1 (Jan. 4, 1965), p. 135; Robert G. Burke, "High Costs, Drilling Problems Don't Slow West Texas Deep Basin Play," OGJ 63:22 (May 31, 1965), pp. 128–38; James F. Massey and John Scott, "World's Deepest Producer," PE 37:9 (Aug. 1965), p. 87; Williamson, Bradshaw, and Roden interviews.

14. Williamson interview.

15. Massey and Scott, "World's Deepest Producer," p. 87; "West Texas Drillers Will Dig Deep Delaware Basin," OGJ 62:15 (Apr. 13, 1964), p. 154; Roden interview.

16. WO 160:5 (Apr. 1965), p. 118; Joseph A. Kornfeld, "Major Finds Spark 42-Rig Play in Southeast New Mexico," WO 166:4 (Mar. 1968), p. 98; Joseph A. Kornfeld, "Carlsbad South Gas Field Sparks New Mexico Play," WO 177:4 (Sept. 1973), pp. 74–75; John R. Kubitz and H. M. Shearin, "Producer-Engineer-Purchaser," JPT 16:7 (July 1964), pp. 719–26.

17. West, Penn, and Hills interviews.

18. Scott, "Oil Country Still Has Prizes," p. 67; Harold Vance, "Bank Loans on Oil and Gas Production," PE 26:11 (Oct. 1954), pp. E4–10; A. J. Pearson, "Some Guides to Proper Loan Selection in Petroleum Production Financing," JPT 15:3 (Mar. 1963), p. 232; C. L. Brown, "Bank Financing of Secondary Recovery Projects," JPT 9:3 (Mar. 1957), pp. 22–25.

19. Major interview.

20. John Scott, "Well Servicers Eye Big Work Load," PE 35:7 (July 1963), pp. 76–84; P. E. Essley, Jr., "What Is Reservoir Engineering?" JPT 17:1 (Jan. 1965), pp. 19–25; John Scott and Dr. Paul B. Crawford, "Oil Recovery in the 1970s: Key to Survival," PE 42:7 (July 1970), pp. 41–42; J. L. Rike, "Work-Over and Completion Technology—A Survey," JPT 23:11 (Nov. 1971), pp. 1375–85; Norman J. Clark, "Independents' Wildcat Opportunities in Secondary Recovery," PE 35:6 (June 1963), pp. 50–55.

21. Hendrix and Leibrock interviews.

22. "Midland Independent Describes Himself as 'Close-In' Operator," IPM 38:10 (Feb. 1968), p. 17.

23. Thams interview.

24. Wood, McShane, and Thams interviews.

25. Wood and Thams interviews; Lincoln F. Elkins and Arlie M. Skov, "Cyclic Water Flooding the Spraberry Utilizes 'Effects' to Increase Oil Production Rate," JPT 15:8 (Aug. 1963), p. 877.

26. Wood and Thams interviews.

27. Brown, "Bank Financing," pp. 22–24.

28. Harold Vance, "Will You Be Able to Stay in the Oil Business?" IPM 32:10 (Feb. 1962), p. 14; W. A. Yeager, Jr., and Craig interviews.

29. Kenneth G. Miller, *Oil and Gas: Federal Income Taxation,* 3rd ed. (New York: Commercial Clearing House, 1957), pp. 204–205; Young O. Mitchell, "Cost Price Squeeze," IPM 32:11 (Mar. 1962), p. 24; Granville Dutton, "The Effects of the 1969 Tax Reform Act on Petroleum Property Values," JPT 22:12 (Dec. 1970), pp. 475–79.

30. Pevehouse interview; IPM 40:10 (Feb. 1970), p. 25.

31. Kennedy interview; C&K Petroleum Corporation annual reports, 1970–82.

32. Kennedy, Pevehouse, Major, and Craig interviews.

33. Frazier M. Stewart, "Oil Drilling Programs, Stimulants to Oil Development," JPT 23:5 (May 1971), pp. 539–40, 542; Bell interviews.

34. Stewart, "Oil Drilling Programs," pp. 543–44; Lowell A. Murphy, "Capital Short? Follow One of These Directions," PE 42:12 (Nov. 1970), pp. 6–7; Miller, *Oil and Gas,* pp. 260–90.

35. Truman E. Anderson, Jr., *Oil Programs Investment* (Tulsa: Petroleum Publishing Company, 1972), p. 66.

36. "Investors Ask Oil Firms for 'More,'" OGJ 62:10 (Mar. 9, 1964), p. 56; Anderson, *Oil Programs Investment,* pp. 103–104; "Independents Jump on the Drilling Fund Bandwagon," OGJ 67:13 (Mar. 31, 1969), p. 31.

37. NYT, May 12, 1970; WSJ, May 11, 1970; "Big John," *Time,* May 25, 1970, p. 91.

38. "A Kingdom Besieged," *Time,* Aug. 3, 1970, p. 66; NYT, Aug. 12, 1970; "High Flyers," *Newsweek,* Aug. 24, 1970, p. 49.

39. "High Flyers," pp. 48–49; "Kingdom Besieged," pp. 66–67; NYT, Aug. 14, 1970; WSJ, Oct. 28, 1969, May 11, Aug. 14, 1970.

40. "Funds Organize Self-Regulatory Body," OGJ 68:2 (Jan. 2, 1970), p. 34; "Congress Gets Bill Regulating Drilling Funds," OGJ 70:25 (June 19, 1972), p. 37.

41. "Funds Slow Growth Rate to 12%," OGJ 71:8 (Feb. 19, 1973), p. 46; "U.S. Drilling Funds Raise 10% Less Money in 1973," OGJ 72:7 (Feb. 18, 1974), p. 34; "Petro-Lewis Head Confident Search Money to Be Available," OGJ 72:19 (May 13, 1974), p. 107; Leibrock interview.

42. Leibrock interview.

43. Anderson, *Oil Programs Investment,* pp. 41–42; Major interview.

44. Kennedy interview; C&K Petroleum Corporation annual reports, 1971–73.

45. "John Hurd Outlines Job Ahead for Independents," *TIPRO Reporter* 12:3 (May-June 1960), pp. 8-9; Alvin C. Hope, "The Incredible Story of Natural Gas Regulation," IPM 35:2 (June 1964), pp. iv-vi; "Breakdown in Competition," IPM 35:6 (Oct. 1964), p. 14. For a particularly helpful analysis of FPC policy during this period, see Sanders, *Regulation of Natural Gas* (see ch. 5, n. 22), pp. 94-112.

46. "Permian Basin Case," IPM 35:2 (June 1964), p. viii; "FPC Hits Gas Men with $85,000 Query," OGJ 61:45 (Nov. 11, 1963), pp. 88-89; "The Questionnaire," IPM 35:2 (June 1964), p. xix; Don E. Lambert, "What's Happened to the War on Federal Paperwork Jungle?" WO 159:4 (Sept. 1964), p. 14; "Survey Is Prime Study in Unreasonable Demands," WO 159:4 (Sept. 1964), pp. 18-20.

47. "Permian Price Approach Irks Producers," OGJ 60:48 (Nov. 26, 1962), p. 52; "Permian Examiner Favors Incentive Price for Gas," OGJ 62:38 (Sept. 21, 1964), pp. 82-85; "Breakdown in Competition," p. 15; "Permian Rate 'Too High and Too Low,' " OGJ 62:48 (Nov. 30, 1964), pp. 28-29; "FPC's Administrative Orgy Called 'Government by Fiat,' Congressional Action Urged," IPM 36:4 (Aug. 1965), p. 12; "FPC Adopts Dual Gas Pricing in Pattern-Setting Area-Rate Case," OGJ 63:32 (Aug. 9, 1965), pp. 51-56; Don E. Lambert, "Needed: A Better Way to Control Natural Gas Wellhead Prices," WO 161:4 (Sept. 1965), pp. 25-32.

48. Sanders, *Regulation of Natural Gas,* pp. 111-21; "Permian Basin Case," p. ix; "IPAA Asks Rehearing of Permian Basin Case," IPM 36:5 (Sept. 1965), pp. 18-19; "FPC's Administrative Orgy," p. 12.

49. Edmund W. Kitch, "High Prices Could End Gas Shortage," OGJ 69:23 (June 7, 1971), pp. 42-43; M. A. Adelman, *The Supply and Price of Natural Gas* (Oxford: Basil Blackwell, 1962).

50. "New Fights over Imports," *Business Week,* May 19, 1956, p. 147; "Independents and Majors Tangle in Hearing on Oil Import Cuts," *Business Week,* Oct. 27, 1956, p. 144; "Oilmen Jeer at Import Quotas," *Business Week,* Apr. 5, 1958, p. 29; NYT, Jan. 23, Mar. 11, 12, 14, 21, 1959; Edward H. Shaffer, *The Oil Import Program of the United States: An Evaluation* (New York: Frederick A. Praeger, Publishers, 1968), pp. 18-22.

51. "John Hurd Outlines Job Ahead," pp. 8-9; NYT, Aug. 20, 1961, May 26, 1964, Dec. 11, 1965; "Your Voice in Government," IPM 23:4 (Aug. 1962), pp. 24-25; Jake L. Hamon, "A Look at the Independent," IPM 37:12 (Apr. 1967), pp. 16-17.

52. "FBI Questioning Texas Producers About ABC Sales," OGJ 60:17 (Apr. 23, 1962), pp. 56-57; "FBI Expands Probe to Include Majors," OGJ 60:18 (Apr. 30, 1962), pp. 40-41.

53. "Texas Independents Fear Widening of Controls," OGJ 61:40 (Oct. 7, 1963), p. 97; "New Burden Proposed for Oil," OGJ 61:41 (Oct. 14, 1963), pp. 115-17.

54. Lambert, "What's Happened to the War," pp. 13–20; "The Questionnaire," p. xix.

55. "Environmental Clearance for On Shore Wildcats Mandatory," OGJ 70:12 (Mar. 20, 1972), p. 41.

56. OGJ 69:34 (Aug. 23, 1971), pp. 37–41; NYT, Sept. 21, 1971; "More Guidelines Emerge Under Phase 2," OGJ 70:4 (Jan. 24, 1972), p. 26; "Price Commission Bars Gas-Rate Hikes," OGJ 70:8 (Feb. 21, 1972), p. 26; "Price Freezes on Crude, Major Products Confirmed," OGJ 70:11 (Mar. 13, 1972), p. 39; "IPAA Seeks 4% Price Boost for Crude," OGJ 70:11 (Mar. 13, 1972), p. 38–39; "Justice Probing IPAA Bid for Oil Price Hike," OGJ 70:12 (Mar. 20, 1972), pp. 28–29.

57. "McGovern Reveals New Energy Policies," OGJ 70:42 (Oct. 16, 1972), pp. 82–84.

58. "Decontrol Hits New Pitch," OGJ 70:10 (Mar. 6, 1972), p. 76; "Permian Wellhead Prices at New High," OGJ 70:45 (Nov. 11, 1972), p. 51; "F.P.C.'s Small-Producer Rule Thrown Out," OGJ 70:51 (Dec. 18, 1972), p. 41; "Ruling Against Small Producers Cuts Drilling," OGJ 71:7 (Feb. 12, 1973), p. 43; "FPC Official Urges Permian Area Rate of 35¢," OGJ 70:51 (Feb. 25, 1972), p. 47.

Chapter 7

1. "Crude Pricing: No Relief for the Confused Producer," WO 184:3 (Feb. 15, 1977), pp. 65–68; "Crude Oil Prices: From Confusion to Despair," WO 188:3 (Feb. 15, 1979), pp. 69–74; "U.S. Crude Prices: Up, Up, and Away," WO 178:3 (Feb. 15, 1974), p. 73; Henderson interview.

2. U.S. Bureau of the Census, Current Industrial Reports Series, *Annual Survey of Oil and Gas, 1974,* MA-13K (74)-1 (Washington, D.C.: U.S. Government Printing Office, 1976), pp. 1–4; R. Steinmetz, "Statistical Summary of Wells Drilled Below 18,000 Feet in West Texas and Anadarko Basin," *AAPG Bulletin,* May 1978, p. 588; "Active Drilling Rigs Zoom to 4-Year High," WO 178:3 (Feb. 15, 1979), pp. 85–86; T. B. O'Brien, "Drilling Costs: A Current Appraisal of a Major Problem," WO 183:5 (Oct. 1976), pp. 76–78; "Rig Activity Is Up and Going Higher," WO 180:3 (Feb. 15, 1975), p. 92; Bell interview; "Crude Oil Prices," p. 70; "U.S. Drilling: Another Good Year," WO 184:3 (Feb. 1977), pp. 70–73.

3. Texas Railroad Commission, Oil and Gas Division, *Annual Reports,* 1969–81; WO, Annual Review and Forecast Issues, Feb. 15, 1977–81; Jim West, "Independents Vital to U.S. Petroleum Supply," OGJ 75:4 (Oct. 24, 1977), p. 86; NYT, Mar. 17, 1972.

4. Robert J. Beck, "Demand, Imports to Rise in '83," OGJ 81:4 (Jan. 31, 1983), p. 78; Philip C. Crouse, "U.S. Crude Prices: No Improve-

ment in 1982," WO 194:3 (Dec. 15, 1982), p. 143; U.S. Bureau of the Census, Current Industrial Reports Series, *Annual Survey of Oil and Gas, 1980,* MA-13K (80)-1 (Washington, D.C.: U.S. Government Printing Office, 1982), p. 1.

5. "Call for Gas Decontrol Hits New Pitch," OGJ 70:10 (Mar. 6, 1972), p. 76; Stephen G. Breyer and Paul W. MacAvoy, "Regulating Natural Gas Production," in Robert J. Kalter and William A. Vogel, eds., *Energy Supply and Government Policy* (Ithaca: Cornell University Press, 1976), pp. 181–88; Sanders, *Regulation of Natural Gas* (see ch. 5, n. 22), p. 141; "Permian Rate Ceilings Hit 35, 23¢/Mcf," OGJ 71:23 (Aug. 13, 1973), p. 51; "Higher Prices Trigger Increase in Gas Drilling," OGJ 71:34 (Aug. 20, 1973), pp. 15–20.

6. "U.S. Drilling: Another Good Year," p. 70; WO 188:3 (Feb. 15, 1979), p. 82; Sanders, *Regulation of Natural Gas,* p. 141; "Higher Prices Let Smaller Firms Hike Exploration/Development Spending," OGJ 75:44 (Oct. 27, 1977), p. 103.

7. "Operating Costs Up Markedly, IPAA Says," WO 177:7 (Dec. 1973), p. 73; WO, Annual Review and Forecast Issues, Feb. 15, 1969, 1974, 1977, 1979; "Drilling Costs Still Rising," WO 188:3 (Feb. 15, 1979), p. 121; "Drilling Costs on the Rise," WO 192:3 (Feb. 15, 1981), p. 156.

8. University of Texas System Public Auction Sales of Oil and Gas Leases File, Office of the Chief Geologist, University of Texas System Lands, Midland, Tex. These figures are generally higher than bonuses paid to private landowners.

9. University of Texas System Public Auction Sales of Oil and Gas Leases File; MRT, Sept. 18, 1980; Chase Manhattan Bank, *Financial Analysis of a Group of Petroleum Companies,* 1971, 1973–79 (New York: Chase, Energy Economics, 1972, 1974–80); "Capital Investment of the World's Petroleum Industry," WO 187:1 (July 1978), p. 125; Bell interviews.

10. T. J. Stewart-Gordon, "High Oil Prices, Technology Support Austin Chalk Boom," WO 183:5 (Oct. 1976), p. 123; Byerley, Bradshaw, and Anderson interviews.

11. Table B-67: "Bond Yields and Interest Rates, 1929–1982," in *Economic Report of the President, Transmitted to the Congress, February, 1983* (Washington, D.C.: U.S. Government Printing Office, 1983), p. 240; Jim West, "New Drilling-Money Spout Opening for Independent?" OGJ 72:35 (Sept. 2, 1974), p. 16; Peter S. Rose and Thomas W. Cooper, "Oil and Gas Financing: An Appraisal of Current Methods," WO 185:5 (Oct. 1977), pp. 101–102; Pevehouse interview.

12. "The EPA Man Is Calling," IPM 64:3 (May-June 1974), p. 27; T. Don Stacy, "The Onshore U.S., Some Promises and Problems," WO 188:2 (Aug. 1979), p. 41; Laura Pankonien, "The Independent Producer: He Has Reason for Optimism," WO 189:6 (Nov. 1979), p. 61;

Sanford E. McCormick, "U.S. Oil and Gas: An Independent's Point of View," WO 191:7 (Dec. 1980), p. 42.

13. Rick Hagar and G. Alan Petzet, "Hefty Wellhead Prices Spark Drilling in U.S. Tight Gas Sands," OGJ 80:17 (Apr. 26, 1982), pp. 69–73; Sanders, *Regulation of Natural Gas,* pp. 167–189.

14. "Crude Oil Prices," p. 72; Charles J. Holland, Jr., "Drilling for Gas: It's Complicated Now," WO 188:4 (Mar. 1979), pp. 55–56; Barry Russell, "Cost of Government Red Tape," IPM, June 1981, pp. 19–23.

15. "U.S. House Passes Excise Tax on Decontrol Revenues," OGJ 78:11 (Mar. 17, 1980), pp. 59–63; "Senate Clears Massive Crude Excise Tax," OGJ 78:13 (Mar. 31, 1980), p. 57; "Excise Tax Will Impair U.S. Crude Production," OGJ 78:15 (Apr. 14, 1980), pp. 49–53; Main Hurdman & Cranston, *An Analysis of the Crude Oil Windfall Profit Tax with an Emphasis on the Independent Producer* (New York: Main Hurdman & Cranston, 1980), p. 1.

16. Commerce Clearing House, *Crude Oil Windfall Profit Tax of 1980* (Chicago: Commerce Clearing House, 1980), pp. 1–15, 20; Main Hurdman & Cranston, *Analysis,* pp. 6, 23.

17. Craig interview; "Higher Oil and Gas Prices Spark Heavy Drilling by U.S. Independents," OGJ 78:41 (Oct. 13, 1980), p. 107.

18. Witte and Major interviews; "U.S. House Passes Excise Tax," p. 60; Pevehouse interview.

19. Byerley, W. A. Yeager, Jr., Dameron, and Dittman interviews.

20. Petroleum Information Corporation, *The Overthrust Belt* (Denver: Petroleum Information Corporation, 1978), pp. 66–67; "Drilling and Completion Practices in Active U.S. Areas," WO 194:6 (May 1982), p. 111; Steve Lohr, "The Great Oil Rush of the Eighties," NYT, Aug. 30, 1981.

21. John C. McCaslin and Bob Williams, "Where Independents Are Finding New Oil, Gas," OGJ 80:41 (Oct. 11, 1982), pp. 116–41; Petroleum Information Corporation, *The Deep Anadarko Basin* (Denver: Petroleum Information Corporation, 1982), pp. 5–6, 43, 55; Petroleum Information Corporation, *The Tuscaloosa Trend* (Denver: Petroleum Information Corporation, 1980), pp. 33, 45, 61.

22. Stewart-Gordon, "High Oil Prices," pp. 123–26; Wilford Lee Stapp, "What to Look For When Exploring the Austin Chalk," WO 186:2 (Feb. 1, 1978), pp. 55–58; "Independents' Share of Drilling Reaches 88%," WO 194:3 (Feb. 15, 1982), p. 191; Leibrock interview; "Drilling and Completion Practices," p. 121.

23. G. Alan Petzet, "U.S. Industry Eyes Buildup in Oil Output via CO_2 Floods," OGJ 81:1 (Jan. 3, 1983), pp. 39–42; Robert E. King, "Onshore Successes Dominate U.S. Exploratory Efforts," WO 184:7 (June 1977), p. 44; T. J. Stewart-Gordon, "New Pays Develop New Plays in the Permian Basin," WO 186:6 (May 1978), pp. 68–74.

24. "How Higher Prices Extend Producing Life of Stripper Wells," OGJ 71:51 (Dec. 24, 1973), p. 13; Dave Noran, "Independents Are Busy Maximizing Production from Stripper Wells," OGJ 75:44 (Oct. 24, 1977), p. 134; Clyde La Motte, "America's #1 Conservation Tool: Stripper Wells," IPM, Apr. 1980, p. 6; G. Alan Petzet, "How Stripper Operator Makes an Old Lease Pay Off," OGJ 80:41 (Nov. 11, 1982), pp. 113–15; "Raton Basin Commands More Wildcat Attention," OGJ 81:15 (Apr. 11, 1983), pp. 127–28; Wood, McShane, and Thams interviews.

25. *Texas Oil Directory,* 1969–81.

26. Ibid.

27. Ibid; *Midland City Directory,* 1969–81.

28. Grover interview; Flag-Redfern Oil Company annual reports, 1972, 1977; Bell and Craig interviews.

29. Redfern interview.

30. Redfern interview; John J. Redfern III, "Flag-Redfern Oil Company," in Frances J. Bridges, Kenneth W. Olsen, and J. Allison Barnhill, *Management Decisions and Organizational Policy,* 2nd ed. (Boston: Allyn and Bacon, 1971), pp. 46–52, 146; memorandum by L. G. Blodgett, Oct. 1, 1943, Flag Oil Corporation Papers; Flag-Redfern annual report, 1970.

31. Flag-Redfern annual reports, 1973–76; Flag-Redfern, "Progress Report, 1973."

32. Flag-Redfern annual reports, 1977, 1979–80; Redfern interview.

33. Redfern interview; Flag-Redfern annual reports, 1974–77.

34. Flag-Redfern annual reports, 1976–79, 1981; Redfern interview.

35. Flag-Redfern annual reports, 1977–78.

36. Flag-Redfern annual reports, 1978–82; Redfern interview.

37. Major interview; Leslie Haines, "Focus: Aaron F. Giebel," MRT, Aug. 22, 1982; Leslie Haines, "Focus: R. O. 'Jack' Major," MRT, Nov. 7, 1982.

38. Haines, "Focus: Aaron F. Giebel"; MGF Corporation, annual report, 1971.

39. MGF annual reports, 1971–81; Major interview; Geoffrey Leavenworth, "Are Drilling Funds Worth the Bother?" *Texas Business,* Jan. 1981, pp. 62–64.

40. MGF annual reports, 1979–81.

41. Haines, "Focus: Aaron F. Giebel"; Haines, "Focus: R. O. 'Jack' Major"; MGF annual report, 1971.

42. Haines, "Focus: Aaron F. Giebel"; MGF annual reports, 1979–81; Major interview; Laura Pankonien, "The Independent Producer," p. 61.

43. MGF annual reports, 1971–81.

44. Philip C. Crouse, "U.S. Crude Prices: The Future Will Depend on OPEC," WO 192:3 (Feb. 11, 1981), p. 120; Leibrock interview.

45. Atkinson interview; Petroleum Information Corporation, *The Deep Anadarko Basin,* p. 79; Witte interview; Haines, "Focus: Aaron F. Giebel"; MGF annual report, 1981; Jim West and Glenda E. Smith, "Independent Operators Spearhead U.S. Drilling Explosion," OGJ 79:42 (Oct. 19, 1981), pp. 162–63.

46. William K. Stevens, "Young Millionaire's New Goal," NYT, June 18, 1981; Hendrix interview; Bill Deener, "Oil Swindlers Fleece Fortune from Investors," *Dallas Morning News,* Sept. 27, 1981.

47. Deener, "Oil Swindlers"; Roger Thurow, "Oil-Drilling Ventures Hit by Scandal in '70s Lure Investors Again," WSJ (eastern ed.), June 19, 1981.

48. God and Hammer Enterprises, promotional letter, Aug. 19, 1981, authors' collection.

49. Cornwall and Henderson interviews.

50. "Exploration/Development in U.S. Area Is Poised for Upturn Later in 1982," OGJ 80:25 (June 21, 1982), p. 120; Robert J. Beck, "U.S. Oil Demand to Fall Again by 4.2%," OGJ 80:30 (July 26, 1982), pp. 175–76; Richard Wheatley, "Economic Problems Slow Action in Deep Tuscaloosa Trend," OGJ 80:30 (July 26, 1982), pp. 99–105.

51. West and Smith, "Independent Operators," p. 159; "Joint Survey Lists Big Jump in 1981 Outlay for Drilling," OGJ 81:5 (Feb. 7, 1983), p. 36.

52. University of Texas System Public Auction Sales of Oil and Gas Leases File; OGJ 80:23 (June 7, 1982), p. 54; OGJ 80:24 (June 7, 1982), p. 217; "Exploration/Development," p. 119.

53. Don Cowan and Rick Hagar, "Slack Market, Lower Prices Slash Drilling for Deep Gas," OGJ 81:5 (Feb. 7, 1983), p. 24; "Slump Will Change Industry Climate," OGJ 80:40 (Oct. 4, 1982), p. 27; Jim West and Glenda Smith, "Independents Retain Big Share of Drilling Despite Hard Times," OGJ 80:41 (Oct. 11, 1982), pp. 103–12.

54. Atkinson interview.

55. "Sales by Public Programs Hit Record Volumes," OGJ 80:2 (Jan. 11, 1982), p. 133; John R. Braden and Jack R. Morris, "Economic Recovery Act Provides Planning Opportunities for Oil and Gas Industry," OGJ 79:32 (Oct 19, 1981), pp. 246–48; Truman E. Anderson, Sr., "Capital Supply for Independent Operators Is Growing Rapidly," OGJ 75:44 (Oct. 24, 1977), p. 127.

56. Jim Landers, "Economy Drains Small Texas Oil Firms," *Dallas Morning News,* Mar. 31, 1982.

57. Atkinson, Witte, and Lovelady interviews; Cowan and Hagar, "Slack Market, Lower Prices," p. 26.

58. West and Smith, "Independents Retain Big Share," p. 106; Leslie Haines, "An Optimistic Tom Brown Owes Stockholders Positive Report," MRT, Aug. 4, 1982; G. Alan Petzet, "How Independent Operators Cope

with Slashed Cash Flow," OGJ 80:41 (Oct. 11, 1982), pp. 142–49; David C. Sodamann, "Mesa President Sees Tougher Times Ahead for Oil Industry," MRT, Feb. 17, 1983.

59. Rhoda Brammer, "Rough Patch: Independents Are Hurting Financially," *Barron's,* Sept. 27, 1982, pp. 11, 14.

60. Ibid.

61. MGF annual report, 1981; "Public Oil and Gas Program Sales in U.S. Sliding," OGJ 80:12 (May 17, 1982), p. 140; "Public Program Fund Total Seen Down 35% in '82," OGJ 80:50 (Dec. 13, 1982), p. 48; Haines, "Focus: R. O. 'Jack' Major"; "MGF Oil Announced Cutbacks, Restructuring," MRT, Apr. 7, 1983.

62. MGF annual report, 1982; "MGF Oil Reports $80 Million Loss for 1982," MRT, Apr. 7, 1983.

63. Leslie Haines, "Tom Brown, Inc., Down But Not Out," MRT, Aug. 4, 1983.

64. WSJ, July 2, 6, 8, 9, 14, 15, 20, 27, Aug. 3, 20, 31, 1982, Oct. 6, 1983.

65. MRT, Apr. 7, Oct. 7, 1983; WSJ, Oct. 6, 1983.

66. "May: U.S. Drilling Efficiency Improves, Activity Slows," OGJ 80:51 (Dec. 10, 1982), p. 38; Lovelady, Witte, Wolf, Wilson, and Atkinson interviews.

67. MRT, July 17, 1983; West and Smith, "Independents Retain Big Share," pp. 106–107; Pevehouse and Lacy interviews; Don Cowan and Rick Hagar, "Independent Operators Struggle to Survive Tough Times," OGJ 81:14 (Apr. 4, 1983), pp. 41–45.

68. Roden and Atkinson interviews.

GLOSSARY

The following definitions of terms used in this study are offered in nontechnical form and in the sense in which they have been used.

acidizing: The pumping of acid or other chemicals into a productive horizon in order to increase the flow of oil to the well bore.

associated gas: Gas in an oil reservoir, as in a cap above the oil or dissolved in the oil.

basin: A bowl-shaped sedimentary subsurface structure, once the bed of a prehistoric sea.

bottom-hole money: A commitment by holders of nearby leases to pay an operator if he drills to a specified depth.

brokers: Middlemen in the buying and selling of leases, oil, stock, bonds, or capital.

cable tool rig: The earliest drilling rig in American use. It pounds a hole in the earth by repeatedly dropping a weighted and pointed bit, thus shattering rock.

cash flow: Income after taxes and depreciation.

casing: Steel pipe used in a well to support the walls of the hole and to seal off the borehole from fluids.

casinghead gas: Gas produced from an oil well.

casing point: The stage in well completion at which tubing is set from the surface to or through the pay zone.

condensate: Light hydrocarbons produced with natural gas that are separated from it by processing.

core: A column of rock taken from the bottom of a well bore as a sample of the formation.

depletion allowance: A partial federal tax exemption on income from the production and sale of minerals.

developmental drilling: Drilling undertaken to increase production from a known reservoir.

discounted future value: The estimated value of properties at the time of loan repayment minus the costs of borrowing.

downstream: The refining and marketing segments of the petroleum industry.

dry-hole money: A commitment by owners of nearby leases to pay an operator if his well does not produce oil or gas.

enhanced recovery: The stimulation of production from an oil reservoir by chemical or hydraulic means.

farmout: A contribution of lease acreage in exchange for the drilling of a well.

feedstock: Raw materials — crude oil for a refinery and natural gas for petrochemical plants.

fixed costs: The costs of doing business that do not change in response to the volume of business.

fracturing: The pumping of fluids under great pressure into productive horizons in order to create fissures in the formation and increase the flow of oil to the well bore.

gas cap: Undissolved (free) gas above the oil in a reservoir.

gravimeter: A geophysical instrument used to measure differences in the earth's gravitational pull in different locations in order to support inferences about subsurface formations.

high-gravity oil: Oil of high specific gravity, yielding more gasoline and other high-value products during refining.

horizon: A stratum of porous mineral that contains crude oil.

hot oil: Oil produced in violation of the production rules of state regulatory commissions.

hydrofracturing: Enhancing production from a well by injecting fluids under great pressure to open oil-bearing formations.

lease: The site of drilling and other oil field activity; a legal instrument whereby the right to drill for and produce oil and gas on a given tract of land is given to an operator; a legal instrument in which all or part of the rights to subsurface minerals are conveyed.

lease bonus: A negotiable payment by the operator to the leaseholder, made on a per-acre basis when an oil and gas lease is signed.

low-gravity oil: Oil of low specific gravity, yielding more low-value products during refining.

nonassociated gas: Gas found independent of oil.

nonperforming loans: Loans on which neither interest nor principal has been paid by the borrower.

offset well: A well drilled for the purpose of counteracting the production capacity of a well on an adjoining property by tapping into the same reservoir.

operator: The manager of drilling ventures and producing properties.

override: An interest in the revenue produced from the sale of oil and gas. The holder of an overriding interest does not pay expenses incurred in drilling a well and bringing it into production.

participation: Investment in oil and gas ventures.

pay: The horizon of a formation that contains oil or gas.

payout: The recovery of drilling, completion, and equipment costs from the sale of oil and gas.

permeability: The capacity of a formation to absorb or contain oil.

pipeline proration: The allocation of production in terms of the capacity of pipeline systems.

porosity: The quality of a formation that controls the rate at which a liquid can flow through it.

production payments: A financial interest carved out of a working interest in a lease that conveys a share of the revenue from the lease to the owner of the production payment until he receives a sum of money from the owner of the working interest as specified in a loan or sales agreement.

promoter: The gatherer of capital from investors to pay for oil and gas ventures.

proration: The allocation of petroleum production from a common reservoir or source; specifically, the restriction and allocation of production by a regulatory body. The Texas regulatory body, the Railroad Commission, assigned "allowables"—maximum quantities of oil to be produced—to fields and, within them, to leases and wells.

prospect: A lease thought suitable for drilling for oil or gas on the basis of scientific data and the related interpretations.

proven acreage: Leases within the known boundaries of oil fields.

pumper: An oil field worker who tends producing wells and oil tanks.

reef: A reservoir composed of the skeletal remains of marine animals.

reserves: Unproduced oil and gas.

reservoir: A porous, permeable rock formation containing oil and/or gas surrounded by less permeable rock.

residue gas: The gas remaining after liquid hydrocarbons have been removed in a separator.

reversionary working interest: A right to a specific proportion of the revenue from a well after its original cost has been recovered.

rotary drilling rig: A drilling rig that makes a hole in the ground by augering with a bit that is weighted with the attached drill pipe.

royalty: The proportion of the oil and gas produced from a lease that belongs to the mineral owner.

secondary recovery: The extraction of oil from a reservoir in excess of what can be recovered by pumping, mainly through the injection of water, gas, or chemicals.

seismograph: An instrument used by geophysicists to record shock waves set off by explosions or percussion.

shooting a well: The detonation of nitroglycerin or other explosives within a well in a productive sand in order to open it and thus increase the flow of oil to the well bore.

sour crude: Oil that contains large quantities of corrosive sulphur.

spot market: A market for purchase and sale of oil on a short-term basis.

spudding in: Starting the drilling process.

stepout: The extension of the boundaries of a field by drilling on a lease that is near the field, but outside its proven dimensions.

stripper wells: Oil wells that produce less than ten barrels of oil per day.

sweet crude: Oil that has small quantities of sulphur.

tight sand: A low-porosity formation in which oil and gas move very slowly to the well bore.

tool dresser: A worker on a cable tool rig who heats the drill bit and hammers a new edge on it.

trend: A broadly defined productive area.

tubing: Small-diameter pipe through which oil and gas are produced from the well bore.

unitization: The control and management of all leases in a field as if they were a single lease.

upstream: The exploration and production segments of the petroleum industry.

water drive: Water pressure below or on the edges of an oil formation that forces oil to the well bore.

waterflooding: The injection of water into an oil reservoir to force additional oil to the well bores.

wellhead price: The price paid by the purchaser at the point of production, before processing and transportation costs are incurred.

wet gas: Gas that holds liquid hydrocarbons.

wildcat well: An exploratory well in a new horizon or outside the surface boundaries of known reservoirs. A "rank wildcat" is far removed from existing production and known reservoirs.

workover: Pumping out, acidizing, hydrofracturing, or shooting a producing well to unclog the productive formation.

BIBLIOGRAPHY

In addition to the documents, technical studies, records, business papers, directories, reports, and periodicals cited in the notes, several scholarly books are of special value:

M. A. Adelman, *The World Petroleum Market* (Baltimore: Johns Hopkins University Press, 1972).

Stuart W. Bruchey, ed., *Small Business in American Life* (New York: Columbia University Press, 1980).

August W. Giebelhaus, *Business and Government in the Oil Industry: A Case Study of Sun Oil, 1876–1945* (Greenwich, Conn.: JAI Press, 1980).

Robert E. Hardwicke, *Antitrust Laws, et al. v. Unit Operation of Oil or Gas Pools* (Dallas: Society of Petroleum Engineers of AIME, 1961).

Henrietta M. Larson and Kenneth Wiggins Porter, *History of Humble Oil & Refining Company: A Study in Industrial Growth* (New York: Harper & Brothers, 1959).

Samuel D. Myres, *The Permian Basin, Petroleum Empire of the Southwest: Era of Advancement* (El Paso: Permian Press, 1977).

David F. Prindle, *Petroleum Politics and the Texas Railroad Commission* (Austin: University of Texas Press, 1981).

M. Elizabeth Sanders, *The Regulation of Natural Gas: Policy and Politics, 1938–1978* (Philadelphia: Temple University Press, 1981).

Erich W. Zimmermann, *Conservation in the Production of Petroleum: A Study in Industrial Control* (New Haven, Conn.: Yale University Press, 1957).

The following persons generously shared their time in interviews with us. Unless otherwise noted, the interviews were conducted in Midland, Texas, by Roger M. Olien.

Todd Aaron (Feb. 8, 1980)
Joe C. Adams (Jan. 12, 1981)
Roger D. Allen (Jan. 7, 1981)
Payton V. Anderson (Jan. 6, 1981)

Ernest Angelo, Jr. (Mar. 20, 1979)
W. H. Armstrong (Feb. 13, 1979, with W. A. Yeager, Sr.)
Jerry V. Atkinson (June 25, 1982)
R. W. Barker (Jan. 14, 1981)
Clyde Barton (Apr. 6, 1979, Kermit, Tex.)
Kelly Bell (Nov. 3, 1978; June 1, 1979; Feb. 4, 1981)
George Bentley (Oct. 11, 1979, Monahans, Tex.)
Roland K. Blumberg (Apr. 29, 1982, Seguin, Tex.)
Don L. Bradshaw (Feb. 17, 1981)
Jno. P. Butler (June 6, 1978; July 29, 1981)
L. G. Byerley (Jan. 5, 1981)
Ford Chapman (May 27, 1980)
Donald Combs (Oct. 30, 1981)
John Cornwall (Feb. 25, 1981)
Earle M. Craig, Jr. (Feb. 12, 1982)
Rodger S. Dameron (June 27, 1982)
Ben Dansby (Feb. 18, 1981)
Paul L. Davis (June 24, 1982, with J. Conrad Dunagan)
Don W. Dittman (Apr. 6, 1979, with George Mitchell, Kermit, Tex.)
George P. Gibson (Jan. 28, 1981)
W. H. Gilmore, Jr. (Jan. 13, 1981)
Arden R. Grover (June 14, 1982)
Bernold M. Hansen (June 17, 1982)
Charles F. Henderson (Jan. 30, 1981)
John H. Hendrix (May 23, 1980; Jan. 2, 1981)
John M. Hills (Jan. 14, 1981)
Van D. Howbert (Feb. 3, 1981)
Lee Jones, Jr. (Oct. 12, 1981, Colorado City, Tex.)
William D. Kennedy (Mar. 2, 1981)
James W. Lacy (July 22, 1982)
Watson W. LaForce, Jr. (Jan. 29, 1981)
William A. Landreth (Mar. 19, 1981, with Diana Davids Olien, Fort
    Worth, Tex.)
Robert M. Leibrock (Jan. 13, 1981; Mar. 22, 1983)
Mrs. Thomas Linebery (June 15, 1978, with Diana Davids Olien)
Ike W. Lovelady (June 29, 1982)
R. O. Major (June 8, 1982)
W. H. McGarr (Oct. 30, 1981)
Hamilton E. McRae (June 21, 1982)
Joseph B. McShane (Jan. 21, 1979, Monahans, Tex.)
E. Richard Neff (Jan. 12, 1982)
William D. Noel (Feb. 12, 1981, Odessa, Tex.)
A. "Shorty" O'Donnell (Oct. 30, 1981)
Joseph I. O'Neill, Jr. (June 28, 1982)

Bruce Pearson (June 21, 1982)

William Y. Penn (Jan. 19 and 21, 1981)

Mr. and Mrs. J. H. Penson (Mar. 14, 1981, with Diana Davids Olien, Dallas, Tex.)

B. J. Pevehouse (Aug. 20, 1982)

Mrs. H. N. Phillips (Nov. 1, 1977, with Diana Davids Olien)

George A. Plummer (Jan. 28, 1981)

William H. Pomeroy (June 25, 1982)

H. J. Porter (Aug. 26, 1981, Houston, Tex.)

John J. Redfern, Jr. (May 1, 1980; Mar. 26, 1982)

Edward E. Reigle (July 15, 1983)

W. F. Roden (June 29, 1982)

Joseph G. Sauer (Jan. 5, 1981)

Eric Schroeder (Mar. 14, 1981, with Diana Davids Olien, Dallas, Tex.)

Mr. and Mrs. Tom Sloan and Mrs. T. N. Sloan (June 23, 1982, with Diana Davids Olien)

Maria Spencer (Jan. 25, 1978, by Diana Davids Olien)

John H. Swendig (May 28, 1979)

William H. Thams (Dec. 16, 1980)

John W. Thomas (Oct. 27, 1981)

Robert C. Tucker (Feb. 20, 1981)

Charles Vertrees (Jan. 22, 1978)

Mrs. Charles Vertrees (Jan. 22, 1978, by Diana Davids Olien)

W. W. West (Sept. 23, 1982)

J. C. Williamson (Feb. 16, 1982, near Jal, New Mexico)

William B. Wilson (Apr. 5, 1982)

T. L. Witte, Jr. (June 14, 1982)

Dean E. Wolf (June 22, 1982)

B. Oliver Wood (Jan. 20, 1981)

W. A. Yeager, Sr. (Feb. 13, 1979)

W. A. Yeager, Jr. (June 10, 1982)

INDEX